ALFRED RODRÍGUEZ
RUTGERS UNIVERSITY

AN INTRODUCTION TO THE
EPISODIOS NACIONALES
OF GALDÓS

1967
LAS AMERICAS PUBLISHING COMPANY
New York

863
P43z

Manufactured in the United States of America

CONTENTS

CONTENTS

INTRODUCTION

The *Episodios Nacionales* have drawn relatively scant attention from modern critics. Moreover, even when favorable, critical opinion has tended to relegate Galdós' historical novel to a literary limbo. Histories of Spanish literature contain laudatory but token references to the *Episodios Nacionales,* and special studies of Galdós too often dispose first — and quickly — of the novelist's most persistently cultivated literary form (1872-1912). This critical approach has merely helped spread the misleading notion that the historical novels are nothing more than a stage of literary apprenticeship.

The present study, first conceived and written as a doctoral dissertation, is intended to serve as an introduction to this vast segment of Galdós' work. The cursory analysis of the *Episodios* found in general studies of Galdós is, of course, useful, as are the numerous minute studies that exist of the historical or literary sources of specific Episodios; but our entire approach rests on the premise that Galdós' historical novel lends itself to separate, all-inclusive study, that only a critical approach along these lines could, in fact, hope to clarify its objectives and analyze its artistic qualities.

The validity of our basic premise has recently been confirmed by the appearance of Hans Hinterhäuser's *Los Episodios Nacionales de Benito Pérez Galdós* (Gredos, Madrid, 1963), a monographic study of Galdós' historical novel. The appearance of Hinterhäuser's book, a most valuable contribution to Galdosian studies, did not deter us from publishing our own study, for not too surprisingly — when the length, vastness and complexity of the subject matter are considered — the two vary significantly in terms of outline, goals, critical approach, and specific conclusions. Most important, in this respect, is the distinct intent of the two studies. Hinterhäuser's monograph, which focuses on the *Episodios Nacionales* from a general and theoretical level, is clearly intended as an initial probe — setting up projects and criteria for future studies — into an untended segment of Galdós' literary production. It does little, in terms of outline and presentation, to function as an introduction to the same. The fol-

7

lowing study, beyond any number of specific differences, is clearly distinguished from Hinterhäuser's by its sequential organization and chronological presentation, both intended to offer the pace and the format of an introduction to the *Episodios Nacionales*. It is an introduction that the new interest in Galdós — and specifically in the novelist's historical works — has made imperative, both for the nineteenth century specialist, who can scarcely hope to re-read often or retain this vast segment of Galdós' work, and for the student of Spanish literature in general, who requires a meaningful context for the few Episodios that he will ever read.

Our focus on the *Episodios Nacionales* as a homogeneous segment of Galdós' literary production offers a simple division into two parts. The first, consisting of two chapters, will consider questions pertinent to the work as a whole, matters of generic classification, genesis, and historical approach. The second, which consists of three chapters, deals critically with each of the five Series of *Episodios Nacionales,* and stresses literary development and technique.

The first part will underscore the distinguishing features of Galdós' work within the broad category of historical fiction, and then employ these features as basic criteria for determining the genesis of the *Episodios Nacionales* within the trajectory of the novelist's artistic development. In treating the various issues that are inseparable from a form of the novel that overlaps, by definition, into an independent branch of knowledge, the relationship that exists between Galdós' fundamental view of History and his techniques as a historical novelist will be clarified.

In the second part of the study, each Series of the *Episodios Nacionales* will be dealt with as a literary unit, as a set of solutions to the specific problems of literary expression or historical representation facing the novelist. Personal, circumstantial, and purely aesthetic factors will be analyzed as they apply to each of the literary units. The sequence of unit studies will reveal an ascendant line of artistic complexity and refinement, offering both a timetable and a comparative outline of Galdós' development as a historical novelist.

A study of the basic elements of novelistic fiction — in five extensive and consecutive literary units, involving some forty years of the artist's creative endeavor — will undoubtedly bring out factors in his growth as a historical novelist which will contribute, in turn, to a fuller understanding of Galdós' overall development as a creative writer. The diversity found in the *Episodios Nacionales* — of literary forms and techniques, of characterizational formulas and implementations, of linguistic appropriations and innovations — will constitute a useful addition to the knowledge already available concerning Galdós the novelist.

Finally, there will be certain clear limitations to our study, for a presentation of the scope outlined is not feasible except within specified limits. To begin with, the individual Episodio cannot be made the unit of detailed investigation, for the analysis of forty-six separate novels is well beyond the possibilities of an introductory study. In addition, selective criteria will have to be employed in a number of areas — characterization, for example — in which a more exhaustive approach is simply prohibitive.

PART I

GENERAL PROBLEMS AND BACKGROUND

These initial chapters deal with areas that are somewhat peripheral to the treatment of the *Episodios Nacionales* as art. In clarifying a variety of preliminary questions, they are intended to provide a background to Galdós' historical novel and an initial, synthetic idea of Galdós as a historical novelist. No claim is made to an exhaustive treatment of the various questions dealt with, for the subjects involved offer almost unlimited possibilities for further research.

The first chapter deals with three separate but interrelated questions: the relation of History to Art, little more than an acknowledgment of the traditional problem, the defining features of Galdós' work within the category of historical fiction, and the probable genesis of the *Episodios Nacionales*. The second chapter presents Galdós' concept of History and the nature of his didactic intent, and then employs these as a guide to understanding his practical approach to the past — sources, objectivity, selection — and his special manner of adapting a historical content to novelistic expression.

DEFINITION AND EXPLANATION

History and Art

The possible relationships that may hold between History and literature have long been a subject of controversy. The following paragraphs merely offer a summary of the question.[1]

History deals with what has occurred, while Art, however dependent on specific aspects of reality, may create what has never actually taken place. This simple outline of goals and possibilities constitutes the initial step to the Aristotelian distinction between History and Art.[2] From a distinction that does not itself separate mutually exclusive elements, the classical mind proceeded to a polarization of philosophical values that were inherent in its world-view. History merely reflected the succession of particulars in time, while Art expressed ideal universal categories.[3]

This manner of separation was strictly adhered to by numerous literary theorists of the Renaissance[4] and the alleged incompatibility between History and Art remained largely unaffected for centuries. With the gradual development of a philosophy of history Western thought abandoned the rigid distinction. Hegel's 'Idealist' Aesthetics eventually reflected an attitude which Romanticism had been implementing for years with a mass of historical fiction.[5]

In time, objections to the compatibility of History and Art arose from the opposite quarter: "En los mismos años en que Walter Scott imponía su manera a todas las literaturas europeas

---

1 For a more comprehensive presentation: E. Bernbaum, "The Views of the Great Critics on the Historical Novel," *PMLA*, XLI (1926), 424-441.

2 G. F. Else, *Aristotle's Poetics*: The Argument (Cambridge, 1957), pp. 301 ff.

3 K. Löwith, *Meaning in History* (Chicago, 1949), p. 4.

4 A. Alonso, *Ensayo sobre la novela histórica* (Buenos Aires, 1942), pp. 112-116.

5 G. Lukacs, *The Historical Novel*, trans. Hannah and Stanley Mitchell (London, 1962), pp. 19-30.

ya se discutía la incompatibilidad entre fantasía e historia."[6] Once considered unforgivable because History merely revealed phenomenal aspects of reality, the fusion of the two elements soon came to be regarded as detrimental to the new-found majesty of History itself. This new attitude is evident in the accusations provoked by the novels of Sir Walter Scott, and may even be found to underly Manzoni's critical judgments.[7]

More recently, Croce's new Idealism has suggested a fundamental tie between History and Art, a position strengthened, however ironically, by the development of a marxist aesthetic of the novel.[8] But the question of compatibility has remained a controversial one. So much so, that the matter is dealt with at length in most studies of the historical genre.[9]

The Historical Novel and the Episodios Nacionales

A piece of prose fiction may be defined as a historical novel if its elaboration suggests a primary goal of reconstructing history.[10] The Episodios Nacionales undoubtedly conform to this definition, but their subsequent classification as historical novels is of little practical value, since the criterion employed accommodates such vastly different novels as Ivanhoe, Salammbô, Notre Dame de Paris, and War and Peace.

As each generation contributes new forms and perspectives to the enrichment of this literary 'genre', a more precise general definition becomes less and less feasible. But patterns of variation do emerge within the broad category of historical fiction, and these patterns provide grounds for the establishment of useful subcategories. Literary criticism has proceeded along these lines, using a novelist's particular approach to History and the corresponding manner of historical reconstruction as basic cri-

---

6 E. Anderson Imbert, "Notas sobre la novela histórica en el siglo XIX," *Estudios sobre escritores de América* (Buenos Aires, 1954), p. 108.

7 See J. T. Hillhouse, *The Waverley Novels and Their Critics* (Minneapolis, 1936), pp. 94 ff.; and A. Manzoni, "Del Romanzo Storico," *Opere* (Milano, 1953), pp. 1056-1114.

8 B. Croce, "Teoria della Storia," *Filosofia, Poesia e Storia* (Milano-Napoli, 1952), pp. 444-445; and see Lukacs, *The Historical Novel*.

9 Alonso, *Ensayo*, p. 9 and H. Hinterhäuser, *Los Episodios Nacionales de Benito Pérez Galdós* (Madrid, 1963), pp. 223-232.

10 A. T. Sheppard, *The Art and Practice of Historical Fiction* (London, 1930), pp. 12-14; M. Kantor, "The Historical Novel," *Three Views of the Novel* (Washington, 1957), p. 30.

teria.[11] In this sense, the *Episodios Nacionales* are susceptible of more precise definition.

The following pages present and study the salient characteristics of the *Episodios Nacionales* as historical novels: Galdós' exclusive use of recent history, his specifically historical reconstruction of History, the national basis of his historical view, and his perception of History as social evolution.[12] The task of distinction will be facilitated somewhat by our use of a widely recognized form of historical fiction — the historical novel of Romanticism, hereafter referred to as the 'Romantic Novel'[13] — for comparison and contrast.

Some of the features underlined in this manner will clearly distinguish Galdós' historical novel; others, no less important for the precise definition of the work, are common to most modern historical novels and only slightly, if significantly, altered in Galdós' literary elaboration. Each characteristic stressed is offered, finally, in the context of European literature and thought, thus making it possible to view the *Episodios Nacionales* in the broadest perspective.

The *Episodios Nacionales* deal exclusively with nineteenth-century history. Amado Alonso has conveniently segregated a large group of novels of this type from the more traditional forms of historical fiction.[14] The novelists grouped in this way, including Galdós, rarely move further back than the French Revolution in their historical selection. This criterion of distinction is valid, since the 'Romantic Novel', for example, usually foregoes recent history as an art source.[15] In effect, between Scott and Galdós and between Galdós and Hugo or Manzoni, the most obvious difference is the area of history selected.

The marked departure from the present that so frequently characterizes the 'Romantic Novel' may be attributed, among other things, to the fundamental escapism that is often spoken of in connection with Romanticism.[16] The historical novel that

11 See, e.g., Alonso, *Ensayo,* p. 128; and Lukacs, *The Historical Novel,* pp. 81-88.
12 See G. Gómez de la Serna, *España en sus Episodios* (Madrid, 1954), p. 37.
13 L. Maigron, *Le roman historique à l'epoque romantique* (Paris, 1912).
14 *Ensayo,* p. 145.
15 Maigron, *Le roman historique,* pp. 3, 155-56.
16 E. Auerbach, *Mimesis,* trans. Willard Trask (New York, 1957), pp. 411-412.

13

deals with recent events is clearly related, on the other hand, to the preference for contemporary subjects that signals the advent of Realism. This change in sensibility is gradual but complete. Balzac's admiration for Scott is followed, for example, by Zola's utter bewilderment when confronted with the master's weakness for the English writer.[17] Between Scott and Balzac, in any case, the focus of the modern novel shifted from the past to the immediate present. Balzac, and later Tolstoy, set the norm for the historical novel of Realism, and a general trend ensued.[18]

Amado Alonso's useful list offers a distinct type of historical novelist, interested primarily in the present and consequently selecting only those events that were related to it. Everything that pre-dated the French Revolution, that touched but remotely on the post-revolutionary world, ceased to exercise fascination; while the recent past — viewed as an embryonic present — monopolized the writer's attention.

The works of Scott or Hugo, different as they may be in themselves, indicate the historical scope of the 'Romantic Novel'. These writers invariably selected a specific moment from the past, and their complete works often reveal a patch-work of isolated historical reconstructions. Each novel reproduces a specific segment of history, but continuity between these segments was alien to the novelist's conception.

Most historical novels are similar to the 'Romantic Novel' in this respect, involving the abstraction of a definite unit of time from the current of History. But the *Episodios Nacionales* present a fundamentally different conception. A rigorous chronological sequence between novels suggests Galdós' primary concern with presenting a historical continuum. In the perspective of nineteenth-century Spanish history, the *Episodios Nacionales* are more than just forty-six novels written over a period of forty years. Perhaps their most distinguishing trait as historical novels is this basic unity of conception.

What interested Galdós was the 'becoming' of modern Spain, and by merely reconstructing any specific moment of history,

---

[17] See H. de Balzac, "Avant-Propos," *Oeuvres Complètes,* I (Paris, 1912); and E. Zola, *Balzac,* no translator listed (Madrid, 1890), p. 69.

[18] Lukacs, *The Historical Novel,* pp. 84-85; and with respect to Spanish letters, see R. Brown, *La novela española. 1770-1850* (Madrid, 1953), p. 36.

even with several of his own Episodios, he could not have hoped to depict a process of historical development into the present. Consequently, Galdós' focus on the past as a continuum crystallizes in the novel as a chronological sequence of causally related events.[19]

This conception of the past in genetical relationship to the present, distilled from Vico's 'verum-factum', Voltaire's lay eschatology, and the historical thought of Kant and Herder,[20] became a fundamental postulate of the last century's view of reality. It, above all, makes exact and appropriate the usual reference to the nineteenth century as the Age of History, for reality was conceived as a development in time and only knowable, in fact, when viewed in the various phases of its realization. This fundamental 'historicism' is summarized by Tilgher as follows: "Il secolo XIX concepiva la realtà come Storia, e la Storia come progresso."[21]

This genetical view of the world is clearly manifested in the literature of the period. The reality reflected in art no longer imparts a static sensation, an assumed permanence in time. With Realism, it becomes synonymous with development. Present and causal past are fused in perception, the former lacking sense and substance without the latter.[22] Balzac, for example, rejected the flamboyant historical embellishments of Romanticism, but his literary works invariably presented reality as historical development.[23]

Nationalism is inseparable from modern historical thought. The nineteenth century envisioned historical development in terms of national entities, with peoples — whole peoples in an age of democracy — as the protagonists in an endless drama of progress and fulfillment. The subject of the historical process depicted in the *Episodios Nacionales* is Spain. The omnipresent national entity is never forgotten, never overshadowed by the

19 J. S. Pons, "Le roman et l'histoire. De Galdós à Valle-Inclán," *Hommage à Ernest Martinenche*. (Paris, 1939), p. 381.

20 B. Croce, *La filosofia di Giambattista Vico* (Bari, 1922), p. 257; Löwith, *Meaning in History*, p. 104; R. G. Collingwood, *Idea of History* (New York, 1956), pp. 89-99.

21 *Storia e antistoria* (Modena, 1928), p. 18.

22 G. Poulet, *Studies in Human Time*, trans. Elliott Coleman (Baltimore, 1956), pp. 31-32.

23 F. Brunetière, "La signification historique des romans de Balzac," *Honoré de Balzac* (Paris, 1906).

innumerable events, plots, and characters contained in the forty-six novels.[24]

The fact is that the 'Romantic Novel' also features a national setting, and even a degree of national pride.[25] But these general similarities often cloak intrinsic differences. One such difference issues from the nature of the Romantic's historical selection, for distant epochs are not adequate — under penalty of glaring anachronism — for expressing the diverse facets of modern nationalism. Many 'Romantic Novels' are consequently limited to indirect outpourings of national feeling. The *Episodios Nacionales*, on the other hand, give full expression to the democratized awareness of national values that distinguishes the nineteenth century.

In *Trafalgar*, from the very onset of the work, the reader is made to witness the birth of national consciousness in an unsophisticated man of the people. Araceli's awakening to Spain, complete with the 'mystique' of the past century's religion of nationality, sets the tone of the *Episodios Nacionales*:

> Me representé a mí país como una inmensa tierra poblada de gentes, todos fraternalmente unidos; me representé la sociedad dividida en familias, en las cuales había esposas que mantener, hijos que educar, hacienda que conservar, honra que defender; me hice cargo de un pacto establecido entre tantos seres para ayudarse y sostenerse contra un ataque de fuera, y comprendí que por todos habían sido hechos aquellos barcos para defender la patria, es decir, el terreno en que ponían sus plantas, el surco regado con su sudor, la casa donde vivían sus ancianos padres, el huerto donde jugaban sus hijos, la colonia descubierta y conquistada por sus ascendientes, el puerto donde amarraban su embarcación fatigada del largo viaje, el almacén donde depositaban sus riquezas; la iglesia, sarcófago de sus mayores, habitáculo de sus santos y arca de sus creencias; la plaza, recinto de sus alegres pasatiempos; el hogar doméstico, cuyos antiguos muebles, transmitidos de generación en generación, parecen el símbolo de la perpetuidad de las naciones; la cocina, en cuyas paredes ahumadas parece que no se extingue nunca el eco de los cuentos con que las abuelas amansan la travesura e inquietud de los nietos; el campo, el mar, el cielo; todo cuanto desde el nacer se asocia a nuestra existencia, desde el pesebre de un animal que-

---

[24] See Appendix I.

[25] G. Díaz-Plaja, "El manifiesto romántico de Ramón López-Soler. Con una nota preliminar sobre la influencia de Walter Scott, "*Introducción al estudio del Romanticismo español* (Madrid, 1942), Apéndice I.

rido hasta el trono de reyes patriarcales; todos los objetos en que vive prolongándose nuestra alma, como si el propio cuerpo no le bastara.[26]

The expression of national development is also conditioned by the limited scope of the 'Romantic Novel'. The literary reconstruction of isolated segments of the past is not conducive to a depiction of continual development, and thus often limits the illustration of nationality to a repetitive stress on fundamental ethnic and idiosyncratic peculiarities. The *Episodios Nacionales*, on the other hand, are especially organized — as a historical continuum — to offer a dynamic vision of national development, a 'becoming' that transcends any mere set of permanent national traits. Spain is envisioned, in Galdós' work, both as a set of traditional values, shared to some extent by all Spaniards, and as a dynamic complex of future possibilities, to be forged from the very conflicts that arise between Spaniards. This dynamic national entity is individualized to some degree in each character and each generation depicted.[27]

The introduction of a new social awareness into the methodology of the historical sciences is commonly attributed to the 'Romantic Novel', to Scott in particular.[28] This eventually transformed modern Historiography, which is characterized by a social perspective in keeping with the progressive democratization of nineteenth-century life.[29] Modern historical novels, following upon Scott's spectacular innovations, focus on a complete society as the object of artistic representation. In a sense, historical fiction incorporates a conscious sociological end.[30]

With respect to the *Episodios Nacionales*, good evidence of

26 B. Pérez Galdós, *Obras completas*, 3rd ed. (Madrid, 1950-1951), I, 241. All subsequent references to Galdós' *Obras completas* will be to this edition.

27 J. Schraibman, "Patria y patriotismo en los *Episodios Nacionales* de Galdós," *Boletín Informativo del Seminario de Derecho Político*, XXVII (August, 1962), 171-186; and see A. Lazaro, "España en su novelista: Galdós," *La verdad del pueblo español* (San Juan, Puerto Rico, 1939), pp. 67-84.

28 A. Reyes, *El deslinde* (México, 1944), p 101; and see G. P. Gooch, *History and Historians in the Nineteenth Century* (London, 1952), p. 435; and Maigron, *Le roman historique*, p. 208.

29 For Galdós understanding of the evolution outlined in this paragraph, see his acceptance speech as a member of the Spanish Royal Academy, *Discursos de la Real Academia Española*, 7 y 21 de febrero, 1897 (Madrid, 1897), pp. 26-27.

30 Lukacs, *The Historical Novel*, pp. 30-63, a Marxian interpretation of Scott, clearly reveals, despite its overemphatic stress on economic factors, the social consciousness that preludes the novel of Realism.

this phenomenon is their penetration into areas of national life that Galdós never again treated so extensively: the blood aristocracy, the arts, and rural Spain.[31] Another indication of the novelist's sociological intent is his jurisdictional dispute with Mesonero Romanos. The latter, an important source of information for Galdós, reserved the literary highlights between 1814 and 1833 for his own *Memorias de un Setentón,* while alloting the political history of the same period to Galdós. The novelist's reluctance to depict the reign of Ferdinand VII without incorporating everything of significance led to his breach of the limits stipulated by Mesonero Romanos.[32]

The sociological emphasis of the 'Romantic Novel' is readily differentiated, in most cases, from Galdós' orientation in the *Episodios Nacionales.* The Romantic's reconstruction of isolated segments of the past, however complete each segment may be in itself, limits the presentation to a society as it existed at a given moment in time. The *Episodios Nacionales,* conceived as a continuum, add dynamic force to a broad sociological scope. In Galdós' work the beliefs, the entertainment, the food, everything, in short, that constitutes a society is presented in the successive stages of a long evolution. It is this genetical view of society, the perception of History in terms of social development, which underlies Galdós' creation of the modern Spanish novel.[33]

Genesis of the Episodios Nacionales

Works advanced as precursors of the *Episodios Nacionales* invariably reveal some similarities to Galdós' historical novel. The degree of affinity and its importance to the genesis of the *Episodios Nacionales* can be determined, in each case, by a comparison with the characteristics underscored in the previous section. As noted there, the 'Romantic Novel' may be completely disregarded in this connection, a ruling that applies both to the

---

[31] See, e.g., G. Dendariena, "El pueblo de Madrid y las novelas de Galdós," *Galdós: su genio, su espiritualidad, su grandeza* (Madrid, 1922), pp. 3-20.

[32] E. Varela Hervias, *Cartas de Pérez Galdós a Mesonero Romanos* (Madrid, 1943), pp. 41-45.

[33] J. F. Montesinos, "Notas sueltas sobre la fortuna de Balzac en España," *Revue de Littérature Comparée,* XXIV (1950), 309-338.

Spanish Romantics who tried to imitate Scott and to those writers who revived a similar trend in Galdós' own day.[34]

Pedro Antonio de Alarcón, author of *Historietas Nacionales,* is Galdós' best known predecessor in the area of historical fiction,[35] but he is not a precursor of the *Episodios Nacionales.* A difference and a similarity are immediately apparent in their respective works: both employ nineteenth-century history, yet the *Episodios Nacionales* are novels and Alarcón's works are short stories. The one similarity noted — for Alarcón's stories reveal none of the other features pointed out in Galdós' historical novel — fades, moreover, when one considers the two novelists' basic treatment of the same period of history.

The quantity and quality of Galdós' documentation attests to a primarily historical intent. Alarcón, on the other hand, has little use for textual history; his sources are invariably folkloric and his intent primarily anecdotal.[36] Recent history only appealed to the writer when it offered pseudo-historical anecdotes, for which he was not averse to searching in epochs as remote as the sixteenth century. In effect, Alarcón's 'historical' selection could only find literary expression in short tales, which reveal little that would justify considering their author a precursor of the *Episodios Nacionales.*

Alonso Cortés has pointed out a group of lesser known novelists (Agustín Príncipe, López Montenegro, and others) that provides more ample grounds for comparison.[37] According to Alonso Cortés, the commercial success of such late novels as *Memorias de un liberal — Fernando el deseado* (1860) might have influenced Galdós' decision to fictionalize Spanish history. But even if this were true, it would hardly constitute grounds for attributing to such works a substantial role in the genesis of the *Episodios Nacionales.*

Much more pertinent, in this respect, is the historical scope of some of the aforementioned novels that deal with nineteenth-

34 See G. Zellers, "*La novela histórica en España,* 1828-1850 (New York, 1928); and E. Allison Peers, "Studies in the Influence of Sir Walter Scott in Spain," *Revue Hispanique,* LXVIII (1926), 1-160.

35 E. Huerta, "Galdós y la novela histórica," *Atenea,* LXXII (1943), 101.

36 J. F. Montesinos, *Pedro Antonio de Alarcón* (Zaragoza, 1955), pp. 49-80.

37 N. Alonso Cortés, "Precursores de Galdós," *Quevedo en el teatro y otros ensayos* (Valladolid, 1930).

century history. The literary reconstruction of the War of Independence, or of the entire reign of Ferdinand VII, brings to mind Galdós' presentation of a historical continuum in the *Episodios Nacionales*. The difference, although of degree, is nevertheless basic. The large segments of history depicted in such novels as *Historia pintoresca del reinado de Isabel II* are clearly circumscribed by specific historical limits, a war or a reign. There is little evidence, therefore, of anything resembling Galdós' conception of the recent past as continuous development into the present. However large, the segments are offered as isolated units of time, the author showing little or no concern for their causal organization as an embryonic present.

This fundamental difference in conception between the novels listed by Alonso Cortés and the *Episodios Nacionales* precludes any important similarity between the two in their depiction of nineteenth-century history as social evolution or national development. In neither area do these predecessors of Galdós offer the dynamic qualities that characterize the *Episodios Nacionales*. There is very little evidence, therefore, to support the contention that these works are, in any strict sense of the term, precursors of Galdós' historical novel.

It has been suggested that Erckmann's *Romans Nationaux* were the model for the *Episodios Nacionales*.[38] Although there are obvious similarities — the general title, the use of recent history, and the first-person narrative — they are not conclusive, and a more precise determination of the French writer's influence on Galdós is indicated.

Although the two works deal with recent history, a basic difference, albeit of degree, is evident. The historical continuity that distinguishes the *Episodios Nacionales* is neither as constant nor as relevant an aspect of Erckmann's novels. Even when considered a literary unit, the *Romans Nationaux* lack the cohesion and the scope of Galdós' historical fiction. A good example of this is Erckmann's abrupt passage from one heroic epoch (the Napoleonic era) to another (the Franco-Prussian War), which certainly renders historical continuity impossible.

The two works also differ significantly in their expression

---

[38] L. Louis-Lande, "Le roman patriotique en Espagne, *Episodios Nacionales*, par Galdós, Madrid 1873-75," *Revue des Deux Mondes*, XIV (1876), 936; and E. Gómez de Baquero, *Novelas y novelistas* (Madrid, 1918), p. 14.

of nationalism. Erckmann's militant pacifism led him to de-emphasize the nationalist fervor that underlies much of the history he treated. *Madame Thérèse*, for example, focuses on the French Revolution from a foreign point of view, and *Le conscrite de 1813* deliberately contrasts the peaceful values of life to the disruptive abuses of aggressive nationalism. Unlike Galdós, Erckmann was blind, for the most part, to the impact of nationalism on the formation of modern European states.

The manner and breadth of social representation is another factor that sets the two works apart. Erckmann's novels make no effort to incorporate some very important strata of nineteenth-century French society.[39] The *Romans Nationaux* reveal little interest in encompassing all the social forces that moulded nineteenth-century European history, and nothing could differ more from Galdós' intentions in the *Episodios Nacionales*.

It is clear, in general, that Erckmann did not seek to reconstruct the 'becoming' of a modern nation. He consequently lacked both the basic view of History and the broad historical scope identified with Galdós' work. The Spanish novelist's familiarity with Erckmann's novels may account for the similarities noted earlier, and perhaps even for Galdós' elaboration of the past in terms of specific historical episodes, but all this is insufficient, as we have seen, to justify considering the *Romans Nationaux* an indispensable model for the *Episodios Nacionales*.[40]

The absence of direct literary precedents makes it necessary to view the genesis of the *Episodios Nacionales* in a broader perspective. We have noted, in pointing out the main characteristics of Galdós' historical novel, that there exists, in most cases, a direct relationship with the basic features of Realism: a preferential focus on recent history, a genetical view of reality, an exclusively national interest, and an all-embracing sociological perspective.[41] Initially, however, this relationship offers little more than a loose blueprint, for European Realism produced nothing quite like the *Episodios Nacionales*.

39 Lukacs, *The Historical Novel*, p. 209.
40 For similar conclusions, although reached along somewhat different lines, see E. Gómez de Baquero, *El renacimiento de la novela española en el siglo XIX* (Madrid, 1924), p. 58; and S. de Madariaga, *Semblanzas literarias contemporáneas* (Barcelona, 1924), p. 72.
41 Auerbach, *Mimesis*, pp. 400-434; and for an identification of the *Episodios Nacionales* with the literary realism of Galdós' other novelistic works, see J. Casalduero, *Vida y Obra de Galdós* (Madrid, 1951), p. 50.

The error lies, of course, in seeking absolute correspondences. Balzac was Galdós' first important contact with the literature of Realism, and however much the latter's historical novels may differ from the *Comédie Humaine,* the French writer's works may serve as the basis for an enlightening comparison. Balzac, for example, presented Galdós with a genetical perspective that traced national development in the evolution of representative social institutions.[42] The 'Avant-Propos' to the *Comédie Humaine* reads, in fact, like a call to the Spanish novelist's program in the *Episodios Nacionales*: the artistic reconstruction of the 'becoming' of a modern nation.

To seek more specific correspondence between the two works would probably prove unfruitful, but even Galdós' deviations from the Balzacian outline offer valuable insights into the genesis of his historical novel. The Spanish novelist focused primarily on political history; the French writer, on economic development. The *Episodios Nacionales* were deliberately set in the past, while Balzac's work often touched on the present. The most obvious reasons for these basic discrepancies are, at the same time, the most enlightening: the two novelists lived more than a generation apart and reconstructed essentially different worlds.

The genetical, causal relationship between past and present that underlies both the *Comédie Humaine* and the *Episodios Nacionales* is qualitatively altered by the years that separate the work of the Balzac from that of Galdós. The determining factor is the extent to which each was removed in time from the complex of events that initiates modern European history.

The revolutionary upheavals that mark the beginning of modern French history were still close at hand for Balzac (1829). In the France of 1830 or 1835, one could speak of the French Revolution, the Napoleonic era or the Bourbon Restoration without referring to experiences several generations removed from the present. Balzac could novelize the full 'becoming' of modern France through fictional lives made active, without anachronism, in his very own day. It was quite unnecessary to write historical novels, as such, in order to trace a modern development from its inception.

[42] G. Lukacs, *Studies in European Realism,* trans. Edith Bone (London, 1950), pp. 40-45.

Galdós, on the other hand, could only depict a national development from epoch-making events in the recent past by employing the format of a historical novel. The Spain of 1868-1872 was causally linked, in his vision, with everything since Trafalgar (1805); but the direct bridge between the two, so believably effected in Balzac's day, was virtually impossible in the eighth decade of the century. A historical continuum longer than the active longevity of any believable character made it necessary to set the *Episodios Nacionales* in the past.

The distinction between Balzac's economic emphasis and Galdós' political focus is explained by the nature of the history that each reconstructed.

Balzac stressed what he obviously deemed the most important aspect of modern France, and political factors were often woven into a novelistic fabric that highlighted economic and social evolution. The history of Spain between 1805 and 1868 displayed a totally different complexion. Economic development, so manifestly central in Balzac's France, had no comparable place in the 'becoming' of modern Spain.[43] On the contrary, the latter's modern history is carried out, for the most part, on the ideological plane of politics, and Galdós' political emphasis in the *Episodios Nacionales* merely reflects the essential structure of historical reality.

When Galdós confronted modern Spain, his vision had incorporated the genetical perspective and the artistic methodology of Realism. In order to depict a meaningful causal development, however, Galdós had to begin by setting his work in the immediate past. The special character of Spain's modern history required, moreover, that his primary stress be political. The combination of these factors leads, inevitably, to the creation of historical fiction.

All that precedes must be viewed, finally, in the light of important personal factors, in conjunction with what is known about Galdós, the man and the writer. We shall follow, to this end, a method of successive delimitations, until all meaningful factors, both general and specific, have been touched.

Galdós' inclination toward History is evident as early as *La Fontana de Oro* (1868). It is an unmistakable trait of the young writer, but can be dangerously misleading if over-

---

[43] K. Marx and F. Engels, *Revolution in Spain* (New York, 1939).

simplified.[44] Berkowitz's biography of Galdós stresses the child's early and enthusiastic contact with the history of the nineteenth century,[45] but the writer's decisive inclination is only truly meaningful as a function of his political and intellectual environment.

It is significant, for example, that Galdós reached maturity precisely while Spain was undergoing the severest political readjustment of the century, that his intense preoccupation with Spainish history crystallized during the years of unabated crisis (1868-1872) that preceded the publication of *Trafalgar*. In the words of Gómez de Baquero: "La electricidad histórica del momento comunicó a la obra de Galdós la vocación y el sentido de la historia."[46]

The young novelist's intellectual environment is even more important in this respect. The historical matrix of nineteenth-century thought was gradually introduced, about mid-century, to a Spain that had belatedly awakened to the European community.[47] A study of Rafael Altamira y Crevea, the Spanish historian, traces the subsequent infiltration of 'historicism' into every area of Spain's intellectual life.[48] The new sensibility passed from Milá y Fontanals to Menéndez y Pelayo, and, as part of Krausian philosophy, from Sanz del Río to his many disciples.[49] Galdós lived for years before 1872 in an intellectual atmosphere that Azcárate would shortly consider over-saturated with 'historicism':

> Hubo tiempos en que era preciso demostrar que la pura historia es ciencia. . . . Hoy, si acaso, hay que poner coto a las pretensiones de aquélla cuando se propende a ensanchar indebidamente su propia esfera.[50]

What has been pointed out so far could apply, as well, to any number of Galdós' contemporaries. This calls for a further probe into the novelist's biography, because what surprises in

[44] See, e.g., R. de Mesa, "Gènesis de los *Episodios Nacionales*," *Revista de Libros*, III (1919), 33-46.
[45] H. C. Berkowitz, *Pérez Galdós, Spanish Liberal Crusader* (Madison, 1948), pp. 9, 21.
[46] *El renacimiento de la novela*, p. 54.
[47] See, e.g., J. López-Morillas, *El Krausismo español* (Mexico, 1956), p 191.
[48] *La enseñanza de la historia* (Madrid, 1895).
[49] Ibid., p. 140; and see P. Laín Entralgo, *Menéndez y Pelayo* (Barcelona, 1945), p. 117.
[50] This is found in Azcárate's prologue to R. Altamira y Crevea, *Historia de la propiedad comunal* (Madrid, 1890).

Galdós, for example, is not that he should have read Balzac — a writer known to Spaniards for decades before 1867 — but that only he, in his generation, should have identified himself with the new concept of reality found in that French writer.

Galdós' fundamental liberalism is, in this sense, his most distinguishing personal trait. The group of writers often referred to as the 'generation of 1868' remained largely indifferent to the revolutionary movement that identifies it as an entity. Almost all the literary figures so classified — older than Galdós in every case — had cast their political and social philosophies before the Revolution of 1868, so that only Galdós is adequately identified by that political association.

Galdós' liberalism must be understood in its widest philosophical connotation: the capacity to await and accept innovations, the ability to envision reality (social, political, etc.) in its possibilities of change. This basic attitude, which underlies Berkowitz's biography of Galdós, was an essential prerequisite to the historical perspective offered in the *Episodios Nacionales*, and indispensable, as well, to the writer credited with renovating the Spanish novel.

An insular origin also distinguishes Galdós from most of his contemporaries, for the novelist did not reach Spain until his nineteenth year (1862). Galdós eventually became as peninsular as any Spaniard, with but one important difference: the first impression of discovery on a sensibility free from the blunting effect of prolonged contact. Alongside *El escándalo* or *El sombrero de tres picos*, *Pepita Jiménez* or *Juanita la larga*, *Peñas arriba* or *Sotileza*, the Spain reproduced anywhere in Galdós' work reveals the penetration of a fresh critical vision.

CHAPTER II

HISTORY IN THE *EPISODIOS NACIONALES*

Fundamentals: *View of History, Didactic Intent, and Variations*

The nineteenth century looked upon History, for the most part, as dialectical continuity.[1] Unlike novelists who interpreted its structure in terms of personal 'a priori' concepts,[2] Galdós reconstructed the past strictly within that fundamental view, from which his conception of the *Episodios Nacionales* — a historical continuum — issues directly:[3]

> Cosas y personas mueren, y la Historia es encadenamiento de vidas y sucesos, imagen de la Naturaleza, que de los despojos de una existencia hace otras y se alimenta de la propia muerte. El continuo engendrar de unos hechos en el vientre de otros es la Historia, hija del Ayer, hermana del Hoy y madre del Mañana.[4]

The fact that the novels of each Series are linked by common plots and characters provides an organic basis for the chronological sequence of historical events. Some 370 fictional characters appear in successive volumes, and each helps to underscore the human continuity of History. The Series are themselves linked in this manner, with some 104 fictional beings connecting the five units to simulate the dynamic progression of nineteenth-century Spanish history.[5] The dialectical structure of Galdós' historical continuum is expressly emphasized by the way in which the various Series are interrelated. The Second begins, for example, with the final chapter of the War of Independence, which is the subject matter of the First Series, and ends with the inception of the Carlist War, the subject matter of the following Series. This interlocking of historical epochs projects a fundamental dialectic.

---

[1] See P. Geyl, *Use and Abuse of History* (New Haven, 1955), pp. 31-32.
[2] See, e.g., I. Berlin, *The Hedgehog and the Fox* (New York, 1957), p. 46.
[3] See C. Clavería, "El pensamiento histórico de Galdós," *Revista Nacional de Cultura*, Caracas, XIX (1957), 170-177.
[4] B. Pérez Galdós, *Obras completas*, II, 1372.
[5] For a summary of the function of reappearing characters in the *Episodios*, see Hinterhäuser, pp. 276-284.

Galdós' view of History is not a novelty in itself, but his literary reconstruction in accordance with its specifications was a pioneering venture. No historical novelist before Galdós appears so concerned with reproducing the essential structure of historical reality. This goal, which no more implies the subordination of Art to History than Balzac's novel implies the subordination of Art to Social Dynamics, is evidently within the aesthetic aspirations of Realism.[6]

Didacticism is an essential facet of historical fiction in general. The romantic novelist's treatment of a remote past can be said to teach History, even if it be nothing more than ornamental erudition. Other historical novelists are more specific in their intent, substantiating a thesis, for example, by selecting a moment from the past that appears to confirm their viewpoint. Another didactic approach, which embodies the specific value of History as a method of imparting knowledge in the classical world-view,[7] consists of throwing light on particular aspects of the present by means of concrete examples from the past. This use of History, henceforth referred to as exemplary, involves but one criterion of selection: a basic similarity to the present.

Galdós' didacticism in the *Episodios Nacionales* goes beyond the aforementioned categories. Each volume introduces a personage or reconstructs an event of historical significance, but in addition to rendering History amenable his treatment implies a much broader didactic goal: to facilitate the understanding of the present by tracing the process of its realization. As Ricardo Gullón, one of his most recent commentators, has put it:

> Su intención era manejar la historia como algo vivo, sin arqueología, sintiéndola emocionalmente dentro de sí, operando y formando parte de la patria. Galdós quería hacer inteligible lo pasado para dar sentido a lo presente. La España contemporánea y el hombre español, cuyo conocimiento le importa, no pueden entenderse sin la referencia constante a un ayer contenido dentro del hoy en que el novelista vivía.[8]

This intent can be clarified by a comparative examination of the novelist's diverse efforts in the field of historical fiction.

6 R. Altamira y Crevea, "La mujer en la novela de Galdós," *Atenea*, LXXII (1943), 158-159; and Casalduero, *Vida y obra*, p. 50.

7 A. J. Toynbee, *Greek Historical Thought* (New York, 1952), p. 43.

8 *Galdós, novelista moderno* (Madrid, 1960), p. 151.

None of Galdós' historical novels are in the romantic tradition, that is, completely removed from the present; nor do any treat History as a sounding board for abstract theses. In *La Fontana de Oro* and *El audaz*, however, Galdós selected periods of history with marked similarities to the years 1867-1870, in which they were elaborated:

> .... me ha parecido de alguna oportunidad en los días que atravesamos, por la relación que pudiera encontrarse entre muchos sucesos aquí referidos y algo de lo que aquí pasa; relación nacida, sin duda, de la semejanza que la crisis actual tiene con el memorable período de 1820-23.[9]

In these two historical novels, which precede the *Episodios Nacionales*, Galdós selected his subject matter with an eye to making his readers aware of a specific political situation in the present. The relation thus established between past and present, strictly on the basis of similarity, is exemplary and not causal. The *Episodios Nacionales* were written, on the other hand, for an entirely different purpose. Spanish history between 1872 and 1879 bears little resemblance to that being novelized, precisely during those years, within the first twenty Episodios. It is clear, therefore, that Galdós had no intention of drawing examples from History; but sought, instead, to emphasize the 'becoming' of the present from the past.

It is significant, as well, that *La Fontana de Oro* and *El audaz* are completely independent literary works, instants abstracted from History without regard to chronological sequence or causal relationship. It was not necessary to reconstruct the past as an organically linked continuum in order to bring out a pertinent similarity to the present. This only became necessary in the *Episodios Nacionales*, when Galdós set himself the task of tracing the development of the present from the substance of the past.[10]

Galdós' literary career practically begins (1872) and ends (1912) with the *Episodios Nacionales*. Forty years is such a long period of time that the novelist could have significantly altered his approach to History, the basic view and the didactic intent pointed out above. There are, in effect, some immediately

---

[9] B. Pérez Galdós, "Prólogo," *La Fontana de Oro* (Madrid, 1906).

[10] For somewhat different opinions on this matter, and even a view of these two novels as an integral part of the *Episodios Nacionales*, see J. Torres Bodet, *Tres inventores de realidad* (México, 1955), p. 227; and Casalduero, *Vida y obra*, p. 49.

perceptible differences between Episodios, differences that should be studied in order to determine the extent to which they reflect important changes in the novelist's approach to his subject.

A distinction is frequently made, for example, on the basis of the general literary tone of each Series. The epic tone of the First Series is often contrasted to the dramatic qualities of the Second,[11] a procedure that is readily extended to the remaining units: the Third Series, melodramatic; the Fourth, paradoxical; and the Fifth, farcical. But these essentially literary variations do not indicate any significant changes in Galdós' approach to History.

Galdós did not alter his point of view from Series to Series; but merely reinforced, in plot and characterization, the variety of tones that anyone may perceive in historical works, however objectively documented. And there is no question of Galdós having interpolated anachronistic tones, for History is often adamant in the imposition of certain artistic conditions. It never occurred to Valle-Inclán to create an 'esperpento' dealing with the War of Independence, just as it could never have entered Galdós' mind to press an epic quality onto the reign of Isabel II.

Another distinction, made on the basis of an alleged predominance of either history or fiction, affects the individual Episodios within a Series. *Zaragoza* is used as an example of historical density and *Cádiz*, of the opposite phenomenon.[12] These examples suffice to point up the nature of the difference, which turns out to be nothing more, in fact, than a relationship that must always exist, to some degree, between historical quality and fictional quantity. Galdós grasped the inherent interest of a heroic siege like Zaragoza, and understood that its literary version required a minimum of novelistic stress.[13] He also realized, in the case of the other example noted, that the 'Cortes de Cádiz' lacked sustained interest, that the novelization required a great deal more fictional involvement.

11 See, e.g., Gómez de Baquero, *Novelas y novelistas*, p. 16.
12 F. C. Sainz de Robles, "Benito Pérez Galdós: su vida, su obra y su época," in Pérez Galdós, *Obras completas*, I, 149.
For diametrically opposed views on the relative historical density of the different Series, with which these pages do not deal, see, e.g., Barja, *Libros y autores modernos* (Los Angeles, 1933), p. 593; and R. Altamira, "La mujer en la novela de Galdós," *Atenea*, LXXII (1943), 154.
13 See S. Gilman, "Realism and Epic in Galdós' Zaragoza," *Homenaje a Archer M. Huntington* (Wellesley, Mass., 1952), pp. 171-192.

These differences between Episodios, for the most part matters of literary contingency, reflect no basic changes in Galdós' view of History. Moreover, the criterion of distinction itself — the relative quantity of historical content — prompts a number of serious objections. To begin with, allowances must be made for the nature of the historical subject. A siege like that of Gerona, concentrated in space and extended in time, cannot be novelized in the same way as the battle of Arapiles, geographically dispersed — if preliminary maneuvering is to be included — and relatively concentrated in time. A more serious objection strikes at the very heart of the criterion, pointing out the extreme difficulty involved in separating fictional from historical content in the *Episodios Nacionales*, a question with which we shall deal shortly.

An obvious shift in the presentation of History distinguishes the First and Second Series from the last three, that is, the *Episodios Nacionales* of the first epoch from those written after 1898. History is in both cases reconstructed through fictional characters, but protagonists like Calpena, Fajardo, and Liviano (3rd, 4th, and 5th Series, respectively), unlike Araceli and Monsalud before them (1st and 2nd Series), are not made to identify intimately with the public events of their day. In the later Series, therefore, events are at times narrated from without, as spectacles.[14]

A number of reasons can be ascertained for the relative historical detachment of the last three Series. To begin with, the novelist was dealing with a historical diminuendo. Galdós could readily identify, through actively engaged protagonists (Araceli, Monsalud), with Spain's vital struggle for independence and subsequent clamor for liberty; but he reserved an ironical observer's position, through major protagonists who are spectators, for depicting the listless and undirected history between 1834 and 1880. This attitude, which has its reason for being in the historical subject matter itself, is conditioned by chronology, for the nature of the period between 1834 and 1880 only became acutely evident after 1898.[15]

In the Third and Fourth Series, the phenomenon in question is greatly attenuated by the appearance of protagonists

14 E. G. Gamero y de Laiglesia, *Galdós y su obra*, I (Madrid, 1934), 253.
15 Casalduero, *Vida y Obra*, p. 207.

other than Calpena and Fajardo. Zoilo Arratia, Santiago Ibero, and many others are directly involved in the events depicted, and they effectively carry on the norm of the earlier Series. But in the Fifth Series, in the last four *Episodios Nacionales* particularly, a factor is present that precludes the attenuation just suggested. Liviano, a spectator through and through, fascinates Galdós to the point of excluding all other important characters, and the reason for this lies in the basic similarity, in the chronological coincidence of author and character.[16] Galdós-Liviano recalls events witnessed personally and re-lives himself in the process. The autobiographical prevails over the historical.

In any case, the reasons and qualifications noted once again suggest that the differences studied do not reflect important changes in the novelist's fundamental conception of historical reality.

In commenting upon the last four *Episodios Nacionales,* Casalduero has observed, finally, that Galdós wrote the history of 1874 with an eye to that of 1907. The critic subsequently deduced a basic alteration in the novelist's approach to History:

> Antes hacía depender el presente del pasado, de manera positivista se consideraba el presente como efecto del pasado, la causa; ahora ve como todo el pasado se organiza e interpreta desde el presente.[17]

Such a broad generalization is unwarranted from the critic's observation that Galdós, in the process of re-creating a period of the past, stressed aspects of that past which were similar to events occurring in his own day. The novelist was not averse to emphasizing — in exemplary fashion — the similarities that appeared between past and present in the process of his noveliation,[18] but the only factor of importance is that the past is never altered for the sake of that emphasis, that it in no way ceases to function as a causal explanation of the present.

The Use of History: Sources, Intuition, Objectivity, and Selection

El conflicto entre la información y la invención no existe

---

[16] See, e.g., W. T. Pattison, *Galdós and the Creative Process* (Minneapolis, 1954), p. 8.
[17] Casalduero, *Vida y Obra,* p. 207.
[18] See, e.g., the unpubl. diss. (University of Southern California, 1948) by D. B. Swett, "A Study of the Carlist Wars as a Literary Theme in the *Episodios Nacionales* of Pérez Galdós," pp. 241-242.

cuando los temas son de un pasado reciente, donde los autores pueden ajustarse en lo propiamente histórico al clásico 'famas sequere' y en lo ambiental, cuando más, a unos cuantos toques costumbristas.[19]

Amado Alonso's formula may be valid for novels that employ historical settings as incidental background; but it does not explain the careful documentation of the *Episodios Nacionales,* in which History itself is a primary object.

Galdós relied heavily on the historian, because only the latter's method guaranteed precision and objectivity.[20] This reliance on the history text did not preclude the use of more direct sources. Galdós reconstructed aspects of the past which are not normally found in history texts (fashions and feelings, for example), and newspapers, archives, and literature were often employed to this end.[21]

The novelist's preference for direct accounts of personal experiences led him to favor the published memoir as a source of documentation.[22] Unfortunately, this literary form was relatively scarce in Spain, a circumstance which Galdós openly decried since it forced him to enlist such works as Koska y Vayo's *Historia de la vida y el reinado de Fernando VII,* in which a faltering historical discipline was the price to be paid for the authenticity of personal observation.[23]

This dearth of memoir literature accounts, as well, for Galdós' repeated use of an alternate source of history as personal experience: the personal interview, of which relatively little is known, naturally, since it leaves no traces. There is ample evidence, to be sure, of the direct cooperation between Galdós and Mesonero Romanos,[24] and scattered indications appear of the novelist's interviews with such important personalities as

19 Alonso, *Ensayo,* p. 145.

20 See, among other titles listed in the bibliography, M. Bataillon, "Les sources historiques de *Zaragoza*," *Bulletin Hispanique,* XXIII (1921), 129-141; and G. Boussagol, "Sources et composition du *Zumalacárregui*," *Bulletin Hispanique,* XXVI (1924), 241-254.

21   Berkowitz, *Perez Galdós,* pp. 108-112; and for the provocative suggestion of pictorial sources, see Hinterhäuser, *Los Episodios Nacionales,* pp. 79-88.

22 See Pattison, *Galdós and the Creative Process,* p. 16; and for a list of titles, see Berkowitz, *La biblioteca de Galdós* (Las Palmas, 1951).

23 Pérez Galdós, *Episodios Nacionales,* X (Madrid, 1881), iv.

24 E. Varela Hervías, *Cartas;* and see J. F. Montesinos, *Costumbrismo y novela* (Los Angeles, 1960), p. 73.

Isabel II and Cabrera;[25] but practically nothing is available concerning the countless witnesses that Galdós must have questioned during his travels through Spain.[26] The author's friendship with Sagasta, Cánovas del Castillo, and other important figures of the nineteenth century is another direct source of documentation the significance of which it is virtually impossible to establish with any degree of precision.

The *Episodios Nacionales* integrate and fuse information obtained from the most diverse sources. The descriptive narrations of newspapers and texts, the ideas and sensations of personal memoirs, and the emotion-filled reminiscences of countless witnesses contribute collectively to Galdós' version of nineteenth-century Spain. This naturally reduces the value of compiling Galdós' textual sources, for one cannot achieve a practical distinction between information and artistic elaboration by simply isolating what might have been taken from a specific history book. The novelist's preference for History as personal experience, his extensive use of personal interviews, makes it futile, in effect, to attempt an absolute differentiation between what the author received from outside sources and what was due to his creative imagination. The work of art does not lend itself to a scientific separation of components

Deduction and induction are inadequate, in their usual application, for dealing with unique historical phenomena; while any predominantly intuitive method is repugnant to the basic precepts of methodological objectivity.[27] The scientific study of History proceeds, within these limits, to judgments that are based on data susceptible of verification or proof.[28]

Scientific limitations are especially evident in matters concerning daily life, in the reproduction of those myriad personal details that constitute the human basis of History. The past

25 See, e.g., J. B. Trend, *Origins of Modern Spain* (New York, 1934), pp. 15-16; and Pérez Galdós, *Memoranda* (Madrid, 1906), pp. 17-34.

26 For some indications of this, see Pérez Galdós, *Memorias,* ed. A. Ghiraldo (Madrid, 1930), pp. 57, 223; Varela Hervias, *Cartas,* pp. 45-46, 51; and R. Ricard, "Note sur la genèse de *Aita Tettauen,*" *Bulletin Hispanique,* XXXVII (1935), 475.

27 See, e.g., Reyes, *El Deslinde,* pp. 137-138; and Collingwood, *Idea of History,* p. 190.

28 R. G. Collingwood, *Historical Imagination* (Oxford, 1935), pp. 17-18; and for a thorough discussion of the problem, see E. Nagel, *The Structure of Science* (New York, 1961), pp. 576-606.

yields little documentary evidence in this area, and the historian is justified, as we have seen, in resisting an intuitive extension. The novelist has no such obligation. In fact, it is his business to posit, by the use of his imagination, and intuition, a credible interpretation of reality. In these circumstances, even the historian is apt to recognize the value of artistic intuition: ". . . han sabido acertar con la nota fundamental de una época, mediante la nota artística del conjunto que casi siempre escapa al análisis de los eruditos."[29]

With an artistic sensibility alert to a multitude of intuitive possibilities, and a reasonable check on the intuitive faculty itself, Galdós believably augmented the textual blueprint. This is best observed in Episodios with a great accumulation of textual information, those in which the novelist's intuitive faculty is held in greatest restraint. Bataillon has shown, for example, that much of Zaragoza stems directly from specific sources, that Galdós added nothing in the way of historical content.[30] His contributions were clearly those of the novelist: 1) subjecting the agents of History to elemental human conditions; 2) effecting the realistic individuation of persons and things; 3) establishing the connections that provide cohesion to the historical depiction; and, 4) bringing into sharp focus the fundamental character of the period.[31]

The range and depth of human content that an artistic sensibility may glean from a limited number of facts constitutes Galdós' most important contribution to the history depicted in the Episodios Nacionales. This is most clearly evident in the novelist's handling of historical characters. Galdós' presentation of Cabrera, for example, incorporates human traits often missing from the historian's version of the personage's public activities. The novelist focused on the barbaric warlord in intuited moments of private human behavior, thus raising the historical silhouette to a new level of reality.[32]

An immediate effect of the scientific approach to History is the depersonalization of events and epochs. The scholar must

29 Altamira y Crevea, La enseñanza, p. 240.
30 Bataillon, "Les sources historiques de Zaragoza," Bulletin Hispanique, XXIII (1921), 134.
31 See, e.g., Gilman, Homenaje a A. M. Huntington, p. 179.
32 See G. Marañón, "El mundo por la claraboya," Insula, LXXXII (1952), 1-2.

sacrifice emphasis on what is fundamentally human to precision in the general outline of results. The name and date of a battle, its description in terms of regimental numbers, is all he requires in order to point out the transcendental effects of the action. He cannot be similarly attracted by the psychological state of a representative combatant; nor, if he were, could he actually reproduce it. In attempting to relive the past as personal human experience, the historian would approach the novelist's goal: to recast generic entities (people, soldiers, workers, etc.) into concrete and representative human beings. The novelist literally repeoples History, so that it may again be lived in human terms.

Galdós' intuitive elaborations are neither whimsical nor arbitrary, but issue naturally from the basic difference between historical narration and novelization. It is imperative, in the latter case, to actualize by means of representation. The novelist must fill the void between the historian's lines or fail in the crucial literary task of transforming narration into representation. More complex intuitive operations only occur, as a rule, when inconclusive or fragmentary sources demand a more radical essay of the author's faculties.[33]

Anderson Imbert's remarks on the modern historical novel go directly to the heart of the question of objectivity:

> En los mismos años en que Walter Scott imponía su manera a todas las literaturas europeas ya se discutía la incompatibilidad entre fantasía e historia. El ideal de verdad pudo al fin más; y la novela histórica entró en crisis como género artístico y se transformó en historia novelada.[34]

The ideal of truth to which the critic refers, a crucial factor in the Aesthetics of Realism,[35] led novelists to coincide with historians in a basic criterion of value, and the former to seek historical standards in reconstructing the past.

Galdós' impartial selection of textual sources, his undistorted and precise use of the data they provided, have been demonstrated in a number of studies.[36] An indication of his reputation

33 See, e.g., Varela Hervias, *Cartas*, pp. 22, 45-46, 47, 51.
34 *Estudios*, p. 108.
35 See Lukacs, *Studies*, p. 71; Auerbach, *Mimesis*, p. 428; and for a general review of the question, see R. Wellek, "The Concept of Realism in Literary Scholarship," *Neophilologus*, XLV (1961), 1-20.
36 See, among other titles listed in the bibliography, C. Vázquez Arjona, "Cotejo histórico de cinco Episodios," *Revue Hispanique*, LXVIII, no. 154 (1926), 321-505.

for dealing objectively with History is Gooch's comment: "No survey could ignore the historical novels of Pérez Galdós . . ."[37] And the few who seriously question the novelist's handling of historical reality, critics like Louis-Lande and Contreras, are hardly impartial themselves for chauvinistic and religious reasons, and the extent and substance of their objections must be judged accordingly.[38]

Most noteworthy, however, is the fact that Galdós' objectivity extends to the very process of selection that determines what personages and events are to be stressed. This process is at once the most decisive function in novelizing History and that in which partiality is least detectable. Galdós, although clearly identified with a particular ideology, approached the past with balanced judgment in this respect:

> A él jamás se le ocurrió, al tratar de nuestras guerras civiles, considerar ajena a España aquella parte de la nación donde la realidad política y social se manifestaba con carácter más violento.[39]

This degree of objectivity is best understood as a function of Galdós' didactic intent in the *Episodios Nacionales*, which, in order to reflect the 'becoming' of modern Spain, had to incorporate every significant factor of the developmental process. This indispensable prerequisite — and the fallacy of extending political and ideological prejudices into the past — may have been brought home to Galdós through his friendship with Pereda and Menéndez y Pelayo. Both men were living proof of the other Spain's contributions to Galdós' own environment, forceful reminders that the present, in so far as it included such figures, could hardly be intelligible without a knowledge of the specific past in which they were rooted as thinkers and men.

Galdós' balanced approach to nineteenth-century Spanish history, the express intention to disregard nothing on subjective grounds, did not necessarily require that as a man he renounce any part of his ideology. This is fortunate, for an attempt to do so would surely have failed, or, worse yet, would have deprived the author of an organizing point of view. It is clear that Galdós

---

[37] *History and Historians*, p. 409.
[38] Louis-Lande, "Le roman patriotique en Espagne," *Revue des Deux Mondes*, XIV (1876), 939-940; and R. A. Contreras, "La evolución galdosiana," *Razón y Fe*, XX (1908), 89-92.
[39] Lázaro, *La verdad del pueblo español*, p. 67.

postulated a liberal destiny for modern Spain, and this is reflected in the *Episodios Nacionales*. Although both 'Spains' are vigorously criticized as historical manifestations (governments, leaders, and policies), Galdós' liberalism operates constantly on the abstract level of ideology. In the case of the liberal creed, for example, he attacked only the incidental, the various Spanish versions; while in that of Carlism, for instance, the blow was directed at the very roots. But even this must be qualified:

> Al mismo tiempo, su concepción liberal del mundo, reconocimiento de los contrarios como necesidad interna de toda historia progresiva, hacía que su fachada de novelista comprometido, que siempre supone una mutilación, careciese de la adustez de lo sistemático, de lo rígido y de lo 'ideológico.'[40]

This approach to History, which can hardly be considered partisan, is further attenuated by a practical awareness of the Spaniard's tendency to identify with a leader rather than an ideology, of the difference the Spaniard draws between censoring Carlism, for example, and ridiculing Don Carlos or slandering Zumalacárregui. The *Episodios Nacionales* are notably free from 'ad hominem' expressions.[41] This sets Galdós apart from other novelists who used nineteenth-century Spanish history and explains the measure of tolerance with which Spaniards received even those Episodios which treat extremely controversial epochs.[42]

Publication always imposes the decisive task of selection. All historical novelists are naturally limited, first of all, to aspects of the past that lend themselves to literary elaboration. Beyond this general criterion, however, each is a world unto himself.[43] The problem is simplified at this stage of our study by a foreknowledge of Galdós' didactic intent in the *Episodios Nacionales*. The following criteria of historical selection are readily deduced therefrom: 1) to avoid mutilating historical continuity; 2) to bring into relief the dialectical relationship of successive historical epochs; and, 3) to achieve as representative a historical reconstruction as possible.

40 D. Pérez Minik, "Libre plática con Galdós," *Novelistas españoles de los siglos XIX y XX* (Madrid, 1957), p. 91.
41 See Torres Bodet, *Tres inventores de realidad*, pp. 237-238; and Sainz de Robles, "B. Pérez Galdós: su vida, su obra y su época," p. 147.
42 Sainz de Robles, "B. Pérez Galdós: su vida, su obra y su época," p. 166.
43 For a general view of the problem, see Sheppard, *The Art and Practice of Historical Fiction*, pp. 111-134.

The critic cannot always rely on a direct comparison of history text and literary elaboration, since the novelist's criteria may require the choice of a relatively unimportant element over others of greater relevance in the history text. As it happens, Galdós' views usually coincided with those of the historian, and most Episodios are centered precisely on the historical events that figure most prominently in the text. When the novelist deviates from this general norm, an examination in terms of his criteria of selection invariably reveals a profound grasp of nineteenth-century Spanish history and an unerring appraisal of its literary potential.

A case in point is *Montes de Oca,* an Episodio from the Third Series about which some question has been raised concerning the merits of the personage who serves as the historical nucleus.[44] In effect, the work in question might appear somewhat out of place alongside such titles as *Zumalacárregui, Mendizábal,* and *Espartero.* Its inclusion is understandable, however, in the light of what has previously been established as the author's third criterion of historical selection, namely, the achievement of a representative historical rendering.

Montes de Oca's appeal lies in the opportunity he affords to depict an essential quality of his epoch. Other 'cristinos' were more influential, and certainly more efficient and successful in their political maneuverings, but no other figure of that time so completely personified its spirit. An entire epoch of political romanticism is admirably synthesized in Montes de Oca's quixotic pronunciamento, and Galdós' re-creation of his life and death offers a profound insight into the soul of an age.

The very first volume of the *Episodios Nacionales* is an excellent example of the application of Galdós' first two criteria of historical selection. No specific history text suggested Trafalgar as a starting point. In fact, the only evidence available points to chance as the predominant factor in its selection.[45] It is nevertheless true that the great naval battle is uniquely appropriate to the introduction of the dialectical continuity of the *Episodios Nacionales.* It represents both a beginning and an end, the great 'borrón y cuenta nueva' that introduces modern Spanish history.[46]

44 Gamero y de Laiglesia, *Galdós y su obra,* I, 235.
45 See Pérez Galdós, *Memorias,* p. 56; and Berkowitz, *Pérez Galdós,* pp. 87-88.
46 Huerta, "Galdós y la novela histórica," *Atenea,* LXXII (1943), 102.

The two sieges of the First Series (Zaragoza and Gerona) will provide us with a general idea of the issues provoked by the process of historical selection. No one has questioned their historical significance as events; but the traditional valor of the Iberian city is adequately dealt with in *Zaragoza,* and *Gerona* — which follows it in the Series — might appear redundant. The redundancy is twofold: the elaboration of almost identical events, and their juxtaposition in the sequence of historical reconstructions.

Again, a closer examination reveals Galdós' thorough understanding of the history dealt with in the *Episodios Nacionales.* The two historical sieges are clearly differentiated by the nature of their respective historical agents. The quality of the agent was, of course, crucial to the history-minded nineteenth century, and the subject of far-reaching controversy. The age that placed a premium on the concept of 'people' as a historical entity tended, naturally enough, to deny functional significance to the individual hero.[47] A reaction to this tendency almost simultaneously prompted the opposite view, that of the individual as history-maker.[48]

Galdós' sieges offer a sensible appraisal of both theoretical extremes. In *Zaragoza* and *Gerona,* both the 'people' and the individual hero appear as historical forces, but each is made the primary factor in one of the works. Palafox and Alvarez de Castro embody this qualitative distinction. The first personifies the popular will of Zaragoza, which could have found another in whom to mirror itself, and which would, in any case, have risen to the heroic occasion.[49] Alvarez de Castro, on the other hand, is himself the will to resist, and he dominates Gerona instead of personifying it.[50]

Furthermore, only a contiguous presentation of the two sieges could bring the contrast of historical perspectives into sharp relief, and thus qualify the widely accepted notion of a strictly 'popular' War of Independence. Needless to say, there are additional grounds upon which to support Galdós' selection

47 See, e.g., Berlin, *The Hedgehog and the Fox.*
48 See, e.g., J. Burckhardt, *Judgments on History and Historians,* trans. H. Zohn (Boston, 1958).
49 Pérez Galdós, *Obras completas,* I, 733.
50 Ibid., p. 799; and see R. Alberti, "Un Episodio Nacional: *Gerona,*" *Cursos y Conferencias,* XXIV (1943), 21.

of Gerona, the second and lesser of the two sieges: the special literary value of Alvarez de Castro as a man,[51] and above all, the opportunity it offered to present an instance of Spanish solidarity involving a part of Catalonia.

History as Novel: Perception and Representation

The titles of Galdos' forty-six historical novels are an excellent set of chapter headings for a history of nineteenth-century Spain, since, not unlike the history text, the *Episodios Nacionales* dwell on the exceptional: the battle, the rebellion, the hero. If this parallel were to be drawn out further, however, a basic difference would become apparent in the perception of historical reality that is proper to text and novel respectively.

Any historical occurrence may be focused on a variety of levels: a level of relief, which consists of those who direct it and are most affected by its results; a background level, made up of the countless participants who decide the issue anonymously, as it were; and, finally, even what might be termed a level of indifference, comprising those whose relation to the occurrence is merely fortuitous. All three levels of focus form part of any event that takes place in a human context, last Sunday's wedding or the battle of Waterloo.[52]

The history book deals primarily with the level of relief; but unlike the chronicle of bygone ages, modern Historiography reveals no socio-political limitations. It can focus with equal facility upon a regicide or a popular rebellion; but the historian will endeavour, in either case, to stress the level that is historically most significant, and that for which documented evidence is most often available: in the regicide, the king, his immediate party, and the assassin; in the popular rebellion, the leader, his outstanding henchmen, and those who suffer its fury. Everything else, in either reconstruction, is offered as undifferentiated background.

The novelist, although guided like the historian by great men and memorable events, declined to focus exclusively on the level of relief proper to the history book:

> . . . . yo quiero que aquí, como en la Naturaleza, las pequeñas cosas vayan al lado de las grandes, enlazadas y con-

---

51 Pérez Galdós, *Obras completas*, I, 784-785, 793, 800, 818-820, 843.
52 See Stendhal's version of Waterloo in *La Chartreuse de Parme*, chapts. 2-5.

fundidas, encubriendo el misterioso lazo que une la gota de agua con la montaña, y el fugaz segundo con el siglo lleno de historia.[53]

In keeping with this all-inclusive intent, Galdós' literary elaboration of historical reality incorporated every level of focus.

The resulting interplay of levels requires further analysis. It is erroneous, first of all, to employ personalities as the sole criterion for distinguishing between levels of historical reality. Galdós often introduced important historical figures into a thoroughly fictional, background setting. The case of Narváez in *El siete de julio,* an Episodio from the Second Series, clearly indicates the novelist's technique on such occasions.[54] The well-known personage is made an integral part of the anonymous background of History by introducing him prior to his significant role in the development of an epoch.

When the level of relief is actually presented in the work, that is, when the reconstruction of the past is deliberately channeled through the persons and the actions of the great figures, it is generally managed without a violent departure from the fictional, background level that prevails in the *Episodios Nacionales.* The level of relief, which is normally focused upon for short intervals, is offered as an extension of the background level. This is invariably accomplished through plausible connections between fictional characters, who make up the background level stressed in Galdós' work, and historical personalities, focused upon precisely when their actions affect the development of an age. This convergence of levels of focus, carefully prepared by the author on each occasion, is effectively employed in reconstructing such vastly different historical situations as the secret nightlife of king Ferdinand VII and the feats of Espartero at Luchana.[55]

Galdós rarely focused directly on the level of relief, on the great figures of a period in isolation, for this would have often required a sudden, jarring departure from the prevailing background level of the work. Nevertheless, the depiction of Mendizábal in the throes of political decision, to cite one example, is sufficient proof of its artistic plausibility.[56]

[53] Pérez Galdós, *Obras completas,* I, 1006.
[54] Ibid., p. 1579.
[55] Ibid., I, 1309-1311; II, 765-768.
[56] Ibid., II, 458-460.

It has been suggested above that Galdós worked mainly within what has been defined as the background level of historical reality, preferring to reconstruct the decisive battle through forgotten soldiers. This decision is neither a necessary nor a direct consequence of fictionalization, for there are novels that reproduce the past by focusing exclusively on the level of relief: ". . . in the biographical novel all of the characters have lived; in the best historical novels, such as *War and Peace*, only the history has actually happened."[57]

Galdós had to avoid the limitations of this alternative; he found it necessary, in fact, to focus primarily on the undifferentiated background level of History. The exclusive focus on a prominent person, regardless of how extensively distributed in society his personal contacts may have been, would have seriously restricted the intuitive faculty upon which Galdós relied for incorporating the entire human complex of History:[58]

> ¡Si en la Historia no hubiera más que batallas; si sus únicos actores fueran los personajes célebres, cuán pequeña sería! Está en el vivir lento y casi siempre doloroso de la sociedad, en lo que hacen todos y en lo que hace cada uno. En ella nada es indigno de la narración, así como en la Naturaleza no es menos digno de estudio el olvidado insecto que la incomensurable arquitectura de los mundos.[59]

Success, for Galdós, implied treating the past as a vast network of lives existing simultaneously throughout society, and the effectiveness of his literary reconstruction of Spanish history was to be gauged by the number of human experiences and relationships artistically incorporated into each historical depiction.

The number and variety of elements integrated by the *Episodios Nacionales* attest to the success of Galdós' primary emphasis on the background level of historical reality. It was the only approach open to an essentially intuitive process, since only from within the background level could the novelist's imagination be free to add all the necessary human factors, without altering what the history text specifies concerning great men and outstanding events, and uncover — or creatively discover, whenever necessary — the hidden ties that link 'la gota de agua con la montaña'.

---

57 I. Stone, "The Biographical Novel," *Three Views of the Novel*, p. 14.
58 See Lukacs, *The Historical Novel*, pp. 33-40.
59 Pérez Galdós, *Obras completas*, I, 1199.

Ferdinand VII, his court, and his government disclose no direct association to the earliest germinations of Spanish Romanticism, and the historian, focused on their level, could hardly incorporate the literary movement into his presentation. The fictional characters through which Galdós reproduced the background level of History have no limitations of this kind. They immediately establish the personal contacts — with both the court and the literary group — that make the incorporation of a budding literary movement feasible. Moreover, the depiction is immediately enriched, as it invariably is by the addition of every new facet of a period.

Galdós' view of History, as outlined above, produced a number of characteristics associated with the *Episodios Nacionales*. For example, they are informal, even colloquial in tone. Significant events are treated as part of everyday living, together with incidents from the most ordinary lives:

> Los íntimos enredos y lances entre personas que no aspiran al juicio de la posteridad, son ramos del mismo árbol que da la madera histórica con que armamos el aparato de la vida externa de los pueblos.[60]

Another consequence of Galdós' special view of History is the massive effect that accompanies the presentation, as individual literary figures, of the multitude that comprises the background level of History.[61] The nineteenth century is, to a great extent, the chronicle of that multitude's accession to historical prominence, and the rise of this new historical entity, hitherto anonymous in History, is effectively captured by its overpowering representation in the *Episodios Nacionales*.

The combined effect of the two characteristics noted is the transformation of the everyday existence of an entire people into the substance of History, which immediately brings Unamuno's concept of 'intrahistoria' to mind. As we know, Galdós did not limit himself to the background level of historical reality, but his successful fusion of 'historia e intrahistoria' may actually represent Unamuno's true intention.[62]

---

60 Pérez Galdós, *Obras completas*, III, 761; and for a vivid example, see I, 540-545.

61 See M. Carranza, *El pueblo a través de los Episodios Nacionales* (San José, Costa Rica, 1942).

62 See Torres Bodet, *Tres inventores de realidad*, p. 220; and A. González Blanco, *Historia de la novela en España desde el Romanticismo* (Madrid, 1909), pp. 385-388.

A closer or more meaningful parallel between Galdós and Unamuno's generation is prevented by the latter's basically anti-historical attitude. What these later writers often stressed in the background level of History was 'lo idéntico a sí mismo a lo largo del tiempo',[63] the facets of the past, that is, which are least historical. Galdós, on the other hand, insistently projected the undifferentiated background level, made concrete in fiction, as part of the general flux of History.

In conclusion, Galdós went to the history text for the continuity of events, for factual information as he needed it, but neither re-evaluated facts as a historian nor altered their causal relationships. The novelist merely varied the level of perception, thus releasing his intuitive capacities. And this enabled him to re-create, re-vitalize, and re-people the formless background of the historical canvas, capturing the quintessence of the past in its anonymous dimension.

Galdós' literary elaboration of the past involves, as we have noted, an intuitive extension from concrete historical facts. The novelist's goals entailed the projection, in representative literary trappings, of precise historical situations, attitudes, and relationships. It is convenient, in this connection, to distinguish, if somewhat artificially, between what we shall term the sociological, psychological, and thematic facets of Galdós' technique of historical representation.

The sociological device employed in reconstructing a vast and well integrated historical context is quite apparent in the First Series. The picaresque qualities of Gabriel Araceli, the main protagonist, have been pointed out on several occasions.[64] The most important of them, his easy movement across social classes and institutions, is prompted by the character's lack of restraining ties, family or social. Galdós similarly endowed many of his important protagonists. Although Araceli is perhaps closer to the picaresque model than any other, all are to some extent itinerant, without strong roots, and participate in movements that inscribe an extensive social and geographical trajectory.

Each protagonist of the *Episodios Nacionales* is the center of an expanding social circle, becoming successively and simul-

63 J. Martínez Ruiz, *Doña Inés* (New York, n.d.), p. 7.
64 See Louis-Lande, "Le roman patriotique en Espagne," *Revue des Deux Mondes*, XIV (1876), 936; and Casalduero, *Vida y Obra*, p. 59.

taneously engaged on different levels of society. For example, he may at once be the friend of the popular demagogue's brother and of the reactionary minister's mistress, which creates a believable nexus, but — and this is an important point — on the background level, between the socio-political extremes of the historical context.

This type of ramification guarantees the presence and participation of the protagonist in every sector of society. In fact, it permits much more, because Galdós' protagonist comes to embody an elaborate social network in his varied contacts. Wherever the personal escapade or the public event may lead him, he arrives with the potential of an all-encompassing view: the specific event or situation, to which he is directly linked, and its most distant social and national repercussions, brought forth, in time, by his other numerous connections.

La corte de Carlos IV, an Episodio from the First Series, offers a very complete cross-section of Madrid society (royalty, nobility, artists, people); and it can serve, for this reason, as an example of the novelist's procedure. Galdós must first have intuited an ideal outline of his subject, a reasonably accurate replica of the stratified yet closely interrelated social make-up of Madrid in the first decade of the nineteenth century. This blueprint was then implemented, novelistically, by the itinerant Araceli's wide range of personal contacts, and there results a historical context that is offered as the dynamic interaction of its component elements.

The psychological facet of Galdós' representational technique is actually a function of his literary characterization. The process of elaborating History, of transforming narration into representation, involves, as we have noted elsewhere, the extraction of concrete personalities from the generic categories of the history text (workers, soldiers, etc.). This requisite of novelization opens up an area of historical representation that is untouched, for the most part, by scholarly historians: History as viewed by those living it.

Galdós' extraordinary skill in fixing distinct psychological shades, when coupled with his fecund characterization in the *Episodios Nacionales,* provides a wide range of living perspectives on every moment of history depicted. Even short-lived secondary characters leave behind personal views on historical sit-

45

uations that remain unidimensional, by comparison, in most history texts.

This procedure is fraught, of course, with all the dangers of anachronism attending historical fiction, since the novelist is undoubtedly under strong pressure to project into his characters a knowledge of events that they simply could not have possessed. Galdós' exceptional restraint, in this respect, usually allows little margin for anachronism, and this heightens the value of the representational technique under discussion.[65]

The thematic aspect of the novelist's historical representation consists, largely, in striking meaningful parallels between history and fiction, thus creating analogies that make a number of historical factors directly accessible to the reader. These parallels may be of several kinds, ranging from elaborate symbolism to coincidences that are almost unavoidable.

The Navarro-Monsalud conflict of the Second Series is a perfect example of an elaborate symbolic parallel. The initial encounter of two 'Spains' is expressed, novelistically, through the intra-family struggles of two completely different protagonists: they are stepbrothers, the legitimate one is the 'tradicionalista,' and hate is the basis of their relationship. Galdós undoubtedly saw an illustrative value in casting the historical equation in the guise of a concrete human problem, and Lukacs' commentary upon Scott applies perfectly:

> For him it means that certain crises in the personal destinies of a number of human beings coincide and interweave within the determining context of an historical crisis. It is precisely for this reason that his manner of portraying the historical crisis is never abstract, the split of a nation into warring parties always runs through the center of the closest human relationships.[66]

The elaborate parallelism under discussion has a number of illustrative functions. Not only is the key aspect of an epoch reduced to human terms, but the nature of the literary parallel — which spans the entire Second Series — stresses the quality of permanence. The history book can indicate the variations and the prolongation of a historical conflict by repeated allusions to its existence; but art must avoid reiteration. And Galdós' sym-

---

65 See, e.g., Pérez Galdós, *Obras completas*, I, 354, 471-476.
66 *The Historical Novel*, p. 41.

bolic parallel succeeds, without repetition, in keeping a single political conflict before the reader for ten entire volumes.

A second type of parallel between fiction and history is less symbolic and is not intended to reduce specific historical situations to analogous human relationships. Two concurrent series of developments, the trajectory of a protagonist within the plot and the evolution of the country in the same period of time, bring the tenor of a period of history into sharp focus. The dynamic correspondence between Araceli and the Spain that fought the War of Independence is perhaps the clearest example. The character does not precisely symbolize Spain, but his positive spiritual growth does parallel the country's ascendant effort. The *Episodios Nacionales* abound in interactions of this type, and all the important fluctuations of nineteenth-century Spanish history are reflected in its various protagonists.[67]

A third kind of parallel, the assimilation of fictional and historical characters, results, unavoidably, from Galdós' depiction of an entire historical context. The past reproduced in the *Episodios Nacionales* is made up of a single substance, human experience; and fictional characters are indistinguishable in their attitudes and mannerisms from historical personages. The fictional character's everyday acts, which form the basis of the various plots, are similar to the actions of historical characters, which find their way into the history book. Nothing less can be expected, of course, since both are enclosed within a single determining framework.

As may be imagined, the *Episodios Nacionales*, with over a thousand characters, half of them fictional and the other half historical,[68] offer a high incidence of this type of parallelism, which in some measure makes up for the necessarily inexact sort of coincidence that it entails. Its illustrative value lies in the fact that the reader easily identifies himself with the fictional beings, and thereby gains an insight into the lives of similarly motivated historical personages. One example of this is the insight provided into Spain's era of political romanticism by Galdós' incorporation of a romantic psychology and a ro-

67 See L. Alas, *Galdós* (Madrid, 1912), pp. 316-317; and Sainz de Robles, "B. Pérez Galdós: su vida, su obra y su época," p. 161.

68 See the unpubl. diss. (University of Wisconsin, 1937) by R. G. Barr, "A Census of Characters in the *Episodios Nacionales* of B. Pérez Galdós."

mantic world-view into the characterizational content of the Third Series.

Finally, we shall analyze the problem of representation faced by the novelist who attempts to transmit historical causality in fiction. As noted earlier, the literary elaboration of the past involves selection. Regardless of the criteria employed or the care exercised, only a few events from any causally interdependent series can actually be novelized. Since Galdós' historical novel offers a continuum focused on the background level of historical reality, it is especially subject to the danger of obscuring historical causality. This problem would not arise, for example, in dealing with a literary work that reproduces an isolated instant of history, in which historical causality would be superfluous. It would be greatly attenuated, as well, in a historical novel that focused mainly on the level of relief, in which historical and novelistic causality might coincide.

Galdós' synthesis of factual data and creative intuition crystallizes as a set of incidents that constitute the life of a fictional protagonist. This selective presentation of history through the private motivational apparatus of a specific fictional character tends to establish a bond of interdependence, of causal interdependence, between the historical events novelized and the protagonist's personal causality. This danger is most evident in the First Series, with its single narrator-protagonist. In the absence of a complete series of causally interdependent events, which, as we have seen, is made impossible by the process of selection, a purely novelistic motivational order tends to supersede historical causality.

It must be pointed out that Galdós did not overlook the causal links selectively omitted in his literary reconstruction of nineteenth-century Spanish history. On the contrary, he was well aware of their importance in projecting a meaningful historical continuum, and consequently interpolated the necessary information in dialogue or direct narration. This, however, could only succeed in part, because the causal linkage supplemented in this fashion was altogether subdued by the overpowering immediacy of the history actually re-lived in the work by the fictional protagonist.

In short, nineteenth-century Spanish history might still appear to flow exclusively within the channel marked by a protagonist's personal trajectory, thus greatly reducing the value of Galdós' work as historical representation, if the *Episodios Nacionales* had not been predicated, from the beginning, on an entity that transcends as it incorporates the various fictional protagonists. This entity, whose omnipresence could be stressed without detracting from the presentation of History as personal experience, is Spain. It is the indispensable canvas upon which everything transcribed, whether as direct representation, dialogue or narration, acquires a positional relationship; the transcendent background that automatically organizes the motivational patterns of individual protagonists into the meaningful network of historical causes and effects that underlies the *Episodios Nacionales*.

Galdós emphasized Spain in the vital experiences of Spaniards.[69] He revealed the historical nucleus of the *Episodios Nacionales* in an accidental, novelistic foreground, as the everyday life-adventure of believable Spaniards; and he simultaneously projected the self-same nucleus onto a larger, national canvas, which provided the most diverse individual experiences with historical meaning. By means of the first, Galdós succeeded in transforming historical abstractions into concrete livable realities; and by virtue of the second, the past that was selectively novelized was made to retain an indispensable minimum of historical causality.

[69] See Appendix I.

PART II

THE *EPISODIOS NACIONALES* AS ART

The *Episodios Nacionales* must be organized to facilitate a critical analysis. The author's own division of the work into five Series is basic, of course, but it does not reflect the decisive nineteen year interval between the Second and Third Series. A simple grouping of the five literary units along chronological lines would overcome this difficulty, but it would fail to underscore the distinctive qualities of the Fifth Series. The following division accounts for the Series units, their chronological production, and the innovations of the last *Episodios Nacionales:* Chapter I, First and Second Series (1872-1879); Chapter II, Third and Fourth Series (1898-1907); Chapter III, Fifth Series (1908-1912).

Each chapter entails a Series by Series study of literary form, plot development, characterization, and a miscellany of secondary features: comedy, symbolism and others. The summary of each chapter will permit a general comparison of the Series involved, and offer an opportunity for stylistic commentary.

FIRST AND SECOND SERIES

When the first *Episodios Nacionales* appeared, Spain still lacked modern novelists,[1] and the writer subject to newspaper work or dependent upon political sinecures was yet to be replaced, as in most of Europe, by the independent novelist, capable of attracting and holding a personal public. Genius, a sensibility capable of penetrating the needs of the hour, and even a concerted endeavour to achieve economic independence were required of the artist who would change a state of affairs whereby the most representative art form of the century was kept from fulfillment.

An important relationship exists between the situation outlined and the genesis of the first of Galdós' definitive art forms. Only after conceiving the *Episodios Nacionales* could he truly feel himself a novelist, with works capable of molding a new and loyal reading public from the devourers of translations and serialized pulp.[2] Two intrinsic features of these historical novels may be credited, to a large extent, with this revolutionary achievement: the size of the individual volumes and the regularity with which they appeared.

Once Galdós had established himself as a novelist, critics considered the length of his novels objectionable and an expensive luxury in a country of inconstant readers.[3] The *Episodios Nacionales* reveal, however, that Galdós had begun with works that conformed in length to the tastes and needs of his public. The fact that the first Episodios are less than half as extensive as *La Fontana de Oro* and *El audaz,* which immediately precede

---

1 J. Montesinos, *Introducción a una historia de la novela en España en el siglo XIX* (Madrid, 1955), XV.

2 See M. Menéndez y Pelayo, "Contestación académica a Pérez Galdós," *Discursos de la Real Academia Española,* 7 y 21 de febrero, 1897, p. 45; and Berkowitz, *Pérez Galdós,* pp. 100-101.

3 Alas, *Galdós,* p. 243.

them, indicates a deliberate change on the part of Galdós. In this sense, the incredible rapidity of production that became a hallmark of the *Episodios Nacionales,* and in which Galdós took a special pride, may be seen as a function of holding readers accustomed to serialized 'entregas'.

Finally, the earliest Episodios dealt with a period of history that even today pulsates with emotion. The War of Independence, an era of heroism, purpose, and relative solidarity contrasted pointedly with the confused and divided 1870's upon which it was projected; and it is easy to see why few works of literature have been so favorably received by the Spanish people.

Inherent historical appeal, limited size, and greatly varied subject matter make these first two Series of *Episodios Nacionales* the most widely read and most uniformly acclaimed of Galdós' literary creations.[4] These Series are, furthermore, the first instance of a literary approach to History that left its imprint on Spanish letters.[5] Finally, they provided Galdós with an audience that made it possible for him to become the first of Spain's modern novelists, for it is as 'el autor de los *Episodios Nacionales*', an epithet that derives from these first two Series, that he was to be known throughout his life.[6]

A) First Series

The ten volumes of the First Series dwell on less than ten years of Spanish history, but they are perhaps the most decisive years in the history of modern Spain. Trafalgar closes an era of enmity toward England, Spain's fruitless and negative 'quehacer' in the eighteenth century. The years that follow dissolve the other leg of its century-long stand, a complacent security in the shade of French influence. Both factors, as offered in Galdós' literary elaboration, serve to introduce the War of Independence, the confused agitation from which Spain would crystallize a future direction.

---

[4] See, e.g., A. Del Río, *Estudios galdosianos* (Zaragoza, 1953), p. 105; S. H. Eoff, *The Novels of Pérez Galdós* (St. Louis, 1954), p. 2; Alas, *Galdós*, p. 44; and R. F. Giusti, "La obra galdosiana," *Cursos y Conferencias,* XXIV (1943), 10-11.

[5] Gómez de la Serna, *España en sus Episodios*, p. 50.

[6] See, e.g., J. Martínez Ruiz, *Lecturas españolas* (Madrid, 1920), p. 244.

Literary form

The reader is notified of the First Series' intended formal unity at the very onset of *Trafalgar:*

> Muchas cosas voy a contar. ¡Trafalgar, Bailén, Madrid, Zaragoza, Gerona, Arapiles! . . . De todo esto diré alguna cosa, si no os falta la paciencia.[7]

A unitive plot spans the ten volumes, strengthening the unity inherent in a chronological presentation of history. Araceli's words — quoted above — also proclaim his first-person monopoly of the narrative function, another powerful unifying factor.

The convergence of chronological presentation, unitive plot, and first-person narration results in an extraordinary degree of Series unity.[8] Chronological sequence is an invariable characteristic of the *Episodios Nacionales,* and one deeply rooted, as we have seen, in the very conception of the work; but the other two factors noted, novelistic structure and narrative form, require further study.

The degree of plot unity encountered in the ten volumes might suggest a serialized novel, except that the First Series also contains plot elements that are restricted to the individual Episodio. Despite the powerful unifying devices worked into the literary form of the Series, Galdós managed a degree of plot sufficiency for each separate volume. The individual Episodio will normally consist, then, of a segment of the unitive plot, which stems from and projects itself into other Episodios, and of an additional plot element — henceforth referred to as subplot — which crystallizes and is resolved within it.

This unity-diversity tension — which is intrinsic to the Series as a literary unit, yet different in each — results in a novelistic structure that is uniquely suited to the task of presenting a great variety of elements within a unified historical perspective. Each Episodio presents a single event, a specific socio-geographic context, while the articulation of all ten novels embodies the historically meaningful totality, the War of Independence.

This novelistic dualism may also be analyzed in the light of

7 Pérez Galdós, *Obras completas,* I, 208.
8 Gullón, *Galdós, novelista moderno,* p. 59.

Galdós' attempt to form a reading public attached to him personally. The continuous unitive plot guaranteed, to an extent, that many readers of *Trafalgar* would go on to the following volumes. But Galdós understood that a restrictive unity, which could divest the isolated Episodio of literary appeal, would limit his public to the readers of that initial volume; and this would account for the novelistic diversification by which each volume stands as an acceptable reading unit in itself.[9]

Unlike those first-person narrations which suggest being written just after or in the very midst of what they relate, Araceli narrates his past as reminiscence, as a contemporary of the first reader (1872).[10] The fact that the first-person narrative form itself results in a weakening of immediacy[11] would hardly be significant were it not added to the effect of this retrospection. It appears, in fact, that an intentional weakening of immediacy was sought by the author, which may be due to the quality of the history novelized in these *Episodios Nacionales*.

By 1872 Bailén, Zaragoza, and all the other moments of history focused in the First Series had already acquired the gloss of what is legendary, semimythical, and remote. Galdós may have found it convenient, even necessary, to sacrifice total actualization in order to retain some of that legendary quality. In these circumstances, a retrospective first-person narrative provides the necessary compromise between the immediacy expected of an artistic representation and the retention of historicity in the subject. An aged Araceli re-lives part of his youth, but always conscious of the fact that it has been consecrated by time. Furthermore, this narrative form, with its active protagonist-narrator projected forward into the reader's day, emphasized the nexus between past and present that underlies Galdós' conception of the *Episodios Nacionales*.

Galdós put the first-person narrative to good use, especially the weak reader-protagonist identification — an effect of the powerful character identity transmitted by the form itself — that is often considered a literary handicap.[12] The unusual degree of credibility thus assumed by the protagonist-narrator

9 Gullón, *Galdós, novelista moderno*, p. 59.
10 Pérez Galdós, *Obras completas*, I, 208, 1180.
11 A. A. Mendilov, *Time and the Novel* (London, 1952), pp. 107-109.
12 Ibid., p. 104.

emphasizes the presentation of History as personal experience, an effect that is further strengthened by the illusion of a legitimate source of first-hand historical knowledge: the memoir. The First Series is written as a detailed literary memoir covering the years 1805 to 1813; and the 'tete a tete' thus established between reader and narrator gives expression to what the author conceived as an important difference between 'what happened' and 'what happened to me'.

Finally, this retrospective memoir form, that is, the active protagonist's own recollections at a great distance in time, permits an unusual degree of historical precision. In all probability, no other form could incorporate, so believably, the general knowledge that transcends the limited perception of a single individual and at the same time relate a very specific experience of History. Araceli's narration of the past as personal experience is offered, without anachronism, in conjunction with the objective work of later scholars.[13]

Plot development

The unitive plot of the Series, with which we shall deal first, must integrate, in the mobility of its protagonist-narrator, a wide range of historical operations, of social and geographical contexts. It is therefore patterned, like the Byzantine Novel of another age, on the separation of young lovers. This is well suited, of course, to a necessarily extensive and episodic story, but two crucial factors — the disparate social identities of the lovers and Araceli's intense patriotism — give the traditional plot outline a distinctly modern configuration.

Even amid his varied patriotic duties, Araceli seeks the fulfillment of his impossible love; and the plot highlights the lovers' various encounters, which provide successive moments of climactic excitement. After each such plot reinforcement, necessary in an extended story of this type, Galdós effected a new separation of the lovers. Given the natural contingencies of war and the powerful social forces that pull the two youngsters apart, these repeated separations are not anti-climactic, indeed they are quite acceptable.

A second dimension of the unitive plot is centered on the

13 Pérez Galdós, *Obras completas*, I, 231-232, 331.

Countess Amaranta and Santorcaz. The relationship between Ines' natural parents, whose own socially disparate love-affair (similar to that of the young protagonists, Inés and Araceli) had ended tragically years before, is reduced to an aftermath of hatred that has an interest and a development of its own. Their bitter conflict over the possession of Inés, whom both had neglected for years, casts a shadow of tragedy, a suggestion of irreconcilable class hatreds upon the lives of the young protagonists.

Amaranta's blood relationship to Inés and the paternal relation of Santorcaz, as well as the knowledge of the tragic past shared by these two, startle the reader successively, and contribute further plot complications. The elemental technique of surprise furnishes additional plot intensifications, analogous to the periodic encounters of Araceli and Inés. The new series of complications woven into the unitive plot are indispensable, as well, to the accumulation of feasible coincidences which the incorporation of a lengthy historical development requires. The fusion of the two plot elements is carried out, consequently, with precise functional effects.

This novelistic framework encloses a relatively simple plot development, which, in typically Galdosian fashion, has love as the prime mover of action. Love, embodied in Inés, is a major factor in the transformation of Araceli from 'picaro' to hero, and its effects are even more pronounced in Amaranta and Santorcaz. The tragic course of these two, of which only the final stages are enacted in the Series, is unalterable; but love transforms Amaranta from cynical aristocrat to understanding mother, and even smooths Santorcaz's bilious ferocity. A soothing force in no way related to romantic passion, love slowly changes everything and everyone in the First Series.

The social differences between the young lovers broaden the base of the plot conflict, since the social classes which they come to represent are pitted against each other. These differences also add significance, within the novel, to the protagonist's patriotic activities, which are absolutely indispensable to the historical reconstruction of the War of Independence. Soldiering, with its possibilities for rapid social advancement in that era, is the one direction adequate to the positive resolution of the plot conflict.

The second dimension of the unitive plot contributes tragic overtones, as we have seen, to an otherwise simple love tale, but also serves to augment the socio-political range of the unitive plot. On the one hand, it provides Galdós with a perspective on the aristocracy of the period (Amaranta); and on the other, with an opportunity to present the historical phenomenon of the 'afrancesado' (Santorcaz). The two represent conflicting extremes, which become concrete in the mutual hatred of the characters.

The contrast between generations, a social conflict resolved negatively in the past and positively in the present, provides the unitive plot with an added level of historical meaning. It serves to indicate a fundamental change in Spain as it entered upon a new phase of its history. The success of the young protagonists, where Amaranta and Santorcaz had failed, is not the result of personal virtue and perseverance alone. A primary factor is the historical atmosphere reconstructed in the Series. And the final disintegration of the old court aristocracy, the political conflict and social turmoil involved in the rise of new classes, are instrumental in the development of the story.

The segmentation of the unitive plot into ten parts is, first of all, a function of the Series as a literary unit. It provides organic nexus, novelistic ties, between historically linked volumes. The manner of segmentation is important, however, for it is often calculated to arouse interest and encourage the reading of the following volume. After reconstructing a major historical event, the story often moves toward a climax that is abruptly cut off by the end of the volume.[14]

The numerous heterogeneous plot elements that are, to one extent or another, independent of the unitive plot have been referred to as subplots. These differ from each other in their degree of independence and in other respects that we shall have occasion to point out. In *Gerona,* for example, the unitive plot of the Series is reduced to serving as the literary vehicle of a completely independent subplot, that centered on Siseta, Nomdedeu, and Andrés Marijuán. In *La batalla de los Arapiles,* however, the two novelistic elements overlap, and Araceli continues the unitive plot while intervening in the subplot that

14 Pérez Galdós, *Obras completas,* I, 469, 559, 667. For a fruitful comparison of this unitive plot and the 'novela popular,' see Hinterhäuser, *Los Episodios Nacionales,* pp. 337-352.

developes about Miss Fly. In *Cádiz,* unitive plot and subplot are practically fused, and both Inés and Araceli play principal roles in the subplot centered on the exploits of Lord Gray; while in *Zaragoza,* on the other hand, the unitive plot — present in the ubiquitous Araceli — does not intervene to any extent, as such, in the subplot that relates the tragic love of Agustín Montoria and María Candiola.

A few Episodios substitute the introduction of unitive plot elements for the customary subplot. In *Bailén,* for example, the initial appearance of Santorcaz and the introduction of the Rumblar family serve the functions of a subplot, although both elements are eventually retained as part of the unitive plot, from which they may not be independent in the long run.

The various subplots are always independent of each other, and most generate a very immediate interest by re-elaborating traditional themes, stressing exotic elements, and combining either or both with a sweeping irony. The need for all these factors, in presenting and stressing independent plot developments that share each volume with the unitive novel of the Series, is quite understandable.

Cádiz introduces the Don Juan theme, which Galdós repeated with alterations and innovations throughout the *Episodios Nacionales.* The stamp of Lord Gray is unmistakable, a Don Juan fashioned on Lord Byron, complete with the nihilistic cynicism that the Romantics — precisely in the years reconstructed — stressed so much in the traditional myth-figure. The culmination of the subplot is sheer irony: the impious foreigner, himself the bastard offspring of a Spanish legend, is killed by Araceli, moved by an equally legendary Spanish concept of honor. The climax of *La corte de Carlos IV* is a Galdosian version, again steeped in irony, of the Shakespearean 'play within a play', brought to the Spanish stage shortly before by Tamayo y Baus in *Un drama nuevo.*[15] So well is this brought off, with the great Máiquez as protagonist, that the artifice is again genuine. *Zaragoza* offers a subplot outline that is even more thoroughly Shakespearean. The impossible young lovers are a Montoria (Montague) and a Candiola (Capulet), and the family feud ends, of course, in tragedy.[16] *La batalla de los*

[15] P. P. Rogers, "Galdós and Tamayo y Baus' Letter Substitution Device," *Romanic Review,* XLV (1954), 115-120.
[16] Gilman, *Homenaje a A. M. Huntington,* p. 188.

Arapiles evokes the romanticized image of Spain then prevalent in Europe; and the novelist's subtle irony transforms Miss Fly's exotic perception of Spanish reality into the believable substance of the story.

A few subplots depend less on the ironic re-elaboration of traditional themes or on the striking impression of exotic elements. These remain close to the pattern of the conventional love story (*Trafalgar*), or constitute a biographical study of some unique personage (*Juan Martín, el Empecinado*). In no case, however, did Galdós intend the subplot to be, in and of itself, the sole appeal of any Episodio. The most conventional tale develops within a historical context that bears an interest of its own, an interest that can be assimilated into the fiction itself. With the tragic Gerona as background, for example, the touching affection of the child-adults Andrés and Siseta sheds all it might otherwise have contained of the pathetic and the trite.

In general, Galdós' fecund imagination created subplots that combine an inherent simplicity and an appealing literary quality. He enlisted, to this end, such interesting human creations as Trijueque and Nomdedeu, such fascinating themes as Romeo and Juliet and Don Juan, and such captivating social circles as the court and the theatre.

The degree of sufficiency that the subplot lends the individual Episodio must also be analyzed as a function of Galdós' reconstruction of a complex historical reality. The unitive plot of the Series, which touches on the most diverse historical events, could not be expected to reflect the distinct quality of each with any degree of directness. The presence of Araceli in Zaragoza, Madrid, and Cádiz provides a unified perspective on those dispersed actions, but the protagonist cannot feasibly become a 'zaragozano' or a 'madrileño'. His relation to most socio-geographical contexts is necessarily adventitious. He shares experiences, but he cannot be truly representative of each.

This representational function is generally fulfilled by the subplot. Developed as part of a specific context, from within it, the subplot enables the novelist to effect an intimate fusion of history and fiction. The subplot of *Juan Martín, el Empecinado* stems directly from the world of the 'guerrilleros', and its protagonist, Trijueque, is an authentic prototype. The subplot of *La corte de Carlos IV* reveals the lax morality of the court aristocracy, whose members participate actively in the story; and that of *Zaragoza* introduces the reader to a family that personifies the city's undaunted spirit.

Even the absence of a legitimate subplot in *Bailén*, for which a literary reason has already been adduced, may be justified in terms of this function. The socio-geographical dimension is virtually eliminated, or rendered unimportant, by the fortuitous occurrence of a battle between people completely foreign to the specific locale.

Characterization

The First Series is the autobiography of its sole narrator. Araceli begins life under conditions that suggest a picaresque destiny, but gradually acquires values that counteract an incipient anti-social direction. The process of change is presented as a complex dialectic of life experiences. In *Trafalgar*, Araceli grasps the first of his positive values, the social concept of 'patria'; but this novel perspective on society is blurred by radical changes in his immediate environment. The aloof behavior of Rosita Cisniega, no longer the playmate and equal of the street urchin who idolizes her, and her eventual marriage to a young man of her own social rank, have the effect of pushing Araceli, once again, into a picaresque pattern of behavior. But no positive experience is lost on the protagonist, and in *La corte de Carlos IV*, shortly after his first encounter with Inés, Araceli gains a redeeming self-respect. And finally, with the advent of war, the protagonist altruistically identifies himself with Spain's struggle for independence. He can thus be said to represent the first generation of modern Spain, without roots, perhaps, in a past that was dead, but far from picaresque in its definitive motivations.

Araceli's personal development is credible, mainly because Galdós chose the proper time and place for each stage of growth. As we have noted, the protagonist experiences the first inklings of patriotism during an ill-fated naval engagement, and he first evolves rules of proper conduct in society as a reaction to an immoral court environment. He learns abnegation and pity in the siege of Zaragoza, and acquires a tolerance for the complexity of human nature in *Cádiz* and *Juan Martín, el Empecinado*.

Araceli's experience of Spanish history, not just a subject to be narrated passively, is always a factor in his development as a human being, and it is this intimate relationship that lends the characterization its verisimilitude.

The one questionable aspect of Araceli's presentation is the range of knowledge he occasionally displays. The uneducated youngster acquires sophistication somewhat more rapidly than one would expect. There is, however, an important saving point. What might be considered questionable in the youngster of the story[17] is suitable enough in the enlightened old narrator of the Series; and many mild discrepancies of this kind, which may be interpreted as the latter's unconscious projection into the former, actually contribute realism to the retrospective form of the First Series.

The first-person narrative is normally limited to what constitutes the narrator's conscious existence, foregoing the rich inner life that other forms of narration explore. This formal limitation is somewhat mitigated by the retrospective character of the First Series, which occasionally permits the old narrator a degree of detached self-appraisal. The protagonist's subconscious life is also projected, on occasion, by means of dream recall,[18] but neither device is sufficiently employed to overcome the formal barrier.

Consequently, Araceli remains a simple psychological entity throughout; and this is fortunate, since a more complicated being would have been less suited to the reconstruction of an era which was essentially forthright in its conscious drives. The protagonist responds to simple and basic emotional stimuli, to love and patriotism; and he is enriched as a person, in typically Galdosian fashion, by both these forms of altruism. Even when a choice must be made between them, both alternatives contribute to Araceli's positive development (tolerant understanding, fundamental honesty); and there can be no better indication than this of his relatively unidirectional growth pattern.

The outstanding impression left by Araceli is that of a self-made man, of the person who rises to the occasion time after time, and gains, from each new enterprise, the unique historical experiences that guarantee his development of a totally

17 See, e.g., Pérez Galdós, *Obras completas*, I, 378, 698.
18 Ibid., pp. 258, 443, 757, 1057-1058, 1164.

new personality. He contrasts vividly, in this sense, with every other character in the Series, both with those incapable of escaping the traditional forms of being and those whose very existence is nothing more than a negative reaction to those forms.

The other three protagonists of the unitive plot represent completely different orders of characterization. Inés, for example, undergoes no important development whatever. She passes from humble poverty in *La corte de Carlos IV* to aristocratic opulence in *Cádiz* without noticeably altering her basic traits: love, understanding and resignation. She clearly embodies the virtues of a feminine ideal, the charming combination of strength and resignation, passion and practical sense.

A static ideal of this type could hinder the development of the novel, but Inés often overcomes this basic characterizational inflexibility in the very exercise of her virtues. She gains extraordinary relief in the mature wisdom with which she tempers her child-adult relationship with Araceli, and in the humble resignation that governs her conduct with respect to Amaranta and Santorcaz. Although Inés remains relatively unchanged throughout, her capacity for love determines most of the character development in the unitive plot.

Santorcaz and Amaranta differ from both Araceli, whose growth is fully recorded in the work, and Inés, whose personality remains virtually unchanged. When Inés' mother and father are introduced, in *La corte de Carlos IV* and *Bailén* respectively, they are fixed personalities, made understandable as the reader gradually discerns the tragic roots of Santorcaz's nihilism and Amaranta's cynical frivolity. In both cases, the relations established in the work with Inés bring about basic personality changes.

Amaranta's contact with her illegitimate daughter produces a radical transformation, which is believable only in terms of the powerful factor involved. The cynical aristocrat explodes in maternal feelings, for years consciously stilled by endless rounds of palatial intrigue and repressed behind an outward show of frivolity. The wayward mother undergoes a fitting expiation, being made to deny her genuine emotions when Inés' presence makes their repression unbearable. From this purgatory, which is uniquely suited to the sinner, Amaranta emerges a surprisingly warm and understanding woman.

The change outlined is grounded in both history and plot. Amaranta's maternal feelings are aroused and reinforced, for example, by the devious attempts of a moribund aristocracy to perpetuate itself at the expense of its illegitimate offspring: the proposed marriage of Inés to the weak and dissipated Count of Rumblar. On the other hand, Amaranta's final consent to the marriage of Inés and Araceli, a commoner, clearly indicates the extent of her evolution, and results from a belated awakening to the tragic lesson of her own life, which is itself encouraged by an atmosphere of change and equality.

Santorcaz, a man twisted by hatred, is the most complex characterization of the four. Broken by the tragic past shared with Amaranta, and having lived many years of exile in France as a result, Santorcaz is sustained by an obsessive will to destroy the religious and aristocratic social order that had rejected him. His fundamental nihilism contrasts vividly with the affirmative attitudes of the epoch.

Inés' father kidnaps her out of hatred, in order to hurt Amaranta by educating their offspring in his consuming passion. And the initial contact of father and daughter has a dramatic quality, as if love and hate were suddenly pitted against each other. When Inés' charitable resignation triumphs, it is again logically grounded in both history and fiction. The turn of historical events spells failure for the 'afrancesado', for his dream of destroying the very foundations of Spanish society, and this allows Inés' love to open a breach in the protagonist's protective wall of rancor. The sick and prematurely aged fanatic succumbs to his paternal feelings, but, until his deathbed, that is the sole extent of his weakening.

Galdós chose to present the 'afrancesado' in the foreground, thus indicating the historical significance of the group; but he refused to disturb, to this end, the illusion of national solidarity that underlies his presentation of the War of Independence. The 'franc-mason' is consequently put together from personal hatreds as well as abstract political beliefs, and clearly motivated by an obsessive need for destructive vengeance that the reader can understand. This greatly attenuates the traitor's prominent insertion into an atmosphere of religious patriotism.

Santorcaz's emotional pattern of behavior so mitigates his political and social nihilism that Galdós can even stress in him — without detriment to the patriotic setting — a degree of love for Spain. Much that the 'afrancesado' says is, Casandra-like, quite true in the perspective of the following Series, and in the end, Galdós served notice of future developments by unexpectedly siding with the traitor Santorcaz over the noble Amaranta.[19]

The protagonists of the various subplots are even more diversified in conception and development. Some, like Lord Gray and Miss Fly, depend for immediate effect on exotic qualities. As foreigners, they are properly endowed, in the surprised narrator's view, with a wide latitude of credibility. Consequently, they do not require extensive delineation, since their exotic essence flows naturally from what they say and do. Lord Gray's poetic sensibility, nihilistic attitude, and sexual recklessness are established without extensive psychological analysis. The same applies to Miss Fly, whose feminine delicacy and juxtaposed masculine independence are instantly fascinating and make any further individuation superfluous.

The two examples, Lord Gray and Miss Fly, also suggest the varying degrees of flexibility possible in exotic characterizations. The author's presentation of the young Englishwoman varies greatly from his treatment of Lord Gray. Her unrequited love for Araceli, her magnificent expressions of wounded feminine pride, suggest a personal dimension that is altogether lacking in her compatriot, who is fixed, once and for all, within the outline of an exotic model.

Several subplot protagonists, such as Andrés Marijuán and Siseta from *Gerona*, reveal no distinctive personality traits. They are prototypes of a characterizational formula that stresses uncomplicated normality. It is clear, in such cases, that Galdós did not intend to attract the reader with any singularity of personal development, but sought, instead, to express a range of representative human reactions to historical situations that are themselves exceptional. Nothing is required of these characters beyond the ability to react to external forces in a convincingly representative manner, a function as important to Galdós' historical reconstruction as that of more complex characters.

No other characterizational formula is as well suited, more-

[19] Pérez Galdós, *Obras completas*, I, 1179-1180.

over, to the projection of the extreme effects of a given historical situation. When timid and uncomplicated human beings are made to react heroically, for example, a special set of factors operate. The very roots of heroism are bared, for the virtue is shaped by a specific set of circumstances from the stuff of everyday people. Its genesis is clearly visible in the work, since it is offered as a function of essentially unheroic personalities.

Finally, there are protagonists who undergo a relatively complex development within the limited scope of a subplot. In Nomdedeu, from *Gerona,* for example, Galdós traced the gradual deterioration of a man faced with unremitting hunger. A physical, almost palpable despair erodes the altruistic core of the humane doctor, and a succession of nervous animal exacerbations, interlaced with recurrent phases of remorse, lead, inevitably, to the loss of all human restraint. The passage from altruistic doctor to egoistic madman is itself fraught with paradox, for Nomdedeu's acquisitions of food — the fruit of theft and even attempted murder — are invariably destined for an invalid daughter, and his actions are, consequently, an endless series of egoistic altruisms.

Trijueque, from *Juan Martín, el Empecinado,* is a study in tragic frustration. Galdós created a priest who stumbles, long after ordination, upon a repressed military vocation. The world of Trijueque's childhood dreams, of Cortez and Alexander, suddenly assumes the character of everyday reality; but only to confine him, despite inborn abilities, to a subordinate position within a small guerrilla band. The protagonist's singleminded interpretation of his destiny, his will to command, produce an innner tension that is released as hatred for superiors, deemed inept and envious. Frustration perverts Trijueque's strength, producing a monster of cruelty and a guerrilla forgetful of his cause.

The character is a stunning combination of ethnic characteristics: uncompromising individualism, extraordinary faith in a personal destiny, indomitable pride, and innate genius for war. All these might define the Spanish conquistador of another age, but are merely seeds of pathological frustration in a priest of the nineteenth century. Only tragedy can stem from Trijueque's firm identification with a destiny he can never fulfill; and, unrepentant to the end, his Judas-like suicide —

more desperation than expiation — is itself an overt defiance of his superior's decision to remand him to his church, far from the cries of battle, as punishment for his treachery.

These exceptionally detailed characterizations have a special value of their own, of course, as studies in human nature, but they are not lacking, for this reason, in very specific representational functions. Both characters analyzed, for example, project attitudes that are dissonant in the general context of the work (egoism and treachery). The realistic projection of such attitudes from within a general atmosphere of selflessness and patriotism is most effectively assigned to forceful and relatively well developed characters.

Two noblewomen, the Duchess Lesbia and the Countess of Rumblar, provide examples of the novelist's combination of characters as a function of historical representation. The Duchess Lesbia personifies the decadent court aristocracy under Charles IV: an embellished exterior that hides a rotten core. The Countess of Rumblar, a provincial aristocrat, begins, on the other hand, by manifesting the pride in duty of an aristocracy at the height of its historic function. Actually, her subsequent role is no more positive than that of the Duchess Lesbia, and Galdós combined two completely different personalities to better emphasize the historical reality of a social estate that had become anachronistic in the modern age. The Duchess displays but one positive quality, a physical beauty that contributes to her moral decline; the Countess' is a dated vitality, based on an unreasoning adherence to the past and on prejudices and outmoded values. The inveterate anachronism of the Rumblar household is extensively described in the work,[20] affording Galdós a permanent expression of a diseased social class.

Secondary characters are so numerous in the First Series that it is useful to separate them into two large groups: those with a primarily novelistic function, and those who most effectively point up special facets of the historical context. A grouping of this kind is necessarily artificial, because many, if not all the characters, belong to both categories.

A few characters from the first group — the Marquesa X, for example — are little more than names; but the great majority exhibit distinguishing personal traits: Cándido Santos de Malvar,

<hr />

[20] Pérez Galdós, *Obras completas*, I, 494-495, 888-890.

the best and most timid of souls; Malespina, the pathological liar; Flora Cisniega, the aging 'cursi'; Lobo, the pathetic expression of economically motivated duplicity; the Marqués X, the comical defender of diplomacy in an age of war; Pepita González, the ignorant actress whose thin veneer of polish barely hides a savage breeding; Mauro Requejo, a petty bourgeois given to avarice; and others.

Galdós emphasized the one aspect of each character that is functional in plot development. So much so, that many of these characterizations are essentially typed, that is, limited in their development to a single facet of personality. Galdós attenuated this, for the sake of realism, by occasionally focusing on other human dimensions of his characters: the vicious Lobo in the amiable company of friends or in the midst of his family, the grasping Requejo experiencing the first inklings of love, and Pepita González in meek submission to Máiquez. The plot connections of these secondary characters encourage their frequent appearance in the company of protagonists and historical figures, and they thus acquire a higher degree of verisimilitude.

The other group of secondary characters is more numerous, for the *Episodios Nacionales* are crowded with personages whose appearances — even when momentary — provide depth and variety to the historical canvas; different ideas, perspectives, and social elements. The rule here, in characters with a primarily representational function, is to introduce a given personality, with little or no further development. As exemplified by Pacorro Chinitas and 'Primorosa', however, this limitation does not detract from the character's individuality nor restrict the depiction of a wide range of human relationships. Galdós successfully conditioned each 'popular' type — otherwise common to Ramón de la Cruz or Mesonero Romanos — with the historically determined attitudes that fix it adequately within a specific context.

Galdós breathed life into every characterization of this multitudinous second group. The first-person narrative, which requires that Araceli introduce every character personally, grants each an initial measure of verisimilitude; but it is Galdós' skillful individuation in the short time allotted to each personage that constitutes the mainstay of the work's effective characterization. The novelist employed all the devices at his command, selecting the element or combination of elements that fixes a believable personality: physical appearance, language, and idiosyncrasies.[21] Thus, people like Pepe Pellejos (Sursum Corda), 'Pujitos', Gorito Santurrias, and Ignacia Rejoncillos (Zaina), to mention but a few, emerge realistically from the anonymity of the history text.

A common, all-pervasive patriotism, strong enough to assimilate even the most diverse personalities, is the catalyst that occasionally forges a collective protagonist. But this collective entity, inimitably handled by Galdós, is only meaningful, identifiable, in so far as the reader is able to recognize a number of believable characters encountered individually beforehand. Moreover, it is the degree of individuality granted to each character from this second group that becomes invaluable to the author in the broad reconstruction of historical events and actions. On such occasions, Galdós may refer specifically to the activities, the fighting and the dying, of persons familiar to the reader. This provides an unusual degree of relief, on the one hand, to every historical description of the *Episodios Nacionales;* and simultaneously forces the reader, on the other, into contact with a past that is re-lived as emotion, for even when minimally developed the secondary characters are real enough to arouse the reader's sympathy at every turn.

Galdós created a wide variety of people in the First Series. Some live out a full literary existence, but entire categories of characters are necessarily destined to incomplete elaboration, to token development. Children, for example, usually constitute one of the aforementioned categories, and can serve to indicate the wealth of values to be found in Galdós' limited characterizations. Araceli himself, 'el Empecinadillo', and especially Siseta's brood, from *Gerona*, suggest the novelist's delicate appreciation of the world of childhood.[22] Galdós' conscious effort to penetrate that world is manifest in the autobiographical elements that are discernible in the characterization of *Gerona*, in which a pair of child-adults, Siseta and Andrés Marijuán, establish — almost as if playing dolls — the home that the former's orphaned brothers need.

21 See, e.g., Pérez Galdós, *Obras completas,* I, 382, 1699.
22 Ibid., pp. 205-206, 218-219, 768, 809-812.

The depiction of historical characters is by no means the least difficult of Galdós' tasks. Sainz de Robles has commented as follows upon the unique problems involved:

> A mí me parece mucho más difícil re-crear un personaje que crearlo. Para crear un personaje basta una poderosa imaginación, servida por un sutilísimo don de observación. Como al personaje creado nadie le conocía, nadie juzgará en él sino su verdad humana y la eficacia de su realismo . . . Para re-crear un personaje . . . se precisa algo más que imaginación. Se necesita intuición genial. Se necesita sensibilidad exquisita.[23]

Some historical characters intervene actively in the novelistic development of the First Series. The most striking examples are Juan Martín (el Empecinado) and Máiquez, who are central to the subplots of *Juan Martín, el Empecinado* and *La corte de Carlos IV*, respectively. In such cases, Galdós had to intuit believable segments of real lives, the unbroken and undiscolored extension of a historical role into fictional plot functions.

Without unduly disturbing the historical silhouette or the historico-legendary image, as the case may be, Galdós brought familiar, intuited aspects of these real lives into sharp relief. An example of the novelist's resources and procedures is the penetration achieved into the real 'Empecinado', as distinguished from the heroic figure, by reproducing the guerrilla's colorful language.[24] The factual and the intuited elements are so fused, so artfully blended, that a historical personage dealt with in this way often emerges more believable than the legendary image and more fully dimensional than the silhouette often found in history texts.

A number of historical personalities held a special interest for Galdós, and the novelist missed no opportunity to present their public activities. The best example is Alvarez de Castro.[25] Although the hero's limited appearances hardly permit the intuition of distinguishing personal traits, Galdós' artistic devices are still invaluable. No summary of Alvarez de Castro, no attempt to define his stoic valor, can match the laconic 'se hará lo que convenga' with which the novelist indelibly stamps him in the reader's mind.

23 Sainz de Robles, "B. Pérez Galdós: su vida, su obra y su época," p. 170.
24 See, e.g., Pérez Galdós, *Obras completas*, I, 977.
25 Ibid., pp. 779, 784-785, 793, 818-820, 843.

Most historical characterizations, involving the countless minor figures that help create the impression of historical precision, are merely descriptive. This paucity of detail extends, however, to several characters of the greatest historical importance. In subsequent Series, it will be noted that Galdós was not reluctant to present the most prominent personalities of an epoch, intuiting details of their private lives through their contact with fictional characters. His relative unwillingness to do this in the First Series may be due to the legendary quality that enveloped the great men of the War of Independence. In dealing with Castaños, Velarde, or Mina, the presentation of unheroic personal facets, a familiar version, may have been deemed inappropriate.

Before concluding our study of characterization in the First Series, a few general remarks are in order. To begin with, only a very limited number of characters could actually be analyzed. The selection was guided, for the most part, by two criteria: first, historical or novelistic importance; and second, the degree to which a given character embodies a typical characterizational procedure of the author. Secondly, we have considered historical characters only those that appear in history texts with the same name. Lord Gray, 'La Naranjera', Lesbia, Mañara, and any others who may be veiled reproductions of specific historical figures,[26] have been considered literary creations. Finally, no attempt has been made to deal separately with the author's use of established literary models: Don Juan, Celestina, and others.[27] It was deemed convenient to do this in connection with later Series, in which this practice becomes more prominent.

Miscellaneous

1. Comical elements

The humoristic note that forms part of the past century's world-view is an essential element of the modern novel.[28] In the great writers of that age comedy is often the expression of

---

[26] See Berkowitz, *Pérez Galdós*, pp. 97-98; and R. de Mesonero Romanos, *Memorias de un setentón* (Madrid, 1926), I, 71, 313; II, 122-123.

[27] See, e.g., Pérez Galdós, *Obras completas*, I, 920, 953.

[28] B. Croce, *European Literature in the Nineteenth Century*, trans. Douglas Ainslee (London, 1924), pp. 268-269; and Pérez Minik, *Novelistas españoles*, p. 92.

sympathetic identification with human nature.[29] Galdós' art abounds in comical figures and humorous situations, and even here, in the first *Episodios Nacionales,* he employs a number of comical devices that re-appear throughout his work.

One of these is the primarily comical characterization, which is made to embody specific human flaws. There are two good examples in the First Series, and both are related to a long tradition of comedy. Malespina, introduced as a talkative Andalusian, is the pathological liar. The Marqués X is the monomaniac, obsessed with the notion of diplomacy. The two comical types converge: the liar has a pet source of prevarications — the subject of artillery — and the monomaniac must eventually lie in his endless application of diplomacy to life.

Galdós presented each of these characters separately, of course, but later renewed their effect by bringing them together to enact a classical 'miles gloriosus' sequence. Their association in Galdós' mind is no accident, for the two are composed of the same pathetic substance, reacting — each in a slightly different manner — to defend an inflated self-image that reality belies at every turn.

Gross exaggeration is the device employed in creating Santiago Fernández, who is known as 'El Gran Capitán'. The character's stubborn ignorance, his insistence upon the comparative greatness of the trivial, is a preparatory condition. The main flow of comedy stems from a patriotism so fervent that it leads, when coupled with stubborn ignorance, to exaggerations that are paradoxically both heroic and ridiculous. Fernández is, in this sense, a convenient example of the pathetic quality that underlies so much of the novelist's characterizational humor, of the sympathy that arises from his perception of human weakness. Fernández dies heroically, yet ridiculously, as a consequence of the exaggerated patriotism upon which his comical effect is based, and human nature is smilingly glorified in the grandiose quality of its debilities.

Personification is yet another source of comedy. A good example is Restituta Requejo, the personification of avarice. Her physical features, her movements, everything about the woman

---

29 See R. Pérez de Ayala, *Principios y finales de la novela* (Madrid, 1958), p. 46; and F. de Onís, "El humorismo de Galdós," *Revista Hispánica Moderna,* IX (1943), 293-294.

is suggestive. This unequivocal parallel between physical appearance and personality is reinforced by withholding from the character the human qualities that might attenuate the vice involved. Galdós' procedure in this case is actually threefold: the personification effected in the physical aspect of the subject, the de-humanization that reinforces it in the psychological sphere, and, as a final touch, a suggestively cacophonic name.

Galdós also evoked humor by means of anachronism. This is usually prepared by an extreme innocence in the subject. The young count of Rumbler, removed from reality by an absurd education, or Juan de Dios, separated from the world of everyday experiences by an intense timidity, are so ingenuous that their initial contact with reality is necessarily comical. Such characters may outgrow this humorous role, of course, except when the candor is a definitive characteristic.

The humorous possibilities of chronological anachronism are also exploited by Galdós. An example of this is Pedro Congosto, no less humorous for being a composite character, representatively constructed from several historical personalities.[30] His dated uniforms and archaic vocabulary are laughable in themselves, and his quixotic simplicity — which entertains the hope of recapturing the past's heroic spirit in outmoded artefacts — is even more so. Congosto is both pathetic and ridiculous, and the modern reader may even detect an element of satire in Galdós' stress on a delusion that is universal.

The various comical types studied are susceptible, in addition, of situation comedy, of appearances under circumstances that compound their humorous effect. Congosto, the quixotic figure, is presented, for example, in the process of courting a 'Dulcinea', who is none other than the 'cursi' Flora Cisniega; and he is subsequently placed in the hands of Lord Gray, whose intolerance of human stupidity is matched by his disdain for tradition.[31]

The humorous situation is as prominent as the humorous character in the First Series. A note of sarcasm is apparent, for example, whenever certain institutions are presented. An endless round of palatial intrigues reaches a ridiculous level in *La*

30 J. Sarrailh, "Quelques sources du *Cádiz*," *Bulletin Hispanique*, XXIII (1921), 41.
31 Pérez Galdós, *Obras completas*, I, 954-955.

corte de Carlos IV, and the picaresque stamp of the 'Motín de Aranjuez' compounds the satirical effect.[32]

The role of the reactionary elements in the 'Cortes de Cádiz' can serve as an example of Galdós' procedure. The situation, the intervention of real people, the speeches, and the reactions from the galleries are all essentially historical. The reader's identification with the general atmosphere of anti-traditionalism is intensified, moreover, by an added perspective from the plot. Araceli enters into the social life of the reactionary group that gathers in the home of the Rumblar family. With no political motives of his own, he selects and emphasizes what is potentially humorous in the characters gathered there. By recalling such private details in the historical situation described, or vice versa, the novelist elicits a compounded comical effect.

In outlining the subject matter of the Series' subplots, we have noted an extensive vein of irony. Several explanations are possible. It may be, for example, that the ironic twist is a necessary factor in maintaining the interest level of the subplots involved, the development of which is always necessarily limited.[33] On occasion, however, the irony appears to reflect a Galdosian attitude. This is particularly evident in *La batalla de los Arapiles,* which crystallizes, as we have seen, about an ironical projection of 'romanticized' Spain. It is a Cervantine irony, undoubtedly, and reminiscent of 'la razón de la sinrazón.'

The abundance of humor found in the First Series is surprising, for a heroic-legendary atmosphere makes difficult the esthetic integration of comedy. This demanded of Galdós an extraordinary tact, a careful avoidance of discordant juxtapositions. Perhaps the best example of the tightrope involved is the case of Fernández, 'El Gran Capitán', in which Galdós came closest to an impossible fusion of epic heroism and garrish humor. In general, the type of humorous situation encountered in *La corte de Carlos IV* would be incongruent in *Zaragoza* or *Trafalgar.* Within the epic event itself, the only humor possible is that which stems from a sympathetic perception of fundamental human failings. The comedy created by means of the old mariners in *Trafalgar* or evoked by the character of Candiola in *Zaragoza* is of this type.

<hr/>

32 Pérez Galdós, *Obras completas*, I, 414.
33 For a view of the First Series as a parody of the 'novela popular,' see Hinterhäuser, *Los Episodios Nacionales*, pp. 352 ff.

2. Symbolism

It is convenient to begin with Eoff's clarification of the problem inherent in the treatment of Galdosian symbolism:

> Admittedly, there is always justification for seeking an ulterior meaning in Galdós' novels, which is sometimes hidden and sometimes plain to the eyes. The question is how best to arrive at this meaning. Shall the setting, the events, personages and personal relationships be viewed as symbols of the author's generative ideas, or shall the characters first of all be regarded as living creatures whose natural behavior within a network of circumstances constitutes a story on which to base a judgment?[34]

The first alternative could lead to an unconscious distortion of art in the process of facilitating a symbolic possibility, or to an unbalanced emphasis on a symbolic relationship that constitutes a single facet of the literary work. The second alternative avoids these pitfalls, certainly, but can itself obstruct, by omission, the full and immediate comprehension often afforded by symbolic relationships.

In the *Episodios Nacionales,* symbolism is very often either associated with characterization or crystallized as a function of historical illustration. For this reason, it is perhaps most appropriate to risk the pitfalls of the first alternative noted above, and to stress the symbolic possibilities as they appear in the sequence of the work.

The most characteristic device of Galdosian symbolism is immediately evident in the First Series. Several names establish the essential characteristics of their bearers: Lesbia, the promiscuous Duchess, Mañara, her philandering gallant, the naive Cándido Bueno de Malvar, and many others. In the First Series, however, name symbolism hardly touches any of the main protagonists, and cannot be compared either quantitatively or qualitatively with the norm of later Series.[35]

A number of scenes in the work invite symbolic interpretation, as a form of historical illustration. *Bailén* begins, for example, with a heated discussion of the recent French invasion. The debaters, however, are most unevenly matched. Santorcaz's unimpeachable facts predict the defeat of Spain with relentless logic. Fernández, the comically exaggerated patriot, is only sus-

---

34 *The Novels of Pérez Galdós,* p. 21.
35 See Casalduero, *Vida y obra,* p. 60.

tained by a profound ignorance of recent military history. His defense of the Spanish position is no more than an accumulation of irrational or laughable statements.[36] This blatant 'razón de la sinrazón,' for it is nothing else in the least informed reader's eyes, admirably synthesizes the nature of Spain's heroic resistence. In *Trafalgar*, the 'old' Spain that succumbed there forever is personified in the battle itself by 'Mediohombre', the old sailor who has left part of himself in every naval encounter of the previous century. The 'new' Spain, which emerged from that heroic effort, is present in Araceli. The last scenes of the battle — the former's confession with the latter before dying, or the latter's doubtful survival — are rich in symbolic possibilities.[37]

Other scenes that might be remembered in this respect are the rat war of *Gerona;* the coincidence of Nomdedeu's death and his invalid daughter's full recovery, which suggests the disintegration of old Spain in the very historical situation which hardens a new Spain to life; and the combination of guerrilla types in *Juan Martín, el Empecinado,* which presents, in capsule form, the various shades of Spain's nineteenth-century plague.

The First Series introduces fewer symbolic relationships than it might have because the first-person narrative is generally unfavorable to the esthetic integration of symbolic connections. The fact that everything described or narrated must first have passed through a specific character's mind detracts from the verisimilitude of relationships which cannot suggest having been 'fixed' and still be effective.

B) *Second Series*

The Second Series reconstructs twenty years of Spanish history, but the fact that it covers a longer period than the First Series has no effect on the novelization. Galdós did not employ a quantitative criterion in determining the limits of a Series, but simply accommodated the literary unit to a dialectically meaningful period of history. In the present case, this encompasses the final spasms of the War of Independence, the complete reign of Ferdinand VII, and the initial moments of the crisis brought on by his death.

36 Pérez Galdós, *Obras completas,* I, 474.
37 Ibid., pp. 267-268.

The rigorous unity contrived by the literary form of the First Series is substantially weakened in the Second Series. The unified perspective induced by the novelist's chronological presentation of History has its effect here, of course, as it does in every Series; but there is a distinct reduction in the degree of Series cohesion derived from narrative technique and novelistic structure.

Galdós began by abandoning the exclusive first-person narrative, which naturally eliminated, in the Second Series, the unipersonal configuration of the First. The impersonal narration that characterizes the Second Series — for an occasional use of the first-person memoir technique does not substantially alter the work's impersonal character — allows the writer to focus on a variety of elements without the encompassing nexus that a specific (first-person) narrator's mere existence entails.

All Series require, as literary units, sufficient novelistic cohesion to reflect the fundamental unity of a definite period of history. But they also require, as we have seen, a degree of novelistic diversification, indispensable to a realistic depiction of the great diversity that makes up even the most homogeneous epochs. In the light of this necessary but flexible dualism, the novelistic structure of the Second Series constitutes a dissociative step.

Instead of a single unitive plot, which had to be integrated Episodio by Episodio into a series of tangentially developed subplots, the Second Series crystallizes a unitive nucleus from the relatively independent novels of Monsalud, Bragas, Navarro, and Jenara.[38] The Series is centered on a single nucleus of four lives, but no one of these, nor all of them combined for that matter, is comparable, in its unifying effect, to Araceli's monopoly of the First Series.

The basic independence of the four protagonists guarantees the Second Series an unprecedented degree of plot diversification; while a careful interlocking of their trajectories provides the needed measure of Series unity. After *El equipaje del rey José*, for example, Monsalud disappears and Bragas assumes the main role. The new plot, which carries through *Las memorias*

---

[38] Gamero y de Laiglesia, *Galdós y su obra*, I, 77.

de un cortesano de 1815 and *La segunda casaca,* retains important connections with the lives of the other three protagonists,
and the omnipresent third-person narrator can readily abandon
Bragas' memoirs when these converge with Monsalud's resurgent
activities. The same technique is later employed to incorporate
Jenara's personal memoirs.[39]

This novelistic structure of the Second Series ascribes the
illustrative functions of the First Series' subplots — with few
exceptions that shall be touched upon immediately — to more
complex plot developments, themselves sufficiently coordinated
to forge a degree of overall Series unity. This provides both a
method of plot diversification that has greater artistic possibilities and a Series unity that is unencumbered by such restrictions
as a unipersonal narration and a single, overextended unitive
plot.

The exceptions noted above consist of a few plot developments that are tangential to the unitive nucleus, that is, to the
interconnected trajectories of Monsalud, Bragas, Navarro, and
Jenara. These tangential plot elements — henceforth referred to
as novelistic microcosms, to avoid confusion with the subplots
of the First Series — represent a point of similarity between the
novelistic structures of the First and Second Series, but can
actually serve as the basis for a clear functional distinction between those two structures.

The geographical dispersion of the history novelized in the
First Series (a condition that implied sharp idiosyncratic, cul-
tural, and social differences as well), and the author's concern
with events rather than ideological conflict, required the integration of many representational subplots, mutually disconnected
and only circumstantially related to the continuous unitive
plot.[40] The Second Series, on the other hand, deals with a period
of history that is relatively compact in terms of geography,
and the novelist emphasized ideological conflict rather than
scattered military actions. This made it possible to reconstruct
almost an entire era from within a single nucleus of related
novels; but not quite, and this accounts for the few novelistic
microcosms found in the Series. These simply assume representational functions in areas that were not susceptible of presen-

39 Pérez Galdós, *Obras completas,* I, 1383, 1615, 1635.
40 See above, pp. 59-60.

tation through the plot activities of the four main protagonists: the lowest levels of society, in *Un faccioso más y algunos frailes menos;* and the political activities of rural Spain, in *Un voluntario realista.*

Plot Development

The ideological clash novelized is itself inherently dramatic,[41] and it is reinforced, as such, by concrete plots that embody ideological abstractions. The novelist made little use of the violent aspects of the conflict, of the numerous liberal rebellions that mark the period. Galdós' historical selection is clearly directed, instead, to the fundamental political problem, which is highly susceptible of moving dramatization: the personal conflicts of individuals, which find an outlet in the ideological arena of nineteenth-century Spain.

The four lives that constitute the unitive nucleus of the Series begin by sharing a common point of origin: Puebla de Arganzón. This intimate relationship, established from the onset, permits the development of each life to touch upon the other three. The outline is not unlike that of any number of Galdós' contemporary novels: a society peopled by characters who are focused in succession, but who appear throughout as part of the human context of the work. Only a contemporary novel as long as *Fortunata y Jacinta,* of course, could incorporate the elaboration of so many protagonists over such a long period of time.

In the Second Series, Galdós focused preferentially on Salvador Monsalud, who possesses characteristics conducive to an interesting and illustrative plot. He passes, for example, from 'afrancesado' — a stigma attenuated by the character's manly gratitude — to liberal archconspirator, a personal evolution that reflects one important facet of the transition between the War of Independence and the reign of Ferdinand VII.

The political nucleus of Monsalud's novel, which facilitates the necessary discussion and analysis of the period's liberal rebellions, calls to mind Llanos Gutiérrez's *Sandoval,* written in English during the very years novelized by Galdós. The similarity is interesting, but there are manifest differences. Monsalud's political evolution — from reluctant French sympathizer to disil-

---

[41] Gómez de Baquero, *Novelas y novelistas,* p. 16.

lusioned liberal — is, to begin with, much more complex than that of Sandoval, the hero of an openly tendentious novel. Besides, the development of Galdós' protagonist often transcends the narrow sphere of political activity. Three women, for example, are woven into his hectic existence, and each draws out new facets of a rich human creation. Through Jenara, Andrea, and Soledad, women of striking social and personal differences, Galdós offered a full cycle of heterosexual relationships: from the comradery of filial devotion (Soledad) to the adulterous liaison (Jenara).

Monsalud's protracted conflict with Navarro — his stepbrother — and his condescending friendship for Bragas complete the substance of the novel. The first, a rivalry of boys over Jenara and of men over her and everything else, holds the reader until the tragic climax of the last Episodio. Monsalud's weakness for Bragas, in whom he recognizes incurable egoism, is, on the other hand, the work's most important avenue of humor. Monsalud's novel, thus composed, features a disconsolate succession of disappointments, a combination of his own failings and Spain's inability to fulfill a liberal destiny. In the end, however, Soledad awaits the man matured but unbroken by exile and failure; while the death of Ferdinand VII, which coincides with this, contributes a final note of political optimism.

Navarro's trajectory in the Series is much less complex. It is never focused, in fact, for the length of a whole Episodio, which does not detract from its importance. Navarro's existence, independently depicted in short segments throughout the work, is an indispensable part of the unitive nucleus. His relations with Jenara, his unfaithful wife, and with Monsalud, her detested lover, influence the development of their lives at every turn. Together with Monsalud, the 'afrancesado' turned conspirator, this 'guerrillero', turned paladin of reaction, personifies the transition between historical epochs.

Navarro's novel features very little personal development, hardly more than the cumulative reinforcement of a constitutional despair. His inalterable nature resists evolution, the very substance of literary development, and his novelistic existence is consequently reduced to the illustrative dimension of an embittered struggle for political reaction.

Jenara's life, on the other hand, is a delirious striving for impossible goals, a typical Galdosian depiction of feminine existence. As a spiteful woman-child, Jenara rejects Monsalud, the 'afrancesado' youth, and abruptly marries Navarro, the brave 'guerrillero.' But her flighty, adventuresome personality is incompatible with the stolid inalterability of her chosen mate, and the willful woman she becomes is drawn to Monsalud, whom she had once proudly disdained.

Jenara's attraction to the liberal conspirator easily overcomes her weak ideological and religious restraints. She is led on, above all, by a set of circumstances that conspire to impede the satisfaction of her will. These novelesque circumstances, woven into the sequence of historical events,[42] build into a climax of adulterous passion. The long-postponed encounter, one of the most moving ever drawn by Galdós, is momentarily illumined by the sparkling rebirth of childhood dreams; but it ends abruptly (the flimsy substance of an illusion from the past, the willful fulfillment of an elusive desire) with the appearance of Navarro.

Jenara's ungovernable passions intensify every avenue of novelistic development in the Series. Her unscrupulous behavior is the cause, for example, of Monsalud's long, almost tragic separation from Soledad; and her actions aggravate the mutual animosity of Monsalud and Navarro, making her husband's hatred unappeasable. Jenara's movement through the work, even when it does not directly affect her fellow protagonists, is a permanent source of interest: when the beautiful coquette conspires for the reactionary king, for example, or when the emancipated female seeks out the romantic youths of the era.

The meteoric rise of Bragas' political fortunes has all the earmarks of satire. From a humble administrative position in the ill-fated government of Joseph Bonaparte, the unprincipled young man attains the highest posts in the successive governments of Ferdinand VII, both reactionary and liberal. The vices that mar his personality, egoism and duplicity, coincide admirably with the requisites for success in that corrupt milieu.

The two novels that contain Bragas' major appearances are narrated in the first-person, a form that reinforces their satirical intent.[43] Galdós reproduced, in this way, the very tone of taunting hypocrisy with which the opportunist proclaims the altruism

---

[42] Pérez Galdós, *Obras completas*, I, 1656-1696.
[43] Ibid., p. 1271.

of his motives. The greater Bragas' efforts in this direction, the more efficient the satire; for the quality of his actions forces itself unmistakably from behind his hasty veil of sham.

Bragas is patterned on the 'picaro' but placed in social circles that are not the rogue's traditional setting. This change in context reflects the overall modification with which Galdós re-vitalized that literary 'genre'. The traditional 'pícaro' is just another tragic figure in the modern novel; an anti-social being, criminal or pathological non-conformist, explained and understood by means of a pertinent psycho-sociological presentation. But the roguish act, if it is to retain an ethical connotation, must flow from the free perversion of a pronounced capacity for good. This is precisely what Bragas' running commentary on himself, and on his achievements, provides.

It is noteworthy, first, that Navarro Villoslada used a similar approach in *Historia de muchos Pepes;* and that Galdós' creation in *Las memorias de un cortesano de 1815* is exactly what the perspicacious Mesonero Romanos would have attempted in dealing with the same period of history.[44]

The world of fiction that crystallizes from the interaction of these four lives offers both the most important political attitudes of an era and a panoramic cross-section of Spanish life. Bragas, the political opportunist, introduces the sphere of government, both its administrative side — utterly corrupt in the period dealt with — and the more intimate facets of royal activities. Jenara, the royal conspirator between 1821 and 1823, makes accessible the romantic circles of the day. Navarro, the reactionary, introduces the rural, popular, and religious nuclei that fused into the wave of political regression flowing from the War of Independence. Monsalud, the liberal, covers the political intrigue of a full decade, with settings as varied as the masonic lodge and the rural cloister.

As we have noted elsewhere, this central novelistic outline, however extensive, cannot directly incorporate every element of the historical environment, and much that is of importance must be represented in novelistic microcosms. These, like the subplots of the First Series, reveal various degrees of development, and

---

44 Berkowitz, "Galdós and Mesonero Romanos," *Romanic Review*, XXIII (1932), 201-205. Hinterhäuser (*Los Episodios Nacionales*, p. 311) has also seen a stylistic similarity to Miñano's *Pobrecito holgazán*.

may be ordered by their closeness of association to the unitive nucleus of the work. In general terms, the novelistic microcosms are fewer than the subplots of the First series, but are more often extensively developed.

Soledad's personal experiences, for example, never achieve the autonomy of those associated with the four main protagonists, but some of her activities are relatively independent of Monsalud's novel, within which they generally crystallize. At one such juncture, in *El terror de 1824*, Soledad is brought together with Sarmiento and Benigno Cordero to forge a somewhat independent plot. Soledad's ideal charity — caring for Sarmiento, a liberal fanatic who had abused her reactionary father — and Sarmiento's bewildered gratitude are at the center of a story that introduces the embryonic middle-class of Madrid (Cordero) and offers a view of the notorious political repression of 1824 (Sarmiento).

The novel of José Armengol and Sor Teodora de Aransis is farther removed from the world of the unitive nucleus. The full development of these two characters in *Un voluntario realista,* which contrasts with Monsalud's adventitious and disguised appearance, results in a degree of plot autonomy that is unusual outside the unitive nucleus of the Series. Armengol and Sor Teodora, immersed in a rural, religious atmosphere that is natural to them but not to Monsalud, determine the pace, the tone, and the content of the novel. The frustrated sexton and the tragic nun, desperately seeking a fresh lease on life, are swept into the vortex of a stillborn political movement. Both are destroyed by uncontrollable circumstances and hopeless passions, and disintegrate as readily as the reactionary move against Ferdinand VII that offered, in preluding Carlism, a taste of power to the frustrated warrior and of life to the vegetating nun.

The novelistic microcosm with fewest links to the unitive nucleus of the Series, in *Un faccioso más y algunos frailes menos,* takes place in the nether world of 'Tablas', 'Pimentosa', and father Gracián. The combination of characters is explosive, generating the friction that sparks the destruction of a jesuit house by hysterical mobs. Plot development is rather sketchy, but suffices, in general, for a close view of the human elements involved in the historic tragedy.

In conclusion, the Second Series combines elements that are

invariably appealing in novelistic literature: a bitter ideological conflict, pertinent to almost any epoch and steeped in human passions; the difficult life of an idealist, mysterious, frustrating, and adventurous; and a comical opportunism that is political satire and often verges on caricature. Within a Spain seething with conspiracy and periodically rocked by political upheavals, Galdós interlaced the lives of four completely different people. In the situation in which Monsalud sacrifices time and energy, Bragas achieves his materialistic ends; and while a tragic Navarro opposes his inscrutable countenance to a century's progress, his wife Jenara unscrupulously pursues the fancies of her impassioned will. This, together with novelistic microcosms of moving interest, makes the Second Series an extraordinarily absorbing literary creation.

The esthetic combination and presentation of the numerous elements outlined above was undoubtedly the novelist's most trying task. Galdós employed to these ends, upon which the artistic quality of his work depended, all the literary knowhow at his disposal.

The Series begins, for example, with an excellent introduction, and several literary devices contribute to its effectiveness. We have already stressed the historical insight revealed in beginning with the final phase of the preceding epoch. Galdós did equally well by the fictional content. *El equipaje del rey José* immediately introduces the four major protagonists of the work, spells out the nature of their relations, and thus provides a blueprint, as it were, for the development of the entire Series.

No less efficient is the manner of easing the reader into the new fictional environment. Galdós employed, to this end, the stock of characters already his in 1876. The first six or seven persons encountered in *El equipaje del rey José* are known to the reader of Galdós.[45] The name Monsalud is itself familiar, as is the context of the main protagonist's initial steps in the work.[46] There opens up for the reader a world that is familiar, offering the most comfortable accommodations for the Series-long journey.

Another factor that is crucial to the esthetic integrity of the work is the repeated coupling of the Series' various plot threads. Galdós' skill is particularly evident in his treatment of those

45 Pérez Galdós, *Obras completas*, I, 1183-1186.
46 Ibid., pp. 1193-1194.

that make up the unitive nucleus of the Series. The re-appearance of Monsalud in the trajectory of Bragas, for example, is made to heighten the interest with mystery, while simultaneously preparing a new sphere for Bragas' opportunistic activities.[47]

The successive interpolations of Jenara's memoirs constitute a much more comprehensive example, and allow us to underscore some important complementary qualities of Galdós' artistic coupling of plot threads. Each segment of the first-person narration is contrived to relieve the monotony of the work's characteristic third-person narrative and focus upon specific historical situations with the personal intimacy of the memoir; while each interruption of these memoirs allows an omniscient third-person narrator to fill in everything that Jenara's limited experience omits.[48]

An extended unitive plot, consisting of relatively few active elements, requires — as noted in the First Series — a number of periodic intensifications. These are often provided by elemental devices of pulp literature. The second Series, which boasts a much more complex novelistic development, can do without the latter. The few that appear in the Second Series are employed for special effects, and are unobstrusively woven, above all, into the novelistic structure of the work. The fact that Monsalud and Navarro are kept ignorant of their blood relationship, for example, nourishes a Series-long expectancy, adds human interest, and makes the symbolic function of the two characters feasible.

The segmentation of the novelistic content in the ten volumes of the Second Series is suited to the literary unit's new structure. Contiguous Episodios, for example, need no longer take up an interrupted plot thread, and novelistic breaks between volumes can remain outstanding much longer. This is possible, of course, because the interpolation of another of the four related plots does not constitute a complete dissociation of novelistic matter.[49] Such postponements serve, in fact, to interlace simultaneous plot developments, and constitute a structural device that underscores the novelistic interconnection (unitive nucleus) that characterizes the Second Series. These changes in

47 Pérez Galdós, *Obras completas*, I, 1353-1354, 1382-1383.
48 Ibid., pp. 1615, 1635.
49 See, e.g., ibid., pp. 1270, 1350.

the segmentation of fictional content do not perceptibly alter the novelist's goals as outlined in our study of the First Series.[50]

Characterization

The First Series can offer what one human being, Araceli, limited as he is, knows or learns about himself and others. The Second Series, a third-person narration in the main, has fewer limitations on the number and quality of its perspectives on people. This offers greater characterizational possibilities, a potential that is implemented in the Series by a novelistic structure that features the full development of numerous protagonists and a historical reconstruction that highlights different ideologies, political alignments, and worldly attitudes. The result is a generation of Spaniards, of complex individuals, captured in its divided reactions to a specific historical context.

Monsalud is not merely a prototype of the liberal conspirator. Political activities permit him to become identified intimately with the events of his day, but he is, above all, a believable human being. His relationships within the Series reveal both the drive of a vital political idealism and the individual human contours that limit it. The dedicated liberal can thus pay dearly for the freedom of a reactionary prisoner, and even forfeit his own while abetting the escape of a royal conspirator.[51] Individualizing strokes of this kind contribute qualifying overtones to Monsalud's political identity, and are yet made realistic within the fictional fibre of the work: Soledad's father is the reactionary in question, and Jenara herself is the royal conspirator. What matters, however, is that Galdós placed the idealist in situations requiring personal rather than political decisions, facing real problems as a man and not an abstraction. The humanitarian idealist is realistically endowed, moreover, with a measure of human weakness. Monsalud's sexual activities, for example, produce victims to point out his failings and add a facet of anguished remorse to the characterization.[52]

Monsalud is, in general terms, a compendium of attractive traits. He is idealistic, intelligent, and amorous; and to this disarming array of qualities is added a melancholy romantic mien

50 See above, p. 57.
51 Pérez Galdós, *Obras completas*, I, 1489, 1622-1624.
52 Ibid., I, 1535-1536; II, 225.

that derives from the hopeless discrepancy between his political dream and the march of History.[53] Monsalud's instant appeal is thus assured, but what holds the reader after its initial effect is the fundamental realism noted above, the human dimensions gradually unveiled as he develops.

This development, which consists largely of the gradual dissipation of unrealistic dreams, greatly enriches Monsalud as an individual. The character experiences and perceives the barriers that Spanish life and temperament represent to the fulfillment of his liberal ideals, and his reluctant acceptance of this historical situation is a gauge to his realistic development.[54] Without radical changes to tax the credibility of the reader, a slow accumulation of experiences turns the ingenuous child into the politically wise and cautious youth, and the latter is replaced in turn by a mature, somewhat cynical, but still essentially humane ex-conspirator.

Galdós created the perfect hero without sacrificing realism in development or presentation. Monsalud's character is well suited to an age of altruistic ventures and repeated disappointments, but subject to a normal process of development and rarely encountered outside the shell of his human condition.

Bragas is deliberately made to contrast with Monsalud. Their simultaneous appearance in *El equipaje del rey José* establishes a characterizational polarity — altruism, egoism — that the remainder of the Series repeatedly confirms. In addition to this personal difference, the two must be considered distinct characterizations. Bragas, despite his various political mutations, displays a degree of inflexibility that suggests typification. A literary creature whose actions are always predisposed, whose psychological make-up discourages a range of alternative responses, is a typed characterization. Bragas is fashioned, to this end, from the fewest possible motivational elements, all in some manner directed towards a single goal. Lacking personal value conflicts, he responds automatically to life.

The literary device of typification makes it feasible to present a whole segment of humanity in one creation; and, in effect, Bragas typifies the plague of opportunists endemic in Spanish politics. But the integration of a type-character like Bragas into

[53] See, e.g., Pérez Galdós, *Obras completas*, I, 1491.
[54] See, e.g., ibid., p. 1419.

the very heart of the Series' unitive nucleus required the use of special devices: the character presents himself in a first-person narrative, an effective guarantee of credibility; and his realism is frequently reinforced by the company of important historical figures.[55]

The success of Bragas' characterization is predicated, in the last analysis, on a delicate balance between automatism and individuality. Without a measure of individuality, Bragas' automatic behavior would appear anachronistically puppet-like in a historical setting; while too striking an individuality could detract from the typicalness that provides Galdós with an incomparable subject for illustrative satire. Bragas must consequently show personal characteristics, but these must then fall closely into line with his single-track (egoistic) response to life: childish fears, pompous vanity, etc.

Navarro, like Bragas, hardly evolves at all. Galdós' first sketch of the character, in 1813, reveals all the personality factors that would shortly constitute a reactionary temperament: an uneasy suspicion of all innovation, a deep-rooted aversion to all things foreign, and a religious adherence to everything 'castizo'.

Navarro's life is a perennial struggle against the invasion of new forms, a frustrated attempt to stem the tide of History. The staunch reactionary — with the peculiar grandeur of a Miltonian Satan — is Galdós' most successful depiction of despair as the mainspring of personality. No other Galdosian creation is so completely permeated by bitterness. Navarro's inflexible approach to life, typical of an extreme reactionary, precludes sensitivity and warmth in him. Furthermore, this inability to forgive, forget, and evolve with life is implanted by the author in an existence conditioned by hatred: childhood frustration in his love for Jenara (Monsalud); death of father (French-Monsalud); death of in-law (Liberals-Monsalud); infidelity of Jenara (Monsalud).

The disintegration of this composite of hate, despair, and insensitivity is imminent; and Navarro's role in the Series, a struggle against History, against evils that stem from his own personality, constitutes a believable and interesting set of causes. The death of his father and of Jenara's grandfather (Baraona)

---

55 Pérez Galdós, *Obras completas*, I, 1286, 1314-1315, 1320-1332.

deprives Navarro of all intimate human ties. He is insecure in his marriage, which is childless, and insensitive to Jenara's imaginative flights, in which he cannot participate. Navarro fails to kindle the warmth he desperately needs and his wife Jenara, hardly the long-suffering type, not only leaves him, but seeks out Monsalud. The worst evils that could befall a traditionally oriented Spaniard appear, at first, to glance off Navarro's twin shields of insensitive strength and unrelenting political drive. They gradually take their toll, however, and the character finally passes from despair to madness, and thence to a release, in death, from his gnawing bitterness.

The initial similarity to Bragas is superficial, of course, for Navarro transcends the limitations of a typed character. A fundamental immutability is, in his particular case, more in the nature of a personal attitude than of a characterizational condition. Navarro is never drastically limited, furthermore, in the range of his motivations (profound love, bitter hatred, and political altruism), and his experiences in the work provide, as we have seen, an air of tragic grandeur.

Jenara is the first of a feminine pattern of characterization that was to become identified with Galdós. She is the antithesis of the ideal of feminine virtue, and deviates from this traditional concept by assuming the masculine prerogative of an active existence. Jenara's differentiating characteristics are the will to pursue her own dreams, regardless of their fluctuating nature; and the strength of character to forge a life independent of men, be it father, husband or lover.

Jenara combines extraordinary resolve with boundless imagination, the precise combination that produced many of Galdós' exceptional feminine creations. Like most of these, her flaw is ethical, since an impulsive, self-centered drive for life's promises invariably undermines the restrictions which society places upon feminine behavior. The transgression is often, in Galdós, the sign of a powerful feminine character, one that finds a permanent place in the author's world of fiction.[56]

Jenara is best analyzed by contrasting her with Soledad Gil de la Cuadra, the other feminine protagonist in the Series, who is incidentally treated at greater length. Soledad's virtues gain

[56] Jenara is the only character from the Second Series that Galdós brings forth as late as the Fourth Series. See Galdós, *Obras completas*, II, 1440-1441.

immediate favor with the reader, but she remains a weaker literary creation than Jenara. The innocent creature fallen into an evil world enchants, but does not captivate as a human being. The fact is that virtue reduces Soledad's capacity for uninhibited reaction within the novelistic context. Although not unrealistically limited in this sense, for she evolves believably as a person (matured by love and the experience of adversity), Soledad's development is invariably channeled by an 'a priori' moral condition.

Jenara knows no such limitations. She literally casts her own life, fully and in all its extremes, from the passions, conflicts, and political alternatives that accumulate in the work. She interests, above all, as an individual, as a complex of potentialities. While Soledad demands our unconditional approval, Jenara may be accepted or rejected, she is problematical and possessed of an ambivalence that generates interest.

Galdós' great achievement in the characterization of Jenara is the degree of realism attached to a personality in whom will and imagination combine to force the most radical alterations. The novelist accomplished this, for the most part, by a careful preparation of the circumstances attending Jenara's introduction to the work. Her instantaneous passage from sweetness and love to bitter hatred for Monsalud, in *El equipaje del rey José,* is set in an atmosphere of a profoundly patriotic and religious animosity toward everything French or 'afrancesado'. This unexpectedly violent reaction, somewhat attenuated by the circumstances described, establishes the believable vital tone of the character.

José Armengol develops outside the unitive nucleus of the Series, but is a protagonist in his own right. His characterization recalls that of Trijueque, for he too is a man whose innate being is tragically perverted by life. The protagonist of *Un voluntario realista* is more fully drawn and more complex than Trijueque, adding a sexual dimension, altogether lacking in the guerrilla-priest, to an overall vital frustration.

Armengol is a born warrior, coming alive in the midst of decisive action; he is, furthermore, a being impelled by powerful sexual needs. An ironic but fateful combination of circumstances places such a man in the role of sexton to a nunnery. A desperate sadness, but with paradoxical overtones of irony, is the prevailing note in the personality of Armengol, alias 'Tilín', a pejorative expression that humorously underscores the tragic contrast between a humble life-function and the need for a heroic destiny.

Un voluntario realista, unique in the Series for its rapidly paced narration, offers a summary outline of Armengol's formative years, then depicts the moment of his rebellion under cover of the reactionary movement that preluded Carlism. Both the character and the movement fail miserably, pathetically, thus combining to project the tone of that historical moment. Carlism would have another day, but 'Tilín', frustrated as well in his love for Sor Teodora de Aransis, is broken in spirit. In an overtly Dickens-like scene, a bewildered and beaten Armengol becomes the nun's pathetically innocent sacrifice upon the altar of her unconfessed passion for Monsalud.[57]

Sor Teodora, co-protagonist of *Un voluntario realista,* is one of the few nuns treated at length by the author. She, in particular, is well linked to his world of fiction through Doña Perfecta.[58] The retrospective narration of Sor Teodora's convent existence is basic to the characterization: the childish motives that led to the cloister, the gradual weakening of that impetus, and the vegetative life into which she is finally immobilized by a closed destiny. As in the case of Armengol, the Episodio captures the moment of rebellion.

This revolt, of the life that still pulsates and the woman that still lingers in the nun, is never overt in Sor Teodora. The reactionary movement that penetrated the rural cloisters of Spain allows the nun to become directly involved in conspiracies, thus reactivating her petrified existence in a manner compatible with her state. The resurgence of the woman is precipitated by Armengol's newfound boldness and by the presence of Monsalud, who saves himself from the vengeance of Navarro, on this occasion, by surreptitiously hiding in the nun's cell.

In the end, when Monsalud is finally captured, Sor Teodora, who has herself been forcibly taken by a desperate Armengol, reaches the decisive moment in her reactivated existence. With all the emotional conviction of her sex, with much of the resolute unscrupulousness that readers can recall in another of her blood,

57 Pérez Galdós, *Obras completas,* II, 98.
58 Ibid., p. 229.

Sor Teodora, playing God, substitutes Armengol's death for that of Monsalud. No amount of religious casuistry can obscure her true motives, and her tragic realization of this — which affords Galdós one of his most moving conclusions — is predicated on her re-discovery of life, of femininity, without having ceased to be a nun.

Galdós understood the powerful literary effect of characters whose lives are marked by the tragedy of a thwarted destiny. Later in his career the writer employed a similar characterizational formula to create such moving figures as Pedro Polo Cortés and Tristana.

Benigno Cordero, co-protagonist of the novelistic microcosm found in *El terror de 1824*, is the typical bourgeois of the era, combining the virtues, the shortcomings, and even the vital tone of the bourgeoisie: a complete dedication to work, a blind faith in its efficacy, and a highly developed sense of what is practical.

To better trace the development of the characteristics outlined, and at the same time establish the historical relation between middle-class and 'milicia nacional', Cordero is initially presented in his hour of heroism.[59] The heroism itself is appropriately middling in 'el heroe de la calle de Boteros', and even this militant attitude gradually gives way to the common sense that constitutes the character's essence. Cordero's post-revolutionary (1823) decision, subordinating ideals and patriotism to the immediate necessities of daily life, is not surprising, and the merchant's resolve is not without its own particular brand of merit in a historical context of destructive extremes.

To this characterizational embodiment of the practical philosophy that is the measure of an entire class, Galdós added two basic and complementary qualities: a fundamental honesty, with himself and others, and a candorous virtue in his personal relationships. These are particularly evident in Cordero's Moratinian role after *El terror de 1824*, in which he sedately renounces — in favor of Monsalud — whatever rights the charity of a middle-aged man could have given him to the love of a young Soledad.

Sarmiento, Cordero's co-protagonist, represents the opposite pole, that of insensate impracticality. A fundamental lack of self-

59 Pérez Galdós, *Obras completas*, I, 1592-1593.

restraint leads Sarmiento, who is basically a good man, to the inhuman extreme, for example, of denying water to the thirsty reactionary Gil de la Cuadra. The temperaments of school-teacher and merchant, so deliberately polarized by the novelist, give expression to the extremes of liberal behavior between 1821 and 1823. Ironically enough, the positive and negative signs are apparently reversed after 1823.

With characteristic extremism, Sarmiento identifies himself absolutely with liberty; and his very sanity is shaken by the events that sweep away the constitutional regime of 1821. In these circumstances, the paradoxical retribution in kindness received at the hands of Soledad Gil de la Cuadra, who takes the crazed old man off the streets, prepares the perturbed character's special role in *El terror de 1824.* Sarmiento's identification with liberty, when coupled with remorse for his own past cruelty, leads to a death that is both a form of martyrdom for lost liberty and a grateful expiation, taking upon himself Soledad's guilt for delivering clandestine liberal mail.

In addition to the process of his noble, even grandiose death — both in deliberate contrast to that of Riego and as an incomparable example of the idiotic proceedings of 1824 —, the character interests as one of Galdós' earliest psychopathological creations. He is the product of a Cervantine formula that would later supply the novelist with many exceptional characterizations: a monomaniacal fixation on one concept, which eventually leads to a hallucinatory ambivalence expressed by contiguous and opposite mental states, madness and sanity.

The characters that live out the novelistic microcosm found in *Un faccioso más y algunos frailes menos* are less elaborate. The group consists of 'Tablas', the shiftless 'matón' that so often forms part of popular Spanish settings; his common-law wife 'Pimentosa', whose feminine brand of ferocity establishes the popular version of the 'chula'; father Gracián, a well-meaning but overly-intrusive priest, reformer of social conditions that 'Tablas' (who will lead the assault on the jesuit's monastery) finds very much to his liking; and the child Romualda, who is as pathetic a creation as Marianela.

The grouping of secondary characters along functional lines, carried out in our study of the previous Series, is less useful here. There are hardly any characters with one primary function, either novelistic or representational, since Galdós produced even such special effects as comedy without relying on specialized characterizations.

The familiar secondary characters initially encountered in *El equipaje del rey José* disappear after introducing the Series. The new historical environment is gradually peopled with more representative figures, who often cluster into groups like that studied above from *Un faccioso más y algunos frailes menos*.

Another group of this type features Andrea, one of young Monsalud's loves, and Falfán de los Godos, who eventually marries her. The former, a timely expression of the sensuous and spoiled criolle, acts out the whole range of passionate romantic extremes, chasing Monsalud from pillar to post before consenting to her loveless marriage. The rich husband, as pompous as his name suggests, cuts a ridiculous figure throughout the work as an inept Don Juan.

Together with these, as Andrea's legal guardian, Galdós presented José Campos, the enigmatic head of Spanish Masonry during the liberal interlude between 1821 and 1823. The clustering of characters noted above is functional here, for by weaving numerous relationships about Campos — depictions which range from logrolling with the notable politicians of the day to wrangling over Andrea's future with Monsalud, which also bears political overtones — Galdós was able to reconstruct, intuitively, the obscure personality of an important historical figure.[60]

Other well-drawn secondary characters are Urbano Gil de la Cuadra, a pusillanimous individual fired to anguished manhood by the knowledge of his deceased wife's trysts with Monsalud; Pedro Guimaraens, an example of just the opposite, a man of such masculine bluntness that he recalls another country squire depicted many years after in *Nazarín;* and Primitivo Cordero, in whom Galdós captures the very essence of the 'milicia nacional'.[61]

As several critics have noted,[62] a large number of Galdós' creations in the Second Series are characters whose personalities are expressed, in large part, through physical description. A familiar Lobo can hardly be improved upon, for example, as

60 See Varela Hervias, *Cartas*, p. 22.
61 Pérez Galdós, *Obras completas*, I, 1563-1564.
62 See, e.g., Carranza, *El pueblo a través de los Episodios Nacionales*, p. 23.

Chaperón's rodent-like clerk in the legal slaughter of 1824, and Canencia, another familiar character from the First Series, is a specimen expression of the masonic society's formulistic 'rigor mortis' in the period 1821-1823. New to the world of the *Episodios Nacionales* are Felicísimo Carnicero, as mummified a creature as the Carlist ideas with which he nourishes what little there is to his meager existence; and Romo, the royalist volunteer of 1823 who is the personification of granite heartlessness.[63]

This device of characterization is not new at this point, but it does have an extraordinary high ratio of incidence in the Second Series, a fact that invites the following comments. The practice is normally limited to secondary characters, and Galdós is rarely obvious in its application. When he is, as in the case of Romo, for example, it is generally with a special effect in mind.[64] Moreover, the novelist's creations under this characterizational formula — even those that are most obviously included — retain the degree of verisimilitude that is necessary to function capably within a realistic historical setting.

The very young again receive special attention. Armengol's childhood, for example, is a masterful depiction of a semi-savage thrust suddenly into the quiet of a nunnery.[65] Romualda, the crippled offspring of 'Tablas' and 'Pimentosa', is broken as only a child may be by the absence of affection, by an atmosphere of brutal insensitivity. And Galdós, with the depth of human sympathy that most critics have found in his humor,[66] ingeniously identifies her torment with a slow and painful movement up and down endless stairs. Only in her death is there a note of release.[67]

The Galdós-Mesonero correspondence referred to earlier is especially meaningful with respect to the Second Series, and furnishes some important insights into Galdós' historical characterization in general. Some of the questions put by the novelist, for example, suggest a genuine interest in the intimate lives of

63 Pérez Galdós, *Crónica de la quincena*, ed. W. H. Shoemaker, (Princeton, 1948), p. 51.

64 Pérez Galdós, *Obras completas*, I, 1461; II, 149.

65 Ibid., II, 11-14.

66 See, e.g., Del Río, *Estudios galdosianos*, p. 20; and Dendariena, *Galdós*, pp. 151-160.

67 Pérez Galdós, *Obras completas*, II, 315.

specific historical personages.[68] This serves to confirm the novelist's norm of reproducing, in so far as possible, the man instead of the historical image. In the letter dated October 25, 1876, Galdós wrote: "¿Y Don Víctor Sáez, que si no figuró hasta el '23 me conviene presentarlo desde ahora?"[69] In effect, Galdós introduced him earlier than warranted by his place in the history text, and the value of this procedure, often followed by the novelist, can be measured in the characterization of Don Víctor Sáez. When the personage's moment arrives, according to the history book, he is already an integral part of the historical environment and a more rounded human being than the usual sketch of him.

The Second Series has no major historical figure in an important novelistic role. Only Campos has an ample plot function, but he can not compare, in this sense, with 'el Empecinado' from the previous Series. This may be because the period of history novelized in the Second Series offers few historical characters with novelistic potential, that is, people who could interest the novelist as individual human beings. The picturesque and moving career of Riego might have attracted Galdós, but he was always revolted by the circumstances of the hero's death.[70] Furthermore, the novelist's historical selection deliberately avoided a perspective from the periphery of the Peninsula, and this fact, which shall be discussed at length shortly, eliminated any number of attractive subjects: Lacy, Porlier, Torrijos, and others.

Nevertheless, the Second Series offers a great number of effective historical characterizations. Ferdinand VII, for example, is admirably portrayed in scenes that are essentially tangential to the Series' plot development. The flaws that made him a singularly unsuccessful ruler are revealed in the everyday conduct of the individual, and the man that emerges explains the failure of the king. Galdós also presented a number of the better known intriguers who gathered around Ferdinand VII. The best characterizations in this group are those of Ugarte, whose every word and gesture exemplifies the fiscal corruption of the era; Chaperón, the weak psycopath with whom History iden-

---

[68] Varela Hervias, *Cartas*, p. 21.
[69] Ibid., p. 23.
[70] See, e.g., Pérez Galdós, *Obras completas*, II, 1058.

tifies the brutal repression of 1824; and Calomarde, the submissive reflection of the king's own brand of political duplicity. In each case, the novelist intuited revealing perspectives on their private lives, and all achieve a degree of realism within a distinctly burlesque outline.

Once again, in dealing with the characterization of a Series, we have chosen a relatively small number of characters from a very large group, and again with the criteria employed earlier.[71]

Generally speaking, this is a richer characterization than that encountered in the First Series. A greater number of fully developed protagonists, a prevailing third-person narrative, and the dramatic character of the historical period are all conducive, as noted earlier, to this result. Furthermore, in the Second Series Galdós avoided exotic characterizations, which tend to leave a residue of strangeness, and visibly reduced the number of characters presented simply for their uncomplicated normality. The beneficial deletion of both these types is due, in large part, both to the nature of the history novelized and to changes effected in the literary form of the Series.

Miscellaneous

1. *Comical elements*

The Second Series contains an unusually high incidence of humor, perhaps the highest to be found anywhere in Galdós' work. The years between 1814 and 1833, diametrically opposed in tone to the epic heroism of the War of Independence, often invite satire. The petty and the grotesque — for the liberal squabbles and Ferdinand's personal rule amount to nothing less at times — combine to produce a historical reconstruction permeated with comedy. The result of this is several novels that are unique in Galdós' creative repertoire, in which humor is a primary goal: *Las memorias de un cortesano de* 1815 and *La segunda casaca.*

Bragas, the protagonist of the novels mentioned, is an ideal subject of comedy, for the ways of the rogue are always rich in humorous possibilities. When roguish acts serve to project

---

71 See above, p. 70.

the essence of a historical situation, the picaresque framework acquires overtones of satire. Satire has been encountered before in the *Episodios Nacionales*,[72] but the difference between the first two Series in this respect is basic. Both give expression to satirical perspectives in first-person narrations, but the position of the narrator 'vis a vis' his subject matter is the essential variable. Araceli, it will be remembered, remains alien to the elements satirized; whereas Bragas' commentary issues from a basic identification between observer and observed, between the first-person narrator and the aspects of his world that promote a satirical effect. It is this identity that forces the narrator (Bragas) into a defense of what is defenseless, and consequently intensifies the satire of the Second Series.

The perverse relation between Bragas' successful political career and the means employed in its promotion is an inexhaustible source of satire. This moral discrepancy, reinforced by the protagonist's hypocritical attempts at self-justification, is further compounded, and made universally applicable, by Galdós' deliberate inversion of the picaresque norm. Bragas moves in the highest social circles, which abound in picaresque types like himself. His invariable success, which incidentally is exceeded by that of innumerable others in public service, proclaims the subversion of all values, which is precisely the effect intended.

Bragas is so apt in his opportunistic role that Galdós extended the range of comedy to situations that invite raw, caricaturesque humor. One need only recall the catastrophe that puts an end to Bragas' short-lived engagement as royal procurer, an incident that produces the type of raucous laughter associated with the frustration of villainy by virtue.[73]

A source of humor employed for the first time in the *Episodios Nacionales* is the Cervantine characterization of the monomaniac, for a measure of comedy is the inevitable effect of Sarmiento's fluctuations between sanity and insanity. The student Rodriguín, a cascade of macaronic Latin, represents another traditional form of humor.[74]

Other comical devices found in the Second Series have either been commented on earlier or are treated in other sections of

---

[72] See above, pp. 72-73.
[73] Pérez Galdós, *Obras completas*, I, 1343-1346.
[74] Ibid., pp. 256-258, 310.

this study. Sufficient evidence has already been adduced, however, to justify one broad generalization: the Second Series features forms of comedy that are susceptible of complete integration into the historical reconstruction. Indeed, they positively further — as is the case with Bragas — the literary projection of an era's mood and temper.

2. Symbolism

A new emphasis on symbolism is manifest in the unitive nucleus of the Second Series. The various protagonists are far from being mere symbols, of course, but each life, however personal in its development, actually reflects a specific sector of the political spectrum: the liberal, the reactionary, and the opportunist. In this symbolic outline of fratricidal struggles over ideology, Jenara may be identified with Spain itself. She embraces reaction (Navarro) as the consequence of an alien invasion, then feverishly pursues liberalism for years (Monsalud), but only to lapse, finally, into a feeble Romanticism.

The Series contains, in addition, any number of scenes that invite symbolic interpretation: the collapse of Carnicero's ancient house happens to coincide, for example, with the initial failure of Carlism;[75] and the tragi-comical narration of Lucas Sarmiento's death clearly parallels the disastrous and shameful end of the liberal interlude (1823).[76]

An intensification is particularly evident in the Series' use of name symbolism, which becomes so widespread, in fact, that its literary function must be analyzed. It is immediately apparent, to begin with, that the device is not merely informative, nor even primarily so. The reader, in most cases, could hardly fail to perceive the quality stressed by an appropriate name. A number of other functions, readily deduced from the quality of the names themselves, appear more important.

First, let us deal with the direct and positive association that most of the names in question establish with their respective bearers: Salvador Monsalud, Navarro, Soledad, and others. The author, apparently aware of the value of reader participation, is obviously affording him the satisfaction of discovery. This moment of discovery, often a flash of insight at some point in

75 Pérez Galdós, *Obras completas,* II, 276-277.
76 Ibid., I, 1703-1704.

the character's development, forms a cordial nexus between author and reader, and incomparably fixates the literary creation in the latter's mind.

Furthermore, name symbolism is an intrinsic part of Galdós' characterization, which almost invariably attempts to satisfy a conception in terms of social or political factors through real and profoundly human creations. Name symbolism often serves, in these circumstances, as the catalyst that binds the mutually exclusive characterizational ends of typification and individuality. Of course, name symbolism is never the only factor put in play to this end by the author; but it is one of the most obvious, and undoubtedly one of the most effective. Navarro or Monsalud, for example, are freer to evolve a very personal manner of being — which adds to their realism and contributes to their interest value as human beings — because of an ever-present name association that channels all personal development into a specific area of representation.

To these overall functions of name symbolism, finally, a large number of the novelist's appellations bring a distinct comical quality. Even the manner of conceiving these different names — which always feature a positive relation with the personality of the bearer — is a source of derivative humor. Some names are onomatopoetic, Falfán de los Godos; others, like Bragas, refer to base realities; still others are neologistic conceits, Pipaón; and some, finally, are created by redundant juxtaposition, Benigno Cordero.

An additional function of name symbolism, and one in which the author's irony has an important role, breaks with the norm of positive association between name and bearer. Galdós occasionally polarized the two, name and personality, and thus stressed a negative aspect by dint of contradiction. Generosa (Jenara) is the only notable example in the Second Series. Indeed, the device is rare in Galdós, and usually limited to major feminine creations: either in direct contradiction, Perfecta, Fortunata; or in suggestive opposition, Isidora or Camila.

In conclusion, the ideological conflict reconstructed in the Second Series encouraged the integration of a symbolic framework, and Galdós used this opportunity to an extent compatible with the literary character of the *Episodios Nacionales*. Moreover, the Second Series represents a decisive step in the use of name symbolism, a literary device that distinguishes the work of Galdós within his generation.

3. *Geographical determination*

The First Series takes place, for the most part, outside Madrid; the Second is definitely centered about the Spanish capital. The geographical dispersion of the War of Independence justifies the former, but the urban concentration of the latter is not as readily explained, since much of historical significance — which Galdós sacrificed in avoiding a perspective from the periphery of the Peninsula — occurred outside Madrid.

A possible explanation of the urban concentration noted may be Galdós' main source of documentation for the period. Mesonero Romanos' personal experiences were limited, for the most part, to the Madrid region. One can only hazard a guess, however, as to whether Galdós centered his reconstruction in Madrid in order to reap the full benefits of that precious source, or only utilized the latter after having employed other criteria to decide the geographical reference of the work. The first two Episodios of the Series, set in Madrid though written without the benefit of Mesonero's memory reserve, seem to indicate the latter; while the published correspondence between Galdós and Mesonero can certainly be interpreted to suggest the former.[77]

In any case, the geographical location of the Second Series reflects a particular interest in Madrid, an interest that would soon become a recognized characteristic of the Galdosian novel. The use of Madrid as the reference point for the entire nation, a major tenet of the *Novelas contemporáneas,* is already evident in the Second Series, and constitutes a realistic approach to a period of history characterized by urban predominance.

C) *Summary of Chapter I*

The adaptation of so vast a period of history into the amenable form of the novel is certainly a remarkable feat. The range and complexity of illustrative elements (social groups, classes, institutions) is unique in Spanish literature, for the first twenty *Episodios Nacionales* offer a broad and concrete panorama of early nineteenth-century Spain. On the other hand, a precise

---

[77] See, e.g., Montesinos, *Costumbrismo y novela,* p. 73.

reconstruction of history is not in itself a guarantee of high literary quality. On the contrary, it is likely to result in defective aesthetic integration. The attempted fusion of numerous and heterogeneous elements may result in the anti-esthetic disproportion one finds in many Spanish novels of the romantic era, or in the fragmentation of 'costumbrista' literature. In either case, novelistic development is weakened or impeded.

There is never any doubt, however, that artistic integration and balance is the prime condition of the *Episodios Nacionales,* despite the author's interest in precise historical reconstruction. Our studies of literary form and plot development in the First and Second Series confirm Galdós' aesthetic control of the myriad elements incorporated therein. An imaginative capacity of the highest order was essential to a large scale integration of this type; the ability to conceive themes to fit the needs of historical representation and at the same time organize them, volume after volume, as interesting and instructive narrative.[78]

As a rule, Galdós presented the variegated components of his panoramic view of the Spanish scene in terms of concrete individuals, creating, to this end, a larger body of characters than anyone else in modern Spanish fiction. Once again, however, quantity does not guarantee quality, but our studies of characterization in these two Series indicate Galdós' mastery of the numerous alternatives of character presentation and development in the historical novel. Moreover, the novelist's fictional creations, whatever their degree of elaboration, attain a distinct individuality, a fundamental credibility within the historical context reconstructed. Galdós employed, to this end, every device at his disposal: gradual plot involvement, personal relationships (with historical and other fictional characters), personification, language, idiosyncrasies, and even tics.[79] And the novelist almost always succeeded, finally, in avoiding the psychological anachronism from which so many historical novels suffer.

[78] For objections to Galdós presentation of history in terms of specific human problems, as an integral part of plot, and an adverse judgment concerning the suitability of the plots created by the novelist to that effect — both criticisms answered in large part by this study —, see Gómez de la Serna, *España en sus Episodios,* pp. 204-205.

[79] For the novelist's comments on the nervous tic in characters, see *Obras completas,* I, 1699; and, for a summary of Galdós' use of 'muletillas' to fix personality in the *Episodios,* see Hinterhäuser, *Los Episodios Nacionales,* p. 308.

Some general observations will help clarify the difficulties attending character development in the *Episodios Nacionales*. The novelist who deals with the present finds it unnecessary to stress, in his characters, a background reality that is familiar to the reader. Indeed, his creations may be extremely atypical without detracting from the background world that is a given quantity. The opposite is true of the novelist who reconstructs a past that is unfamiliar to his readers. The former can permit himself completely introspective characters, all but totally divorced from any real environment; but this is a privilege not enjoyed to the same degree by historical novelists, whose characters must be intimately identified with a historical reality which they alone can adequately transmit in the novel.

The representational function of characters developed within the historical novel also sets conditions for the selection of human types. Lukacs has noted, in the process of analyzing Scott's penetrating insights, that the protagonists of great historical novels are middling characters, that is, individuals close to the psychological mean of the epoch reconstructed.[80] The greater representational possibilities of such protagonists — who need not be, and in fact must not be unidimensional — is indisputable, and our study of protagonists like Araceli and Monsalud clearly indicates Galdós' understanding of the problem.

Characterization is further complicated in the *Episodios Nacionales* by the need to integrate historical figures. These appear, like their fictional counterparts, in varying degrees of development. Their assimilation into a literary work requires the dilation of the history text's silhouette without blurring its precise outline or the re-personalization of a legendary image without distorting its essential core of truth; and then the fusion of the intuitive and the factual into as seamless a unity as that possessed by creatures that spring whole from the writer's imagination.

Galdós' tact, fine intuitive capacity, and sense of artistic finish transform the difficulties cited into positive factors, and his historical re-creations are so believable that they can often contribute verisimilitude, by association, to his fictional characters. Moreover, Galdós' presentation of historical figures follows in the tradition of the best historical novelists since Scott,

[80] Lukacs, *The Historical Novel*, pp. 33-37.

who invariably perceive the limitations of the historical figure itself for the purposes of reconstructing the past. The great figures are presented, of course, but do not occupy the center of the stage even in those Episodios that bear their names.

Style

Galdós' literary style is rarely a startling or unique manifestation of his artistic personality. All literary expression implies some degree of stylistic consciousness, of course, but many nineteenth-century writers deliberately avoided an overly-personalized style. In an Aesthetic that accommodated historical and sociological goals, that decreed a conscious stylistic effacement, the important criteria of distinction were often literary method and philosophical perspective. Croce's view of this situation is perhaps extreme, but clearly underscores a fundamental attitude of much nineteenth-century art: ". . . the artistic idea is absent, and its place taken by a series of interesting happenings and historical notions."[81] The result was a primarily communicative style, with features directed to the transcription of a reality that was perceived, for the most part, as fixed in its objectivity and susceptible of rational presentation: impersonalism, profusion, and logical compactness.[82]

In the case of Galdós the virtues of such a style may best be appreciated in the context of what it had displaced as art. Alas, in speaking of 'amaneramiento', Spain's nineteenth-century literary blight, commented: ". . . Pérez Galdós, acaso el único, se ha librado de esta lepra general."[83] Galdós' stylistic direction involved a deliberate revolt against literary affectation, and he evolved, to this end, the ideal medium: an identifiable literary style that is free from distracting singularities.[84]

The first twenty Episodios Nacionales conform, in large part, to the literary style outlined above, but with certain qualifications that contribute to the special character of Galdós' historical novel. Two factors are primarily responsible for this distinguishing stylistic configuration: 1) the novelist is subject to a self-imposed quantitative limit; and, 2) he tends to allow himself

81 *European Literature*, p. 73.
82 See Pérez Minik, *Novelistas españoles*, p. 101.
83 *Galdós*, p. 56.
84 Pérez Minik, *Novelistas españoles*, pp. 95-96.

a greater degree of personal identification than in dealing with less stirring contemporary matters.

The first factor, compounded by the need to incorporate a great variety of elements, and by a frequent change of setting, induces a relatively rapid literary development. This contrasts with the halting and digressive pace of other Galdosian novels. For the same reason, we find in these Episodios a relatively light touch, a greater control of verbal prolixity, and fewer extended descriptions. The second factor stimulates an emotional expressiveness far removed, at times, from the stark impersonalism associated with Galdós' prose. This is particularly striking in the memoir form of the First Series, in which a fictional narrator is esthetically interposed between the author and his enthusiasm.

These early Series already reveal Galdós' clear and richly varied prose. There is no question of unintelligibility, nor of flatness; for the literary medium is neither a compound of metaphor and neologism nor a carbon copy of everyday language.[85] It is, rather, a conscious search for the authentic expression of modern Spain, for the artistic synthesis of familiar speech, of words effaced by usage or fresh from the oven of popular jargon, and the rich academic language of the day, forever threatening to become rancid upon the written page.

Galdós raised the living language of the Spaniard to a literary function, and thus re-vitalized — on contact — the overly staid academic expression of his epoch. On a specific occasion, in the prologue he wrote to Pereda's *El sabor de la tierruca*, Galdós conceded this important contribution to his friend from Santander, but nowhere in the author of *Peñas arriba* is the undertaking in question as apparent as in these *Episodios Nacionales*, of which it is truly an integral part. The first-person narrative, which prevails in these two Series, is the most instrumental device of this undertaking. Araceli expresses, for the length of an entire Series, the linguistic reality of an educated man of the people. The memoirs of Bragas and Jenara have a similar effect in the Second Series.

Furthermore, the dialogue everywhere, even when it forms part of third-person narrations, is an inexhaustible source of

---

[85] See T. Navarro, "La lengua de Galdós," *Revista Hispánica Moderna,* IX (1943), pp. 292-293.

linguistic innovation. The accommodation of language to character is, in fact, one of the novelist's most successful ventures in these *Episodios Nacionales;* and the suggestion, through dialogue, of a character's social or geographical origin, is widely encountered in a work that contains innumerable conversations between the most varied characters.[86] Bragas' 'administrative' speech patterns are an example of the author's use of this linguistic device for comical purposes,[87] a refinement that indicates a mastery of the technique.

Galdós weighed the difficult artistic balance between objective clarity and multiform richness, and quite naturally sought syntactic norms among Spain's classical models of precision and fullness, Cervantes above all. The novelist evolved a sentence structure that allowed dependent elements, capable of reproducing the richness of the subject matter, and, as noted by Gullón:

> . . . . oraciones agrupadas en progresión diestramente graduada para conseguir párrafos largos, de gran aliento, en los cuales, gracias a incisos sucesivos, se presentan en buen orden las diversas facetas del tema, las peculiaridades del asunto.[88]

There is very little stylistic evolution between the First and Second Series, written in relatively few years (1872-1879) and without serious interruption. The most striking blight in Galdós' presentation, footnotes that constantly draw the reader away from the fictional environment, is common to both Series, and even more apparent in the Second of these.[89] The variations that may be pointed out are attributable, largely, on the other hand, to differences of form and content. For example, the emotional quality of the First Series, elicited by the nature of the subject matter and furthered by a first-person narration, is greatly reduced in the Second, the subject matter of which is conducive to irony. While the impersonal narrative that prevails in the latter attenuates the digressive tendency brought on by the retrospective format of the First Series, and this permits a more accelerated rhythm of narration.

---

86 See, e.g., Pérez Galdós, *Obras completas,* I, 212-214, 384-385, 400, 404-405, 427, 674-675.
87 Ibid., II, 179.
88 R. Gullón, "Cuestiones galdosianas," *Cuadernos Hispanoamericanos,* XXXIV (1958), 240.
89 There are 70 footnotes in these first two Series, a didactic norm which Galdós wisely suspended in the later Series.

THIRD AND FOURTH SERIES

Galdós explicitly stated his reasons for discontinuing the *Episodios Nacionales* after the Second Series (1879):

> Los años que siguen al '34 están demasiado cerca, nos tocan, nos codean, se familiarizan con nosotros. Los hombres de ellos casi se confunden con nuestros hombres. Son años a quienes no se puede disecar, porque algo vive en ellos que duele, y salta al ser tocado con escalpelo.[1]

A number of critics have stressed other factors that may have influenced the novelist's decision in 1879, and these range from the very personal 'dolor que le producía relatar los horrores de la guerra civil', to the rather objective fact that the historical novel had exhausted its literary appeal by that date.[2]

Nothing appears to us as relevant, however, in this respect, as the fact that Galdós had altered the conditions of his work by reconstructing the period 1805-1834 in the first two Series, thus bringing the historical sources of the present a full generation forward:[3]

> Si damos valor a una ilusión de tiempo, podremos decir que aquellos veintinueve años fueron nuestro siglo décimo-octavo, la paternidad verdadera de la civilización presente . . . .[4]

Spain's development after Ferdinand VII, after 1834, was a feasible subject for the contemporary novel in much the same manner and for much the same reasons noted in our commentary on Balzac's *Comédie Humaine*.[5] And it is noteworthy, in this sense, that both *Doña Perfecta*, which heads the list of Galdós' *Novelas de primera época*, and *La desheredada*, which is the

---

[1] Pérez Galdós, *Obras completas*, II, 317; and for an awareness of the Carlist problem common to both periods, see *Crónica de la quincena*, pp. 119, 130.

[2] See Casalduero, *Vida y obra*, p. 36; Torres Bodet, *Tres inventores de realidad*, pp. 235-236; and Sainz de Robles, "B. Pérez Galdós: su vida, su obra y su época," p. 159.

[3] See above, Part I, Chapt. I: "The Hist. Nov. and the *Epis. Nac.*"

[4] Pérez Galdós, *Episodios Nacionales*, X (Madrid, 1881), ii.

[5] See above, Part I, Chapt. I: "Genesis of the *Epis. Nac.*"

first of his *Novelas contemporáneas,* have roots in the Second Series,[6] which the novelist obviously intended to exploit as the causal link between past and contemporary Spanish life:

> Pero los personajes novelescos, que han quedado vivos en esta dilatadísima jornada, los guardo, como legítima pertenencia mía, y los conservaré para casta de tipos contemporáneos . . . .[7]

The reason for the continuation of the *Episodios Nacionales* at the close of the century (1898) is a more controversial matter. An economic motive has frequently been emphasized; but, although admitted by the author himself,[8] it is not unique, perhaps not even predominant, and is certainly inadmissible as the basis for an adverse esthetic judgment.[9] The striking coincidence of dates (1898) has also been noted by critics,[10] but even this is open to question. An impending national disaster might well have renewed Galdós' interest in the historical genesis of the present; but he could not have foreseen — in 1897, when the Third Series was started[11] — the character and extent of that impending tragedy. Finally, Casalduero has suggested another 'raison d'etre' for these late Episodios, pointing out the experimental nature of the Third and Fourth Series.[12] In effect, Galdós' historical novel, which, if we are to believe the author,[13] retained a loyal public, represented an ideal medium for seeking new directions. The *Episodios Nacionales* were, of all the literary forms exploited by the novelist, the most susceptible of incorporating stylistic alterations, and their demands upon his creativity could be expected to stimulate new levels of artistic expression.

The various reasons listed above carry a weight of their own, of course, but they are most meaningful when conditioned by the fact that Galdós had already produced twenty volumes

---

6 See, e.g., Pérez Galdós, *Obras completas,* II, 231-235.
7 Ibid., p. 318.
8 Pérez Galdós, *Memorias,* p. 222; and see Berkowitz, *Perez Galdós,* p. 243.
9 See, e.g., González Blanco, *Historia de la novela en España,* p. 441; and Contreras, "La evolución galdosiana," *Razón y Fe,* XX (1908), 82-83.
10 See, e.g., Casalduero, *Vida y Obra,* p. 168; and Torres Bodet, *Tres inventores de realidad,* p. 236.
11 See Pérez Galdós, *Memorias,* p. 231; and Gómez de Baquero, *"Paz en la guerra y los novelistas de las guerras civiles," De Gallardo a Unamuno* (Madrid, 1926).
12 Casalduero, *Vida y Obra,* p. 51.
13 Pérez Galdós, *Obras completas,* II, 231.

dedicated to the literary reconstruction of the history of Spain in the nineteenth century. The Third and Fourth Series, when added to those after a nineteen year interval, become an indispensable complement to Galdós' literary expression of a historical continuum.

These late *Episodios Nacionales* are no less valid, in this sense, than the first twenty, which inaugurated the novelist's influence in Spanish letters. One relationship, however, is significantly altered. Just as the first two Series stand as a meaningful genetical background to the *Novelas contemporáneas,* so do the latter announce — conceptually, novelistically, and stylistically — the later *Episodios Nacionales.*

The Third and Fourth Series conform to the general pattern of the earlier *Episodios Nacionales:* ten volume unit, chronological sequence, rapid production, and artistic fusion of history and fiction.[14] Galdós continued to work with a tried and tested literary outline, and with the novelistic method established in the first two Series. The lapse of nineteen years (1879-1898) is felt, however, in the appearance of some basic innovations.

A) *Third Series*

The Third Series reconstructs an era in many ways similar to that of the War of Independence, for the Carlist conflict also required epic resonances, heroic figures, and a degree of popular fervor. But the essential tone and mood of the two epochs had little in common, for between 1834 and 1844 Romanticism swept through Spain, and is ubiquitous in Galdós' treatment of the period.

Literary form

The Third Series offers a great degree of formal flexibility. Most important, in this respect, is the Series' novelistic structure. A single unitive plot (the story of Fernando Calpena's life) binds almost the entire Series unit, but this external similarity to the First Series is deceptive. The cohesive effect of the unitive plot is greatly attenuated in the Third Series, even to the point of allowing completely independent novels. *Zumalacárregui,*

14 See, e.g., Gómez de Baquero, *Novelas y novelistas,* p. 13; and Casalduero, *Vida y obra,* p. 169.

the first volume, establishes this dissociative norm. In each earlier Series, the first Episodio served to introduce the unitive element, the protagonist of a unitive plot (First Series) or the members of an integrated plot nucleus (Second Series); but this procedure is altered in the Third Series, and Calpena, the protagonist of the unitive plot, is not introduced until *Mendizábal*, the second Episodio of the work. *Bodas reales*, the last Episodio of the Series, is also completely divorced from Calpena's world.

The remaining plots, which comprise the substance of the eight Episodios between *Zumalacárregui* and *Bodas reales*, are all linked to Calpena's novel in some way or another, but are in each case sufficiently independent to constitute novels in their own right. Unlike Araceli, Calpena is not omnipresent; and unlike Monsalud, he is not the heart of a nucleus of lives bound by generation and geography. Consequently, even the plots directly linked to his novel develop in his absence, in different regions, and among different age groups. The First Series, it will be remembered, reconstructed a history of battles and sieges in subplots that were conditioned to accommodate a segment of the Series' unitive plot. The Third Series reproduces a very similar type of history through a complex of highly developed plots, partly or entirely independent of the unitive element. This structural flexibility affords the Third Series a much richer novelistic potential.

This augmented plot diversification is due, at least in part, to a basic change in the novelist's goals. The retention of a personal audience, promoted by a closely linked and continuous unitive plot, has, by 1898, ceased to interest the writer.[15] On the other hand, the need to convey the homogeneous quality of a period remains, which explains why Galdós never offered ten completely independent novels in any Series. This function of Galdós' literary unit in the *Episodios Nacionales* is itself subject, however, to degrees of fluctuation. The different periods of history fictionalized reveal, within their overall unity, a wide range of variation. The War of Independence, 'one' people with 'one' mission, required greater unity in novelistic expression than epochs in which two 'Spains' or a variety of political

15 See above, p. 53.

aspirations were in evidence. A definite relation exists, then, between the historical character of an epoch and the degree of formal cohesion found in the structure of its literary reconstruction.

Also pertinent to this new flexibility is the Third Series' use of the epistolary form. Galdós had already employed this narrative technique in *La incógnita,* where a single correspondent creates a limited perspective on reality. The Third Series sought a very different effect from its use of the form, since historical reality allows no limitation of perspectives. In effect, letters are employed to express a striking relativism, with diametrically opposed perceptions of a single reality being expressed simultaneously.[16]

The dissociative effect of this narrative technique is most evident in *La estafeta romántica,* where numerous letters are exchanged in every possible combination of correspondents. Each bilateral exchange offers a distinct nucleus of novelistic content, and the various nuclei are only incidentally connected, in a number of cases, by the reader standing outside the world of fiction.

Galdós masterfully exploited all the literary possibilities of this difficult narrative form. As a rule, the 'document' is interpolated into a narrative sequence, thus combining an impression of authenticity with the immediate satisfaction of a specific novelistic end.[17] Furthermore, the interpolation is often carefully timed to relieve the monotony of the impersonal expression that prevails in the Series. Needless to say, the very use of letters gives an impression of documentation; but what is more important, Galdós hit upon the technique of novelization that best expresses the well-nigh ineffable subjectivity of Romanticism.[18]

Plot development

The Third Series contains six distinct novels. The unitive plot of Fernando Calpena, the most extensive of these, serves to introduce an additional three novels. Zoilo Arratia's story in *Luchana,* for example, issues directly from the world of Calpena. It takes place, for the most part, in the absence of the latter, and

16 See, e.g., Pérez Galdós, *Obras completas,* II, 1163 ff.
17 Ibid., pp. 983, 1234.
18 See Pérez de Ayala, *Principios y finales,* pp. 22-23; and R. Darío, "Una novela de Galdós," *España contemporánea* (Madrid, n. d.), p. 235.

in its own historico-geographical setting, but Aurora Negretti, the feminine lead, is taken from the unitive plot. A chance meeting between Calpena and Urdaneta is sufficient, on the other hand, to lay the groundwork for the latter's completely independent novel in *La campaña del Maestrazgo*.[19] These varying degrees of plot interrelationship do not extend to the novels *Zumalacárregui* and *Bodas reales*, which, as we have seen, only share an occasional secondary character with the world of fiction created about Fernando Calpena.

Romanticism, as noted earlier, underlies the entire conception of the work, and its concrete expression in literature assimilates a great deal of the Series' novelistic content. There is no novelty involved in reconstructing the basic characteristics of a period, and the Third Series is only exceptional in this respect because Romanticism, unlike the political ideologies of earlier Series, represents a comprehensixe world-view, a manner of being from which Galdós' generation had had to differentiate itself.

Romanticism had left a memory of excesses and extravagant actions, but a memory of these things that had been emptied of their original human impulse. Often lacking the sensitivity to perceive and re-activate the human qualities inherent in the world-view of the Romantics — a sensitivity that rebellious generations often lack with respect to their immediate predecessors — realists tended to view Romanticism much as it is still popularly envisioned today, bearing the inseparable connotations of impractical rebelliousness, sentimentality, and exoticism. All these may have been vital and pulsating attitudes in their day, but appeared de-humanized and grotesque to an insensitive posterity.[20]

It is not surprising, then, that Galdós' view of Romanticism should reflect a degree of irony, a humorous incredulity that permeates the entire Third Series. The novelistic content, for example, is organized to evoke a Romanticism perceived from the shore of Realism, a world-view filtered through an alien sensibility. But despite the humorism induced by this perspective, Galdós frequently transcended a de-humanized version of Ro-

19 Pérez Galdós, *Obras completas*, II, 673-688.
20 See, e.g., Pérez Galdós, *Crónica de la quincena*, p. 33; and for a view of Spanish Romanticism as fundamentally insincere, see E. L. King, "What is Spanish Romanticism?," *Studies in Romanticism*, II (1962), 1-11.

manticism. A vivid interest in everything human led him to an indispensable minimum of rapport with an alien world-view, to a literary reconstruction of Romanticism's stand on life and reality that is often sincerely lived in fiction.[21] Galdós went to great lengths, as well, to accommodate a romantic psychology to the history of the period. His success, obvious in scenes like the death of Montes de Oca or the dash of Cabrera into battle, offers a realistic fusion of the spirit and the action of an age.[22]

Calpena's unitive novel contains unmistakable romantic elements: his origin is unknown, there is a mysterious protector, and the indispensable romantic passion: at first sight, overwhelming, and impossible. Aurora Negretti is the perfect complement: the offspring of an impetuous and tragic love-affair, an orphaned prisoner of gloomy commercialism, with uncontrollable imagination, fiery temperament, and even suicidal tendencies.[23]

Galdós evolved a modern novel from elements clearly selected to parody romantic literature. The protagonist's development, which corresponds to the evolution of Spain between 1834 and 1844, eventually transcends the romantic pattern. From a mysterious youth, incapable of resisting the pressures of a romantic age, Calpena evolves into a mature man in control of his destiny. The long process of change entails a humorous parody of Romanticism, with a sobering reality — the real world shunned and disfigured by the Romantics — imposing itself as a decisive factor in plot development.

Calpena's frantic search for his lost ideal (Aurora) leads to Demetria, and it is a dashing act of romantic chivalry — saving Demetria's father from death in a Carlist prison — that paradoxically brings about a different kind of love. Demetria is a real and substantial person, free from emotional frenzy and hyper-imagination. The subsequent weakening of the romantic ideal represented by Aurora is inevitable, and the rest of Calpena's trajectory involves the gradual displacement of Romanticism by reality.

Pilar Loaysa, Calpena's mother and the anonymous protector of *Mendizábal,* adds another dimension to the unitive plot. She

[21] For a different opinion, see R. Gómez de la Serna, *Nuevos retratos contemporáneos* (Buenos Aires, 1945), p. 212.
[22] Pérez Galdós, *Obras completas,* II, 808-809, 1138-1152.
[23] Ibid., II, 480-481, 489.

expiates the 'romantic' sin that had long before resulted in the illegitimate conception of her son. The process of de-romantization is thus doubly emphasized and even made to assume an air of tragedy. The parallel development of a fundamental problem in two different generations has an interesting quality of its own, and is functional at the same time — as noted in the First Series — in sustaining the interest of an extensive unitive plot.

Aurora Negretti, when forcibly separated from Calpena, gives rise to a new plot. In *Luchana,* she confronts an enamoured Zoilo Arratia, as different from Calpena as Demetria is from Aurora. Galdós altered the role of the sexes, but again employed the general outline of the unitive plot. Zoilo cures Aurora of her romantic 'sickness,' imposing an invincible will that paralyzes her dreamy instability.

This new plot cultivates dramatic elements of its own. Three cousins vie for Aurora, who is romantically attached to the memory of Calpena. The three are deliberately arranged by their degree of social polish; from the deaf-mute Churi, primitive in his physical handicaps, to Martín, the gentle 'señorito' of the Arratia family. The first can scarcely compete, and his interest is primarily psychological: but at first Martín offers a formidable obstacle to Zoilo. The decisive factor, well within the bounds of romantic dogma, is the degree of Martín's social integration, which has detracted from his individuality and eroded his capacity to desire with efficient vehemence. Zoilo, neither primitive nor de-personalized, is clearly superior and literally conquers Aurora.

Calpena never intervenes directly in the novelistic development that culminates in Zoilo's marriage to Aurora; but the plot sequel, which transcends *Luchana,* serves to close a chapter of the Series' unitive novel. It encompasses Aurora's last romantic escapade, for which reality's antidote is an overwhelming, almost sensual maternal fulfillment;[24] and offers the long awaited encounter of the love rivals. Alas has noted that the meeting is a striking example of Galdosian irony.[25] Zoilo's long incarceration moves a reasonable Calpena to solicitude, and the tensely awaited encounter is resolved with a whimper instead of a bang.

24 Pérez Galdós, *Obras completas,* II, 1030-1031.
25 *Galdós,* pp. 344-345.

113

The literary function of plot sequels of this kind is important, and we shall find a similar extension in the following novel. The device strengthens the nexus between a given plot development and the unitive trajectory of Calpena, but does so only after the plot in question has received a full independent presentation. This allows for added serial cohesion without unduly subordinating or restricting the development of quasi-independent plots.

The story of *Montes de Oca* is centered on another life introduced through Calpena. Santiago Ibero embodies a romantic commonplace, that of the noble savage suddenly and tragically inserted into an ignoble and complex society. The theme is masterfully adapted to the historical situation, and the incorruptible soldier is first tempted to break military discipline. Far more significant in terms of novelistic development, however, is the subversion of Ibero's straightforward manliness by Rafaela Milagro, the sophisticated and seductive coquette from the capital.

Ibero is able to resist so long as he maintains contact with the simple rural world of Gracia, his first love, Demetria's sister, and the tie to Calpena that later permits a plot sequel. A long separation from this source of his well-being, weakens Ibero's resolve and blurs his sense of values. The protagonist is never equal to the business of surviving in a world of hypocrisy and sham, and he gradually sinks into a state of inactive depression. The plot sequel will reveal his attempt to find solace in religion — a futile attempt — and describe Ibero's recovery of self in re-establishing contact with a world more in harmony with his straightforward, unsophisticated nature.[26]

The fictional content of *Montes de Oca* is greatly enriched by the paradoxical complexity of Rafaela Milagro. As in the case of many other Galdosian women, covetous materialism leads Rafaela to deceit and immorality. Unlike other heroines, however, Rafaela is unexpectedly surprised — just as she hits bottom — in an instant of disinterested and unrequited love for the idealistic Montes de Oca. The brusque transition is ironical, an effective take-off on the Marguerite Gautiers of romantic and pseudo-romantic literature, for Rafaela remains herself in spite of everything.

[26] Pérez Galdós, *Obras completas*, II, 1234-1253.

The plot of *La campaña del Maestrazgo* is unique for its literary alchemy. The nun Marcela and the Carlist officer Santapau (Nelet), who are in no way related to the unitive plot of the Series, suggest a peculiar fusion of elements from the *Quijote* and *Don Alvaro o la fuerza del sino*. Marcela's name and character, her mode of existence, and the story's one-sided love-affair recall the former; while Nelet's unhappy 'star,' his unwitting execution of Marcela's brother, and the tragic climax recall the latter.[27] The alchemy is not complete, however, until a third traditional element is added. The epicurean nobleman Urdaneta, moved to soften Marcela for Nelet, is a masculine re-incarnation of Rojas' character.

All three elements combine to offer a completely new plot outline: the 'ascetic' resistance of Marcela, the unbalanced impetuosity of Nelet, and the surprisingly effective 'celestinism' of Urdaneta. For a tense moment, Nelet's perseverance and Urdaneta's worldly counsel appear to have the upper hand, but the tragic 'fate' that underlies all three literary sources eventually sweeps everything before it.

Galdós obviously counted on the reader's recognition for literary effect, and there is no question, of course, concerning the romantic qualities of the work. Everything in the Episodio is well-calculated, in fact, to elicit a paradoxical verisimilitude. The traditional themes are woven, for example, into a fitting historical context: a paradoxical war of atrocious barbarity, stoic bravery, and religious fervor, and are set in a physical world of equal appropriatenesss: the unchecked Maestrazgo, dotted everywhere with architectural remainders of the Middle-Ages.[28]

The plot of *Bodas reales* stresses rural-urban conflict, a typically romantic theme that is touched upon several times in the Series. This problem of ninetenth-century Spain, combined with another that is closely related to it, namely the mania for civil employment, is made concrete in the situation faced by the Carrasco family.

Bruno Carrasco's economic independence allows Galdós to present the vice of 'empleomanía' stripped of all extenuating circumstances.[29] His blind insistence on residing in Madrid,

27 Alas, *Galdós*, p. 332.
28 See, e.g., Pérez Galdós, *Obras completas*, II, 773, 790, 794, 815-817.
29 For a previous use of this same device, see R. Mesonero Romanos, *Escenas matritenses* (Madrid, 1925), I, 78-80.

mesmerized by his fruitless endeavour, causes the disintegration of a healthy rural family. A colorless but substantial rural life is repeatedly contrasted to the large city's attractive but deceptive illusion. Thrust into the great urban center, the various Carrascos are either too fascinated to resist its temptations or too weak to adapt to its unrealistic demands.

The conflict begins as a humorous altercation between Don Bruno and his wife Leandra, a clash of illusory hopes and practical realism that recalls the famous discussion between a somewhat quixotized Sancho Panza and a thoroughly panzesque Teresa.[30] By the time the volume ends, however, Leandra has escaped from her urban prison into death, Don Bruno is close to bankruptcy, and Eufrasia, their daughter, has lost herself in the darkest recesses of the city. Only Lea, the other daughter, is saved, and sadly disappointed at that.

The story of *Zumalacárregui* consists of the truncated biography of José Fago. Curiously enough, Galdós began the Third Series with the device employed nineteen years before in *Un faccioso más y algunos frailes menos*. Fago, like Navarro,[31] identifies himself with the great Carlist general, thus facilitating the presentation of a military strategy that is the substance of the Episodio. The mental confusion required for an identification of this kind is believably conveyed by the psychic peculiarities of a Pirandellian Fago,[32] whose credible knowledge of the geography involved adds realism to the narration of military history.

The plot of *Zumalacárregui* reveals a decidedly romantic causality, and the very first scene is indicative of this fundamental design. A terrible coincidence, of the type associated with romantic literature, has Fago, the erstwhile seducer of Salomé Ulibarri, long repentant and a priest, confess the girl's father moments before his military execution. The result is a paradoxical reversal of roles. The priest must air his own guilt, and it is Ulibarri, conversely, who must console. The scene is a masterful introduction to the Episodio and the Series. The senseless barbarity of the Carlist War is immediately stressed in Ulibarri's

---

[30] See Alas, *Galdós*, p. 362; and A. H. Obaid, "La Mancha en los *Episodios Nacionales*," *Hispania*, XLI (1958), 42-47.

For Galdós' overall use of Cervantes' masterpiece, see the unpubl. diss. (University of Minnesota, 1953) by A. H. Obaid, "El Quijote en los *Episodios Nacionales*."

[31] Pérez Galdós, *Obras completas*, II, 290-294.

[32] See Huerta, "Galdós y la novela histórica," *Atenea*, LXXII (1943), 106.

condemnation; and the inescapable presence of the past, basic to Fago's novel, is also underscored. The barbarity, the reversal of roles mentioned, and Fago's unbalanced obsession with the past combine to inject an irrational quality into the world of fiction. This quality will persist — attenuated at times, intensified at others — throughout Galdós' depiction of Romanticism and the Carlist War.

Fago's life is another of the author's studies in human frustration. Abandoned by Salomé Ulibarri in the past, the 'calavera' resolved the subsequent crisis by taking religious vows. The priest's morbid fear of encountering subjects from his past suggests, however, that he has repressed a vital identification with it. He is consequently involved in a motivational paradox: a conscious flight from the memory of Salomé, contradicted at every step by an unconscious search for her. The protagonist can hit upon no pattern of existence that is not somehow at cross purposes with itself, and he invariably fails in his escapist extremes.

These are themselves contradictory, military and religious, and leave Fago in a state of powerless bewilderment. He is a poor priest and an even poorer soldier, for despite the Carlist casuistry of his friend Ibarburru, the two directions are mutually repellent. What is more, any progress in either is immediately vitiated by the omnipresent shadow of the past, by coincidences that evoke the repressed image of Salomé. The latter appears only once in the Episodio, but provides a powerful anticlimax to Fago's quiet passing away.[33]

We have presented the six novels in the order of their dissociation from the unitive plot of the Series. Little more is required to demonstrate a greater novelistic richness than anything encountered heretofore in the *Episodios Nacionales*. Furthermore, there is a great deal in the preceding outline to suggest a fundamental change in the novelist's artistic perception. Entire segments, for example, are envisioned through the dreams and hallucinations of literary characters, a psychic emphasis new to the *Episodios Nacionales*. The resultant blurring of objective reality, the stress on paradox, and the accumulation of conflicts that are resolved negatively clearly differentiate the artistic intent of the Third Series.

[33] Pérez Galdós, *Obras completas*, II, 418.

Characterization

Galdós avoided presenting Calpena as an embodiment of romantic characteristics: exaggerated passions, bohemian inclinations, and overactive imagination. On the contrary, he is introduced as a sensible, tactful, and somewhat timid youth. In fact, the entire first part of *Mendizábal* emphasizes "neo-classical" elements,[34] and thus provides a basis for contrast with the imminent surge of Romanticism. It is, in general, a favorable contrast, and Galdós' only concession to that world-view.

The arrangements indicated suggest special goals in the characterization of Calpena. The first of these was to present the romantic qualities as acquired, incidental and not essential to the protagonist's development. This was fundamental to Galdós' humoristic approach to the romantic generation, whose most expressive traits were deemed violently imposed on human nature. The second goal was to present through Calpena, who first assumes and then discards a romantic personality, the parallel evolution through which all Spain passed in that epoch.

The subject was Romanticism, but Galdós enveloped his presentation in a realistic causality. Calpena's immediate environment, biography, and overall human situation are the determinants of his romantic sally. Immersed in mystery (unknown parents, anonymous protector), with only Hillo's inept 'classicism' to check the mounting pressures of the romantic ambient, and without intimate family ties to temper his first passion, Calpena gradually acquires all the characteristics that Galdós' generation identified with a young romantic.[35]

Subsequent volumes relate the curative encounters of an unrealistic personality with the sobering realities of life. The love idyll comes to an end, and the attractive riddle of birth and station is conspicuously resolved in illegitimacy. These blows, deliberately organized as an ironical perspective on a romantic personality, constitute the realistic basis of Calpena's personal formation. The sudden, irreversible termination of an unstable romantic passion — the result of Zoilo's overpowering effect on Aurora — quiets the protagonist's spiritual exacerbation and permits, in Demetria, a more mature and more permanent relationship; and together with the knowledge of his illegitimate

[34] Pérez Galdós, *Obras completas*, II, 445, 482, 530.
[35] See Mesonero Romanos, *Escenas matritenses*, II, 113-129.

birth, Calpena receives a mother (Pilar Loaysa) in whom to stabilize his existence.

Calpena's is a realistic cycle of development; an evolution from impressionable youth, through romantic exaltation, to flexible maturity. Most important, perhaps, is the fact that each successive phase leaves an enrichening residue, that the very extremes he outgrows add depth and character to the colorless youth first encountered in *Mendizábal*. The disillusioned romantic, for example, retains enough imaginative spontaneity to contrast vividly with the insensitive materialism of his rival for Demetria's hand; for Calpena is never reduced to the cold mummification that is the opposite pole of the Romanticism he surmounts.

Demetria, like Inés and Soledad before her, is immobilized, to a great extent, by a specific set of virtues. She is even less effective, novelistically, than her earlier counterparts, for she appears far less than Inés and never crystallizes an independent plot dimension in the manner of Soledad. Indeed, only the surface of Demetria's existence is ever presented in the work; she remains a creature seen but rarely heard. One must remember, however, that Demetria's personality, or apparent lack thereof, functions as a contrast to Aurora Negretti's romantic instability. She is consequently conceived as an example of order, common sense, and evenness of temperament, all of which curtail self-expression.

There is, despite this fundamental lack of self-expression, or perhaps because of it, an undisclosed dimension of Demetria that beckons to the reader. It is only indirectly signalled in the fundamental contradiction — incomparably suggestive of a rich feminine core that remains largely unexpressed — that underlies her role in the work: perfectly capable of seeing the folly of her father's intemperate (romantic) actions,[36] she nevertheless finds similar attitudes and actions irresistible in Calpena. She perhaps best exemplifies, for this reason, Galdós' ability to give interesting contours to otherwise unappealing people, to successfully offer, as Gómez de la Serna has put it, 'las honestas que nadie suele ver sino en la hora trémula.'[37]

Pilar Loaysa's powerful effect in the work is accomplished

36 Pérez Galdós, *Obras completas*, II, 613-614.
37 *Nuevos retratos contemporáneos*, p. 210.

through letters almost exclusively, and anonymous letters at that. Only masterpieces of the epistolary form can make the 'tour de force' possible. Pilar's anonymous letters to her son subtly suggest her age and sex in the delicate quality of her perceptions, and project the image of a select being, of fine intelligence and sensibility, in the sympathetic irony of her judgments.

Pilar is a dramatic characterization, living an inner struggle between the son she cannot recognize and the husband she cannot offend. Her anonymous control over Calpena is a compromise; but when the latter's romantic exaltation breaks that control, the taut equilibrium in Pilar's life is shattered. The character is then presented in open conflict herself. She must resolve the tragic duality of her life, and favors the son over the husband, maternal feelings over social taboos. Letters expressing a delicate sensibility to sorrow convey Pilar's realization of the mental anguish undergone by Felipe, her abandoned spouse, and indicate her remorseful discovery of a marital devotion obscured by years of conflict.[38].

Zoilo Arratia, protagonist of *Luchana,* is new to Galdós' repertoire of characters, for no other creation of his functions so exclusively through volition. The epoch's well-known interest in Schopenhauer and Nietzsche, which Galdós apparently shared,[39] might explain an emphasis on will that in a sense restricts character development. The romantic identification of willful desire and reality is a mental attitude opposed to the dynamics of compromise that enrich other psychological make-ups. Of course, this does not reduce Zoilo's impact as a character in the novel, for the very process by which he overcomes external obstacles is a powerful generator of interest.

Moreover, Zoilo is not a mere personification of will power. Galdós made the reader a witness to the gradual awakening of a strong, insensitive Basque prototype, with powerful external factors realistically combined to this effect. Aurora and the Carlist siege of Bilbao provoke the first enthusiasms of Zoilo's young manhood, and simultaneously offer the resistance that stimulates his distinctive quality. Aurora is particularly instrumental in this, for her delicate sensibility generates adoration

[38] Pérez Galdós, *Obras completas,* II, 944-947.
[39] See Casalduero, *Vida y obra,* p. 154; and Berkowitz, *La biblioteca de Galdós,* p. 63.

in the unsophisticated protagonist. The siege then conveniently offers him a means of scaling the romantic heights of Aurora's fantasy. The exercise of his phenomenal will reflects Bilbao's undaunted stand and is certainly believable in that epic setting.

Aurora Negretti receives little further development in *Luchana*. Reality has closed about her since *Mendizábal*, and has taken the flippant gaiety from her life. Her conflict, a femininity drawn to Zoilo's strength and a conscious romanticism that stubbornly clings to the past (Calpena), is resolved in passivity. In the shadow of Zoilo's will, Aurora's alternatives are visibly reduced and her literary existence impoverished. Her surrender, which is inevitable from the first, again underscores the effect of reality upon a romantic personality, an evolution from sickly exacerbation to robust maternity.

The protagonist of *Montes de Oca* sums himself up with the phrase 'no discurro, creo.' Both Santiago Ibero's weaknesses and strengths stem from his faith in basic concepts: liberty, fidelity, honor. The young officer's primitive, unsophisticated world-view has permitted him to fight and survive, rising through the ranks during the Carlist War; but it is cumbersome in the sophisticated urban society of the post-war years. The conflict depicted is secular, as the latter proceeds to the erosion of absolute values.

Santiago repeatedly applies criteria that are improper to the time and place, a corrupt atmosphere of political duplicity that differs substantially from the crude but honorable battlefields in which he grew to manhood. The consequences are dramatized in his relations with Rafaela Milagro, for the brave soldier is ill equipped to handle a woman unimpeded by restrictive values. The historical nucleus of the Episodio provides the final phase of the conflict that breaks Ibero. The disciplined soldier believes Montes de Oca to be Rafaela's 'great' love, and he is himself enchanted by the noble idealism of his political prisoner. When the dreaded moment arrives, Santiago finds it all but impossible to implement Espartero's mandate of execution. The experience destroys his last refuge from an alien and hostile society. The military code, a last remaining absolute, loses its luster; and Ibero, renouncing this last link to the heroic world of his youth, sinks, confused and beaten, into the morass about him.

The road back, feasible through a fresh contact with the simple values of rural life, is encumbered by the residue of pessimism and distrust left in the once straightforward and confident soldier. The process of recovery is effectively enveloped by Galdós in a humorous parody of ominous romantic prognostications, and is made to gather momentum in inverse proportion to the distance that separates Ibero from Gracia and the rural life.[40]

Rafaela Milagro is young, ambitious, and separated from her husband, conditions that keep her on the verge of rebelling against social restrictions. The naive Ibero unwittingly opens the door to her latent depravity, which is only diverted for an instant, as we have seen, by a romantic paradox. Her moment of great and unrequited love is offered in a hazy imprecision that makes it viable (dealing as it does with Montes de Oca) and underscores the humorism which underlies the author's view of the period: focused from a confused outsider's point of view (Ibero) and as the culmination of a process of dissipation that should have led to anything but sublimity of sentiment.

But for this one instant of paradoxical behavior, which leaves a residual ambivalence in her characterization, Rafaela develops like any number of the novelist's important feminine characters. The key to their personality, as Eoff has noted,[41] is the strength of character, of will, with which they confront life, with which they set aside social and moral restrictions.

Don Beltrán de Urdaneta, protagonist of *La campaña del Maestrazgo,* is a particularly striking character. The decrepit nobleman is sympathetic to such an extent that a life spent in dissipating a vast fortune is readily condoned. Normally, antecedents of this type produce the opposite reaction, but this is carefully avoided here by a prepared set of factors. Urdaneta is old and he is the personification of noble liberality. Above all, his gay hedonism is rendered favorable by contrast with the materialistic avarice of those who oppose his way of life. The sympathy so deftly incorporated into the image of the old profligate might suggest an ironic autobiographical touch.

Urdaneta's efforts to prolong his life of seignorial pleasures is opposed by the formidable combination of daughter-in-law and grandson, embarked on a niggardly campaign of economic stability. The picaresque outlook that this brings out in the

40 Pérez Galdós, *Obras completas,* II, 1240-1253.
41 *The Novels of Pérez Galdós,* p. 92.

innately noble protagonist is undoubtedly a manifestation of Galdosian irony, but the paradoxical combination of roguishness and nobility, believable in the concrete individuality of Urdaneta, is an incomparable example of the novelist's characterizational dexterity.

Incapable of forgetting or postponing his sybaritic dreams, Urdaneta launches a desperate campaign to seek the fabled pots of gold buried by his deceased friend Luco. The opposition of Marcela Luco only heightens the picaresque quality of his behavior, turning his inborn rectitude to trickery and his noble poise to childish supplication. All this notwithstanding, Galdós does not sketch in Urdaneta another noble degraded by adversity, because the protagonist is immersed in a decidedly positive campaign and resolved to overcome all obstacles. Forever on the offensive, alert to his own interests, Urdaneta assumes a controlling, 'celestinesque' role between the impassioned Nelet and the frigid Marcela; but he retains, despite this circumstance, the essence of his nobility: defiant in the face of imminent death and stoically superior in his long captivity under Cabrera.

Marcela Luco, who talks in syllogisms and yet behaves extravagantly, a hybrid of witch and saint that could have come from the pen of Valle-Inclán, is a medieval figure thrust into the nineteenth century. A minimum of self-expression, and that constantly qualified by abstract theological references, makes the nun's pattern of motivation conspicuously imprecise, and envelops her behavior in mystery. Her role in the plot, a reaction to Nelet's amorous advances, is clearly indicative of this, for her immutable exterior suggests nothing of the sharp inner conflict between rational asceticism and passion. Her final inclination toward the latter remains as mysterious in its causality as everything else about the nun. Her impenetrable motivations, when coupled with a rigorously logical expression, project a weird sensation of irrational rationality.

Nelet's romantic 'star' has him encounter the forbidden nun everywhere, until her image assumes the force of inescapable destiny. Unlike Marcela, Nelet provides a realistic pattern of behavior. A downtrodden Don Juan, his self-confidence broken by failure,[42] Nelet strives to refurbish a shattered self-image. Nothing is more appropriate, in a traditional sense, than the

[42] Pérez Galdós, *Obras completas*, II, 820.

conquest of a nun. Incidentally, this is never given as a conscious process in the character.

Nelet's interest lies in the difficult conflict between his fundamental lack of confidence and his pressing need to gain self-esteem. The aid sought from Urdaneta suggests this psychological empasse, manifesting a weak and indecisive approach to the necessary object of conquest. The anxiety generated by Marcela's rejections and subsequent hesitations leads Nelet to an imaginary existence, in which reality is confused with hopes and fears. These, which become the substance of dreams,[43] invade his conscious life, perpetuating themselves in hallucinations which disfigure the world reconstructed in the novel.

The world of *Bodas reales* is prosaic in comparison. Don Bruno Carrasco is tragi-comical in the singlemindedness with which he refuses to accept failure in his occupational quest, but never transcends the typed characterization of the pretender at court. His daughter Lea is an equally simple characterization, in a role made to contrast with that of her sister Eufrasia. Her resolve to marry, plainly and securely, is the single example in the Carrasco family of a saving return to simplicity.

Eufrasia herself is another in the long list of Galdosian women perverted by the splendor of material things. The rural bumpkin, incapable of resisting the city's temptations, is rapidly transformed — with the expert assistance of Rafaela Milagro — into an accomplished urbanite. A simultaneous ethical evolution points up a negative direction, from simple innocence to depraved ambition. Eufrasia's intimate life, the world outside her home into which she flees and in which she is lost, are presented with deliberate incompleteness, lending an aura of mystery to the character's final resolve to break with her family.

Leandra is the most complex characterization in *Bodas reales*, embodying a full scale psychic breakdown. Irrevocably opposed to her husband's city ventures, she remains, in spirit, behind in La Mancha. This fundamental discontent, a deliberate resistance to any form of adaptation at first, becomes a permanent source of anguish. While Leandra maintains some form of real contact with her Manchegan roots, while she yet harbors the hope of convincing her husband to return, the anxiety is bearable. But when the hope withers with time, and a change of address

---

[43] Pérez Galdós, *Obras completas*, II, 820-821, 830.

prevents her frequent visits to Manchegan friends, a psycho-pathological state is precipitated.

Leandra is first immobilized by paralysis, possibly a psycho-somatic expression of her frustrated inability to find a link with the very roots of her existence. Forever seated in her rocking-chair, an oasis in the midst of a hostile environment, Leandra regresses to an earlier and happier period of her life. She gradually loses touch with the real world about her, inwardly re-living her rural activities. The confusion of objective and subjective elements, although humorous at times, clearly reveals the pattern of a mental breakdown.

Leandra's exceptional literary effect issues from the quality of her perturbation, for the subjective world of her daydreams and the real world about her are so intimately bound in her vision that the literary expression itself becomes an imprecise compound of superimposed masses.[44]

José Fago, the protagonist of *Zumalacárregui*, is the oddest characterization in the Series. The reader's first impression of an anguished being, withering under the strain of an unbearable inner contradiction, is a masterful introduction to the character.[45] The nature of Fago's psychological conflict — between his conscious and subconscious halves — precludes an openly dramatic presentation, in which the character's choice, however difficult, is made between palpable alternatives. Fago is per-manently engaged in a confused effort to segregate an obsessive past, which constitutes his hyper-active subconscious self, from a present that demands a very different pattern of behavior. He is never quite successful, and his today never emerges far beyond the shadow of his tormenting yesterdays.

Fago's past conjures itself into immediate reality at every step. The priest, always in flight from what he was, is forever facing what he has never ceased to be. Incapable of obviating the past's stifling ubiquity, which really lives on in himself, the Carlist soldier-priest is paralyzed unto death by its incessant echo.

Very little of that all-important past is made accessible to the reader, and as Galdós probably intended, Fago's psychologi-

44 Pérez Galdós, *Obras completas*, II, 1290, 1329, 1331.
45 Ibid., pp. 321-325.

cal complex cannot be fully deciphered. This constitutes the ultimate imprecision of a fictional world contorted by teluric effects and hallucinatory visions.[46]

A number of characters in the Third Series are sufficiently developed, without being protagonists, to warrant independent study. In the unitive plot, there is Pedro Hillo, a priest, bull-fighting enthusiast, and admirer of Hermosilla! As Calpena's self-appointed mentor in *Mendizábal,* this meek clergyman activates a necessary and often humorous conversation. His credulous wonder serves to exaggerate every detail of the mystery that surrounds the protagonist. An ironic Galdosian twist has a hyper-romantic temperament — wild imagination, exaggerated conclusions — enclose itself in Hermosillan rhetoric. Hillo is initially useful, furthermore, as the malleable tool of Pilar Loaysa, and even adds, on occasion, to the Series' accumulation of hallucinatory states.[47]

Churi, from *Luchana,* is perhaps less functional, but a more interesting literary creation. The deaf-mute, unique in Galdós' repertoire of characters, is introduced with his cousin Zoilo, from whom he varies very little initially. The presence of Aurora Negretti stimulates them both into manhood. Zoilo, as noted earlier, develops his will and fulfills himself; but love only awakens in Churi a deep sense of inferiority. He cannot establish contact with Aurora, and consumes himself without trying.

In an understandable psychological reaction, however, Churi opposes Zoilo's courtship of Aurora. He renounces his own ambitions, but the anxiety generated by a deteriorating self-evaluation demands the failure of his cousin and equal. When his opposition is pushed aside by Zoilo, Churi seeks a natural alliance with Calpena; and when this fails, the character reacts by evolving away from a reality that is unbearable. He thoroughly dissolves the nexus to his human environment, already tenuous given his inability to hear and speak. This process of 'Calibanization' is as believable, psychologically, as the compensatory impulse that characterizes Churi thereafter: a pathetic Don Juan, living for the crumbs of feminine acceptance that can alone soothe his shattered ego.[48]

[46] Pérez Galdós, *Obras completas,* II, 329, 367, 372.
[47] Ibid., pp. 568, 578-581.
[48] Ibid., p. 977.

José Milagro is the heart of the political activity reconstructed in *Montes de Oca* and *Los ayacuchos*. The reader's first glimpse of Milagro, in *Mendizábal*, reveals a typical 'covachuelista', bereft of character by the endless struggle to remain in office.[49] The tactics of subordination and supplication evolved during a lifetime within the 'spoils' system fail, however, and Milagro, the 'cesante', querulous and critical, seems an altogether different person.

The transformation is even more extreme because Galdós ironically injected a note of sincere political conviction, having Milagro identify himself with Espartero and rise, for once, above his chameleon-like reactions to the political pendulum. The once timid subordinate rushes forth into the political arena of Madrid's cafes, and it is he, in the end, who remains altruistic and loyal.[50] Notwithstanding this show of courage and loyalty, Milagro's entire presentation spells irony. The extremely simple character is always vulnerable, allowing the author a full measure of humor at the expense of the political scene of the 1840's. The comical note is even stressed in the character's hour of political victory. The very idea of Milagro as provincial governor is a hilarious indictment of Spanish politics, even when the Cervantine device is not fully exploited.

The presentation of several secondary characters holds an exceptional interest. Negretti, for example, lives a sense of guilt that undermines his very existence. Galdós placed the manufacturer of artillery in the difficult position of witnessing the effect of his cannon on his beloved Bilbao. An anxiety that mounts with every Carlist bomb forces Negretti into a defensive break with reality, into flights of imagination in which he hits — in a form of anachronistic effect favored by the novelist[51] — upon future scientific discoveries.

Salomé, an earthy peasant woman whose name happens to coincide with that of the Ulibarri girl, indiscriminately and as if by instinct gathers to her breast all in need of a consolation that, as Marañón has noted, is essentially feminine.[52] The characterization is spared social embellishments and ethical

49 Pérez Galdós, *Obras completas*, II, p. 457.
50 Ibid., p. 1266.
51 Ibid., I, 264; II, 722.
52 *Vida e historia* (Madrid, 1958), p. 23.

qualms, thus highlighting the feminine attributes common to mother and mistress. Several critics have judged Salomé superfluous to *Zumalacárregui*,[53] but there is no denying that she is indispensable to the set of coincidences that show up Fago's basic flaws and determine his development in the Episodio.

Juana Teresa de Sariñán, Pilar Loaysa's childhood friend-competitor, Urdaneta's authoritarian daughter-in-law, and mother of Calpena's rival for Demetria's hand, destests all three protagonists. Her personality is projected exclusively through a lengthy correspondence (*La estafeta romántica*), but hate, bitter satire, and Machiavellian duplicity emerge with extraordinary precision from her superb letters.[54]

Other secondary characters embody specific human traits. The Andalusian chaplain Ibraim is an endless flow of dull chatter, of empty sound that debases his office. Lopresti is the effeminate man, aptly endowed with the mentality of the eunuch. Serrano, a tubercular government employee who leaves the stain of slander at everyone's door, is a personification of discontent. Centurión, patiently suffering the whims of royal children, is the perfect courtier and haughtily proud of it.

Here, as in the first Episodios, the fictionalization of mass actions (battles, sieges) required the creation of numerous representative characters, concrete individuals who embody, nonetheless, the significant traits of a collective personality. In the Third Series Galdós created such profoundly human, and at the same time representative figures as Baldomero Galán, an 'isabelino' soldier and the aggressive young counterpart of Espartero himself; Ibarburru, a prime example of the religious casuistry of militant Carlism; 'Chomín' and Gorra, members of the innocent generation that shed its blood for Don Carlos; and Eustaquio de la Pertusa, who incarnates the conspiratorial activities of marginal interests.

The focus on children is somewhat reduced in the Third Series, but still remains an important area of Galdós' characterization. The depiction of Leandra's brood, for example, is a delicate intuition of the innocent self-centeredness of childhood, and the girl princesses — Isabel and Luisa Fernanda — are offered as

---

[53] See, e.g., Boussagol, "Sources et composition du *Zumalacárregui*," *Bulletin Hispanique*, XXVI (1924), 262.

[54] See, e.g., Pérez Galdós, *Obras completas*, II, 922.

a synthesis of childish mischief and premature seriousness, accompanied everywhere by the disturbing shadow of an ominous destiny.[55]

The historical characterization of the Third Series reveals a number of important innovations. To begin with, historical personalities intervene to an unprecedented degree in novelistic development. Espartero and Zumalacárregui are so directly associated with specific literary characters that they can believably channel a great deal of plot activity.[56] Fago's military mission under Zumalacárregui — to fetch a cannon — is novelistically appropriate, historical, and humorous. Montes de Oca's presence is indispensable to the plot of *Montes de Oca;* and historical exactness is only retained by placing his activities in a conjectural limbo. Montes de Oca's relationship with Rafaela Milagro, although unquestioned by Ibero, is never more than a possibility.[57]

The Third Series is also exceptional in that all the important figures of the period, Zumalacárregui, Espartero, Mendizábal, Cabrera, and Maroto, receive an unusual amount of space and attention. Zumalacárregui and Espartero, who quickly attained legendary stature, permit little elaboration beyond their fixed historico-legendary images;[58] but the rest, who allow the intuition of more personal and familiar facets, are among the author's best historical characterizations.

Galdós' intuition added intensely personal facets to the particular character's historical function. Mendizábal is a profoundly human expression of a reformer's tribulations in nineteenth-century Spain. Galdós knowingly focused upon him at night in his office, alone, his public mask momentarily discarded, and struggling with the diverse factors of political decision. There are moments of human weakness before the expected political onslaught, and flashes of the dauntless spirit that pushed forward a program of revolutionary reform.[59] Maroto's presentation is even more intimate, fixing admirably on the vacillations and weaknesses, the torture undergone by a man destined to surrender

55 Pérez Galdós, *Obras completas*, II, 1153-1155, 1345 ff.
56 See, e.g., ibid., pp. 525-526.
57 Ibid., pp. 1122-1123.
58 See, e.g., ibid., pp. 410-418, 764-769.
59 Ibid., pp. 522-526.

an ideal consecrated in blood.[60] Montes de Oca sets the tone of the era's romantic politics. His life, believably projected into a romantic plot structure, and his death, in a manner endemic in the period, underscore a historical posture of subjective, exaggerated, and thoroughly impractical idealism.[61] Cabrera is artistically woven into a medieval setting which offers, in *La campaña del Maestrazgo,* an incomparable background for the character's paradoxical combination of warm peasant simplicity and insensitive demonism.[62]

Other controversial historical figures, Don Carlos and María Cristina, for example, are deliberately presented in less detail. But Galdós opened a new area of historical characterization with his lengthy and interesting presentations of Quintana, Bretón de los Herreros, and Miguel de los Santos Alvarez. The latter is of particular interest, for Galdós reproduced his literary style as well as his person.[63]

The first two Series are not comparable to the Third in richness of characterization. This is due, for the most part, to the latter's unprecedented novelistic complexity and to Galdós' probing into new human dimensions. But it is also noteworthy that the Third Series evidences a novel degree of dissociation between literary protagonists and historical events. The individual development of some characters depends less than heretofore upon a direct participation in the history reconstructed. Calpena, for example, is less identified with any sequence of historical events than Araceli or Monsalud before him, and this allows maximum freedom to evolve beyond the confining function of historical representation. But this freedom is by no means universal, and protagonists like Fago or Ibero reveal no new degree of dissociation from history. Calpena himself, it must be remembered, is never so removed from the events of his day as to subvert his realistic integration into a specific historical environment.

The dissociation between some literary protagonists and historical events is logically compensated for, in terms of representation, by a greater use of the historical characters themselves. The Third Series offers more history than usual through the great

60 Pérez Galdós, *Obras completas,* II, 1040-1042, 1052-1056.
61 Ibid., pp. 1148-1152.
62 Ibid., pp. 851-856.
63 Ibid., pp. 898-902; and see Darío, *España contemporénea,* p. 236.

figures of the period themselves, a circumstance that guarantees them greater literary elaboration.

Thus, the scope of the characterization is extended well beyond anything previously attempted in the *Episodios Nacionales*. Galdós juxtaposed, to an unprecedented number of extensively developed historical characters, an equally large number of complex fictional creations. Such characters as Fago and Nelet, with one foot in the world and another in a subjective universe, stand beside the work's Mendizábals, Zumalacárreguis and Cabreras, in all their realism.

Miscellaneous

1. *Comical elements*

We have noted that the Third Series stems, in great part, from Galdós' humoristic perception of the romantic generation's beliefs and attitudes. Parody of this kind, although akin to satire, is neither as intense nor as negative in its approach. Both parody and satire imply an adverse judgment, but the latter feeds on the contravention of universally acknowledged ethical principles, and thus generates hostility; while the former often expresses no distempered attitude towards the object parodied, which rarely represents — whatever else it may — the subversion of a universal ethos.

The parody of Romanticism is by no means exclusively comical, for it also satisfies the important end of historical representation. To an even greater degree than the satire interpolated into the Second Series (the story centered on Bragas), parody facilitates the reconstruction of an era from within itself. Galdós reproduced the basic world-view of the romantic generation in the only manner in which his own generation could understand and enjoy it: in the somewhat incredulous perspective of the parodist, whose reconstruction of Romanticism simultaneously judged and surpassed it.

Another important source of humor is the Third Series' accumulation of peculiar characters, of people unable to differentiate between objective reality and their own subjective projections. Galdós' propensity for psychopathological characterization, although not a device of comedy as such, invariably leaves a by-product of comedy.[64] This certainly applies to the Third Series, in which Galdós utilized the full literary potential of such confused characters as Fago, Nelet, and Leandra to this end.

Other avenues of humor in the Series warrant little further study. The primarily comical characterization is conspicuous, ranging in importance and development from Milagro and Hillo to Ibraim and Lopresti.[65] The humor that stems from name symbolism, Pedro Hillo, Milagro, etc., conforms, as a rule, to the outline presented earlier.[66]

2. Symbolism

Name symbolism remains, despite the nineteen year interval between Series, the most prominent device of Galdosian symbolism. The numerous examples of the Third Series offer no important innovations, but a qualification to this characteristic device becomes evident for the first time. Two examples suffice to indicate its general applicability. Demetria's name suggests her identification with the earth, a nexus to reality that is meant to contrast with the extravagant approach to life of Calpena and Aurora Negretti. The association established in this fashion is a permanent one, and Demetria does not evolve from the symbolic reference. Aurora Negretti, a contradiction that suggests romantic instability, is an example of the opposite phenomenon. Her development in the work, like that of Calpena, is essentially a process of de-romantization, a movement away from the association fixed by name symbolism. This suggests the limitations of the Galdosian device, which can in no way be functional within the mechanics of character development. In fact, character fixation through name symbolism, without regard to later development, may on occasion obstruct the normal flow of the work.

The Third Series contains relatively few symbolic scenes. But the sombre aftermath of the Queen's wedding can compare in suggestive power with the fall of Carnicero's house in the Second Series or the 'Mediohombre'-Araceli relationship in the First.[67]

[64] See F. Bravo Moreno, *Síntomas de la patología mental que se hallan en las obras literarias de Benito Pérez Galdós* (Barcelona, 1923); and L. B. Walton, "La psicología anormal en la obra de Galdós," *Boletín del Instituto Español*, IV (1948), 10-13.

[65] See above, pp. 126-128.

[66] See above, pp. 99.

[67] Pérez Galdós, *Obras completas*, II, 1353.

On the other hand, the Series does not lack more extensive and complex symbolic possibilities, which involve entire plot segments and in which a measure of inexactness is to be expected. The degree of symbolic association ranges from a close parallel, such as that between Carlism and Fago's pathological obsession with the past, to the somewhat remote parallel between the Queen's wedding and Eufrasia's 'nuptials.' The most extreme example of an extended and necessarily inexact parallel is the plot of *Montes de Oca*. The identification of Santiago Ibero with victorious liberal Spain is direct and unquestionable. When the brave soldier's most laudable qualities bring about his deception in Madrid, a parallel is struck with respect to Espartero and María Cristina, the queen-mother and regent.

3. *Geographical determination*

The Carlist War has its own setting, its own geographical and human environment, and Galdós could not reconstruct it with the same degree of urban concentration noted in the Second Series. On the other hand, he could not forego an important perspective from Madrid, in which Romanticism flashed its brilliant short-lived fires. This ambivalence is artistically surmounted in a variety of ways. For one thing, a number of plots introduce the reader directly into the Spanish capital. When this became incompatible with depicting the Carlist conflict, Galdós relied on the epistolary form, justifiably prominent in the Third Series. The novelist found that well-situated correspondents could furnish literary expression to a geographical simultaneity that was essential to the reconstruction of the period between 1834 and 1844.

Much of the Third Series deals, in one form or another, with rural-urban conflict: Rafaela Milagro-Santiago Ibero-Gracia; Aurora Negretti-Calpena-Demetria; the Carrascos. The romantic polarization of evil sophistication (city) and innocent simplicity (country) fits perfectly into the basic scheme of the Series; but there is an unexpected peculiarity. Galdós always favored the rural ideal, thus identifying himself with romantic dogma and appearing to depart, consequently, from the humorous perspective maintained on Romanticism throughout the work. The novelist's attitude, however, is less related to Rousseauian thought than to the neo-christian movement associated with Tolstoy.[68] This particular Galdosian attitude is apparent as early as *Tormento* (1884),[69] and probably reached its climax in *Halma* (1895).

4. *Subconscious content*

There are dreams and hallucinations in previous Series of the *Episodios Nacionales*,[70] but these become more numerous and of greater functional importance with the manner of characterization first provided in the Third Series. Any fictional character may have a dream or suffer a hallucination, but the margin of propensity is clearly greater for such creations as Fago, Nelet, and Leandra.

Subconscious phenomena vary greatly, for the terms 'dream' and 'hallucination', which may overlap in themselves, are susceptible of further scientific subdivision.[71] For the purposes of this study, however, only three literary categories will be useful:[72] retrospectively narrated dreams, directly narrated dreams, and hallucinations. The dream content itself, often pregnant with symbolic possibilities,[73] will only be commented upon as it relates to novelistic development or characterization.

In the retrospectively narrated dream, an awakened subject relates what he recalls of an unconscious experience; and often, although perhaps somewhat unrealistically, such dreams are remembered in some detail. This form of literary externalization prescribes an analytical approach, that is, a judgment removed from the act of dreaming itself.[74] Although such dreams are related to plot, their retrospective format generally precludes any important promotion of novelistic activity.

[68] See, e.g., Pérez Galdós, *Memoranda*, pp. 247-257.
Also see G. Portnoff, *La literatura rusa en España* (New York, 1932), pp. 123-205; and "The Beginning of the New Idealism in the works of Tolstoy and Galdós," *Romanic Review*, XXIII (1932), 33-37.
[69] Pérez Galdós, *Tormento* (Madrid, 1906), pp. 137-142.
[70] Pérez Galdós, *Obras completas*, I, 258, 443, 757, 817-818, 833-834, 1057-1058, 1164-1167; II, 212-213, et passim.
[71] See, e.g., J. Schraibman, "Dreams in the Novels of Galdós," *Literature and Psychology*, X (1960), 91-96.
[72] For a more comprehensive study of dreams in Galdós' work, but limited to his *Novelas contemporáneas*, see J. Schraibman, *Dreams in the Novels of Galdós* (New York, 1960).
[73] See Pérez Galdós, *Obras completas*, II, 416, 820-821, 830, 855-856, 862 868; III, 279, 323.
[74] Ibid., II, 868, 887; III, 201, et passim.

The important literary functions of the retrospectively narrated dream are limited, as a rule, to prophetic anticipations,[75] misleading wish-fulfillments,[76] and perhaps most important of all, to penetrating insights into the subject's mental and spiritual state.[77] It is in functioning as a characterizational device that the retrospective quality possesses a unique value. An inherent analytical approach simultaneously provides a meaningful dream content and the subject's own reaction to it.[78]

The directly narrated dream is related by the omniscient author as it takes place in the mind of an unconscious or semiconscious subject.[79] In the case of an unconscious subject, the relation of dream content to world of fiction is one of identity, since the dreamer's world blots out everything else. In the case of a semi-conscious subject, of which Leandra's daydreaming is a prime example,[80] the objective world and the dream world are superimposed, their presence made simultaneous by the subject's movement from consciousness to unconsciousness. In either case, the direct narration precludes the break with the immediate world of fiction that characterizes the retrospectively narrated dream, and the analytic approach inherent in the latter is lost, since the dreamer can no longer pass judgment upon his own dream. This reduces the characterizational effectiveness of the directly narrated dream, but allows novelistic action to flow more freely from the dream situation.

The most direct literary expression of a subconscious content is through hallucinations. These are invariably narrated in the third-person and at the very instant of their effect upon the subject, who is awake. The reader is momentarily thrust into the character's active disorder, and the fusion of psychological and real phenomena is complete and immediate. It is clear that the hallucinatory state has little characterizational value; but equally clear, of course, that it is the form of subconscious externalization most readily susceptible of translating itself into novelistic action, of pushing the subject to react as if to a set of real circumstances.

75 See, e.g., Pérez Galdós, *Obras completas,* II, 940, 1577.
76 See, e.g., ibid., III, 312, 469-470.
77 See, e.g., ibid., II, 820-821, 830, 868, 887, 1249; III, 175-176.
78 See, e.g., ibid., II, 862, 868.
79 Ibid., II, 329, 372, 855-856, 1614; III, 123-124, et passim.
80 Ibid., II, 1290, 1331.

Finally, Galdós combined dreams and hallucinations, fusing the particular literary function of each. He moved around the analytical, static quality of the retrospectively narrated dream, for example, by reproducing it in the subject's waking life as hallucination.[81]

More important, however, than the literary functions of each form of subconscious externalization is their combined effect in the work. An unprecedented accumulation of subconscious matter alters the heretofore simple realism of the *Episodios Nacionales*. The world of fiction is often perceived, and even simultaneously, on different levels of reality, which tends to reduce the precision and objectivity of the literary expression. The Third Series is, in this sense, an artistic fusion of four simultaneous and distinct dimensions of one reality: the accumulation of events, ideas and attitudes that constitute the history of the period between 1834 and 1844; the same history envisioned in a familiar perspective, as the personal living of concrete individuals; the same, again, in parody, in the humoristic view of an alien generation; and finally, as altered in the process of subjectivization which all reality constantly undergoes within concrete individuals.

5. *Literary tradition*

Galdós' practice of re-elaborating traditional themes and characters was noted as early as the First Series.[82] Only in the Third, however, does the practice become a major factor in novelistic development and characterization. The separate study of the two facets, themes and characters, will facilitate matters, though it should be remembered they are often combined.

Galdós' re-elaborations of traditional plot sequences, such as the Shakespearean elements of the First Series or the Dickens ending of *Un voluntario realista*, are always suitably integrated into a specific historico-fictional setting. The 'play within a play' sequence occurs, for example, in a plot dealing with the theatre and which has Máiquez as a protagonist; and the Romeo and Juliet sequence of *Zaragoza*, in the tragic atmosphere of a city's ill-fated struggle to survive. These examples point up the novelist's intention. Always counting on reader recognition, he provided a dimension of associative interest to particular novelistic develop-

81 See, e.g., Pérez Galdós, *Obras completas*, II, 862.
82 See above, pp. 58-59, 70, 90.

ments. Nothing could be lost in any case, because even the readers who failed to perceive the associational values were treated to literary elements of time-tested interest: the play within a play, the tragic effect of family feuds on young lovers, or the last minute exchange of characters before an execution.

This literary practice is somewhat more complex in the Third Series. In appropriating parts of *Don Alvaro*, Galdós integrated a genuinely romantic nucleus into the literary reconstruction of Spanish Romanticism. There is irony involved, to be sure, but the accommodation of Spanish Romanticism's most extreme literary manifestation assures a formidable illustrative effect. Well done — and *La campaña del Maestrazgo* can claim to be so — a novelization of this type can simultaneously express what an age thought it wished to be, what it thought it was, and what it became for later generations.

The use of traditional character outlines, especially of those native to Spanish literature, is widespread in the *Episodios Nacionales*. But the Third Series contains these in sufficient number and variety to permit a rundown of possible differences in conception. The association to a given literary model may be obvious and direct, as in the case of Marcela Luco; more subtle, or altered to a degree, as in Urdaneta and Nelet; or sufficiently remote to suggest an unconscious association in the author's mind, as in the case of Pilar Loaysa and Felipe, whose names and personalities have a distinct Cervantine resonance.

The most apparent function of this characterizational procedure, a simple matter of literary economy, is somewhat misleading. It is clear that Galdós avoided 'ex nihilo' creation by adopting pre-existent character outlines, but it is not as immediately obvious that their use implied the creative adaptation of a traditional outline to a specific socio-historical setting. How much more time-consuming and difficult it may be to create 'ex nihilo' than to accommodate an anachronistic personality it is almost impossible to say, but an idea of the difficulties involved in the latter may be enlightening.

The credibility of a traditional character outline may appear to offer no problem initially, because the novelist need not insist on the existence of beings who are familiar to every reader. This initial facility is deceptive, as it is in the case of historical characters, with respect to whom the reader possesses a standard against which to measure the novelist's effort.[83] The demands on the novelist are even greater when he deals with traditional as opposed to historical characters, because the reader's yardstick may combine paradoxically opposed criteria: the novelist's successful rendition of the source figure's essence and the suitability of its adaptation to a totally new literary environment.

Obviously, the characterizational procedure in question must be justified by ends other than literary economy. One inescapable effect of Galdós' traditional characterizations is a poignant expression of 'Spanishness', of the essence of Spain that is incarnate in such figures as Don Juan, Celestina, and Don Quijote. Despite their adaptation to specific new contexts, many of the novelist's re-elaborations make his Spain all the more real for their appearance. Furthermore, the practice allows Galdós to choose the most appropriate literary outline for a wide range of fundamental human qualities or combinations of qualities. It is difficult to imagine any original characterization capable of replacing the Marcela of Cervantes (cold, independent, pedantic) in the peculiar novelistic context of *La campaña del Maestrazgo*, or, for that matter, of displacing the special Byronian donjuanism of Lord Gray in *Cádiz*.

The Third Series, already exceptional for its quantitative use of traditional character outlines, reflects a more complex approach to the device. Galdós deliberately brought together three traditional characterizations, for example, within a single plot, which is itself developed along traditional lines. The cumulative effect in *La campaña del Maestrazgo* is one of artistic distortion by anachronism. The impressionistic world of the Episodio, geographically, archeologically, and even historically medieval, is peopled with protagonists who provide, despite their realistic integration, an additional residue of anachronism.

B) *Fourth Series*

The Fourth Series reconstructs two decades of political sham, moral laxity, and economic ferment. The adult reign of Isabel II, a historical diminuendo, is charged with the repellent sinuosities of Sor Patrocinio and echoes with the vulgar ferocity of Narváez. The mood and temper of the last volume of the Third

---

[83] See above, p. 69.

Series, *Bodas reales,* anticipates the prosaic mediocrity that crushed Spanish life between 1848 and 1868.

Literary form

The Fourth Series is the least compact literary unit of the *Episodios Nacionales.* The Second Series, it will be remembered, attained a degree of unity in the artistic interrelationship of all its major plot developments. The Third achieved its own degree of compactness by means of an extended unitive plot, however incidental the nexus between novels. In the light of both of these, the Fourth Series offers an extremely dissociated structure. It contains neither a unitive plot nor a single nucleus of closely interrelated plots.

So independent are the various novels of the Fourth Series that Galdós employed a number of devices to project the impression of serial unity.[84] A measure directed to this end is the perpetuation of exhausted plot elements. Fajardo, for example, ends his novelistic activity, properly speaking, in *Narváez,* the second Episodio of the Series; but he re-appears in passive roles throughout the remainder of the work. The same is true of Lucila Ansúrez, Santiuste, and other protagonists. A related device is the presentation of future protagonists before they assume the main role in a particular novel, as subordinate characters in earlier plot developments. A tie between the various novels of the Series is achieved in both cases, but it is a weak nexus indeed when compared to the unifying effect of active Series-wide trajectories like those of Araceli and Calpena.

Another unitive device is the Ansúrez family, which supplies the Series with a number of protagonists. A family tie definitely affiliates several plots in the work, but without a hint of the strict intertwining of lives employed in the Second Series. To begin with, the Ansúrez family provides only a few of the important characters developed in the work. Moreover, these are dispersed and disconnected in their literary roles, thus reducing the family's cohesive effect to a minimum; just enough, in fact, to draw the most dissociated plots in the Series — those of *Aita Tettauen* and *La vuelta al mundo en la Numancia,* which take place in Africa and America, respectively — into the scope of the literary unit.

[84] See above, page 76.

A third unitive device consists in forging a literary bridge between successive novels. Galdós often saw to it that one plot ended in the context from which the following plot emerged. The most striking example of this is *La vuelta al mundo en la Numancia*, in which Santiuste's episodic trajectory comes to an end and Diego Ansúrez's novel begins.

All these unitive devices are esthetically integrated in the Series' novelistic development. The re-apperance of ex-protagonists, far from being superfluous, will usually involve the performance of necessary and interesting functions. Fajardo's inquisitive nature, his numerous contacts in Madrid, make him a permanently reliable source of information from the capital. Santiuste, once his own trajectory closes, provides the reader with a humorous analysis of nineteenth-century Spanish history. The Ansúrez family embodies a symbolic projection,[85] which more than justifies its varied and far-flung accommodations to the novelistic development of the Fourth Series.

Plot development

The novelistic structure of the Fourth Series could profitably be compared to Galdós' *Novelas contemporáneas*. A specific environment is prolonged in time, and definite segments are focused upon as independent novels. A common spatial-temporal reference accounts for the appearance of elements from one novel on different levels of focus in other novels. The writer's perspective on the historical environment varies with each novel, but the subject reality is always reconstructed intact.

Naturally, the Fourth Series does not offer as many plot developments (perspectives) as the *Novelas contemporáneas*, but it does contain seven different novels, which are, as we have seen, more independent than those which crystallize from a Series' unitive plot, since nothing subordinates or determines their development. These seven novels are just as readily differentiated from the unitive plots themselves, being less extensive and therefore more rapidly developed. Both distinctions noted contribute to their literary effectiveness.

The more extensive novels in the Fourth Series, those centered on Fajardo, Santiuste, and Santiago Ibero, occupy two

---

85 See Casalduero, *Vida y obra*, p. 190.

Episodios; the others, centered on Lucila Ansúrez, Virginia Socobio, Teresita Villaescusa, and Diego Ansúrez, usually culminate in one. Social and family ties between the various protagonists fail, except in a purely structural sense,[86] to subordinate one plot to another. In fact, plot diversity is often more than merely thematic; and between the novels of Fajardo, Virginia Socobio, Santiuste, and Ibero the differences are sufficiently fundamental to require completely different novelistic forms.

Fajardo personally narrates the first two Episodios of the Series. The memoir technique facilitates the introduction of a character without antecedents in Galdós' work, and the first-person is the narrative form best suited to an introductory retrospection that fixes a novelistic context. This initial flashback relates the awakening of young Fajardo to the world about him, the rebellious need for freedom that conflicts with the discipline of a religious vocation. Fajardo's escape from the seminary, his carefree existence in Rome, reveal the author's customary finesse in dealing with youth.

Young Fajardo's picaresque life in Rome, a rootless and aimless freedom, points up the negative poles of liberty: hunger and solitude. Faced with these, the protagonist succumbs. The escape and the return to the seminary, although nothing exceptional in a boy, actually set the pattern of Fajardo's existence. The desire for liberty, for a full life, is soon reborn in the repentant seminarist, and Berberina's opulent charms occasion a new fall. The wise Monseñor Antonelli, whose learned and serene detachment is essential to the renaissance atmosphere impressionistically affixed to the entire Italian episode,[87] then releases Fajardo from the religious vocation of his childhood.

The pattern is set: anxiety for freedom, incapacity to cope with its demands, and flight back to security. The novelistic present takes place in the Madrid of Isabel II, and Fajardo's Spanish experience is characteristically initiated with an orgy of freedom. In time, however, the protagonist is again made to face the realities that underlie liberty. Without the monetary resources to prolong his enjoyable existence in the capital, Fajardo is presented with a dilemma in which a rich but ugly young lady corresponds to the secure seminary of yesteryear. After a short-lived

86 See below, pp. 143-144.
87 Casalduero, *Vida y obra*, p. 175.

resistance, which ends with the death of Antoñita — Fajardo's mistress and only contact with the popular classes of Spanish society —, the protagonist marries into the powerful upper middle-class of the epoch. Fajardo's choice of security in a loveless match is characteristic; but no less so is his post-marital need for freedom and fulfillment, which takes on pathological overtones as the novel ends. The weak protagonist will be encountered repeatedly in the rest of the Series, and always in open conflict with himself, but he can never again interest as a human development.

Fajardo's final obsession identifies liberty with Lucila Ansúrez, the beautiful member of a nomadic family encountered in *Narváez*. His perturbed search for Lucila is a bridge to the latter's own novel in *Los duendes de la camarilla*. A third-person narrative clarifies what Fajardo's obsessed investigation merely suggests. Lucila is in Madrid, but no longer residing in the convent to which she had been recommended, with great foresight, by Fajardo's wife.

The plot that follows is patterned on that of the previous novel. Lucila had no true religious vocation, regardless of how attractive monastic security may have appeared to the wretched and persecuted nomad. When the new protagonist is focused upon, she has escaped from the convent and is fully immersed in life. She is living, in fact, with Bartolomé Gracián, and her passionate first love — for a persecuted and wounded military rebel — is cast in a candorous abnegation that subdues the primitive ferocity of her ansurian blood and attenuates the stigma of an illicit liaison.

This earthly paradise of free existence, and it is just that despite accumulating troubles and inconveniences, is endangered by Domiciana Paredes, Lucila's confidential assistant in the task of providing for her stricken lover. Lucila's only friend in Madrid is a diabolical woman, replete with celestinesque embellishments. Domiciana, too, has left the convent, but a long sojourn in religious life has identified her with monastic furtiveness and duplicity.

The libidinous awakening of the nun is highly effective. Desperate to recover a wasted youth, Domiciana reacts to Lucila's long conversations concerning her lover. The nun's veiled interest in Gracián, whom she has never seen, becomes sufficiently evident to pierce Lucila's candor, but the latter's instinctive defense is no match for Domiciana's astuteness. Lucila loses Gracián, whose mysterious disappearance — although undoubtedly the work of Domiciana — is only clarified in a later volume.

Lucila reacts to her loss with all the violence of her ansurian heritage. She almost succeeds in knifing Domiciana, but the latter, far too wily and determined, frustrates all her attempts at recovery. Reality finally closes in on Lucila, polarizing her alternatives: marriage to Halconero, a rich old man enamoured of her beauty, or an indefinite extension of her fruitless search for Gracián. Her novel ends when, like Fajardo before her, she takes refuge from life in the security of a loveless marriage. The reader will encounter her repeatedly, she will become a widow and remarry in the work, but will never again crystallize a new plot direction.

With Lucila's marriage, Galdós' focus returned to the upper middle-class society of the first two Episodios. In *La revolución de julio,* Fajardo continues the memoirs interrupted by his mental breakdown. He quickly relates the ulterior effects of his crisis, Domiciana's futile attempt to hold Gracián — an ingenious depiction of a Don Juan in the hands of a Celestina — and gradually centers on the life of Virginia Socobio de Rementería, the protagonist of a new novel.

The first-person narrative is almost prohibitive in its restrictions when employed to convey the life struggles of a second party. Nevertheless, this is precisely what Galdós' conception required, that everything known about the feminine protagonist be learned through Fajardo. An unhappily married Virginia (Rementería is a fop and the marriage an economic one) steals away under mysterious circumstances, and everything is left to conjecture in the deliberately limited perspective of Fajardo's memoirs: Why? With whom? Where to?

The opinions, reasons, and judgments voiced in Fajardo's social circles merely project the surface of reality, forging parallel dimensions of novelistic development that are reminiscent of the procedure executed in the complementary novels *La incógnita* and *Realidad.* Fajardo's memoirs incorporate all the hearsay available; but he retains a distinct perspective on the problem himself, which is mostly conjectural at first and then gradually acquires intelligible outlines.

The meaningful clarification of the various enigmas is controlled for suspense, throughout, by Fajardo's exclusive perspective: Virginia's unilateral correspondence with the latter and his own private investigation. The mystery facet of the plot is centered, for the most part, on the identity of Virginia's chosen companion. When the name of Leoncio Ansúrez is brought forth and confirmed, the plot's socio-ethical facet is intensified.

Virginia's elopement with a man of the people stuns the corrupt uppermost levels of society, which react with powerful means of suppression to this disturbance of their vacuous contentedness and hypocritical morality. Virginia and Leoncio, a revolutionary pair, make a stand against society's powerful forces. Their only hope lies in a revaluation of society's values, a hope they place in the Revolution of 1854. They are defrauded, of course, and the plot culminates with the protagonists' new flight from Madrid, in which they are criminally liable.

The plot of *La revolución de julio* contrasts vividly with the two that precede it in the Series. It coincides, naturally enough, with the revolutionary atmosphere depicted in the Episodio, and Virginia represents a complete break with the pattern of refuge from life established by Fajardo and Lucila. She foregoes security in search of liberty and fulfillment, unhindered by the weaknesses that overwhelm similar yearnings in the other protagonists.

O'Donnell centers on a group of familiar characters, with the novelist's perspective gradually focusing on a new protagonist. Teresita Villaescusa is exceptional in that no earlier introduction is made of her. But as part of that circle of familiar people, Teresita acquires a passport, as it were, into the fictional world of the Fourth Series. Beautiful and fun-loving, she deftly avoids the yoke of an exclusively economic marriage which a mercenary mother seeks to impose on her, thus preparing Galdós' probe in a new direction within the security-freedom-marriage framework of the Series.

Teresita's evolution to this end involves a measure of paradox, basic behavioral changes that do not reflect a corresponding alteration in personality.[88] She rapidly evolves from a socially rebellious youngster into Galdós' unique depiction of a 'cocotte.' Three factors provide a degree of verisimilitude to this strange develop-

88 For a study of this characterizational procedure as a function of impressionistic psychology, see Casalduero, *Vida y obra*, pp. 177-178.

ment: the intimate friendship of Valera (Virginia's sister and truly adulterous counterpart), whose extra-marital relationships fix the accepted procedure within a hypocritical society; the sudden death of captain Villaescusa, which leaves Teresita without economic resources; and most important of all, the immoral precedent set by Manolita Pez, Teresita's widowed mother.

Valera's materialistic motives and Manolita Pez's coquettish weaknesses are not new to Galdós' work, but the corruption of Teresita — single and from a middle-class background — is a definite innovation. Her decision to take on a rich lover is mordant irony on the part of Galdós, for that decision constitutes the most honest solution to the materialistic vocation of the period, ethically superior, without question, to economic matches and their subsequent adulteries, however discreet and palatable to a corrupt society.

Moreover, Teresita is far from degraded by her decision, for even her first 'public' venture stresses a fundamental charity.[89] Her subsequent trajectory, from one rich lover to another, furnishes the experience and knowledge that subdues her rebelliousness and reinforces her humane qualities. The successive liaisons score the growth of her concern for others — truly the height of Galdós' paradoxical irony — until this altruistic dimension becomes the very axis of her novel: a hazily envisioned function as the liquidator of the frozen wealth of the rich, a nexus through which long-accumulated riches pass to those strata of society in which accumulation is illusory.

When Teresita's charity rescues Juan Santiuste from hunger and stultifying inactivity, the novel draws to a dramatic culmination. The decision demanded of Teresita, overwhelmed by Santiuste's superficial qualities, is extremely difficult, a choice between love and her vital function within society. It is clear that a life of poverty beside Santiuste, which Teresita might see as her only prospect, does not prompt her rejection of love; nor is this due to her perception of Santiuste's fundamental hollowness, revealed in a later novel. Aided at a crucial moment by another's precise definition of her function as 'liquidadora de la mano muerta española,'[90] Teresita perceives the full implication of her proposed marriage to Santiuste. The unemotional, almost un-

89 See Pérez Galdós, *Obras completas*, III, 163.
90 Ibid., pp. 218-222.

feminine decision that follows is believable and quite in keeping with her strong-willed, rational approach to life.

Aita Tettauen traces part of Santiuste's subsequent life, and deliberately begins in the context of the familiar Halconero family. This presentation, together with Santiuste's role in *O'Donnell*, impresses upon the reader the fact that Santiuste's existence is a never-ending flight from reality, which he can only bear when sugar-coated by his imagination or when mellowed in an atmosphere of domestic security.

The protagonist of *Aita Tettauen* retains the subservient obsequiousness and the flowery imagination that had once affected Teresita Villaescusa, and these appear to arouse similar emotions — basically maternal — in Lucila, who is about to become a widow. This plot direction is suddenly detoured by the Spanish invasion of Africa.

The novel will consist, from this point forward, of Santiuste's episodic confrontation with life. The war in Africa contrasts vividly with the protagonist's evocation from Madrid; and this discrepancy, natural enough to the reader, is devastating to Santiuste. He is quite unable to adjust and is gradually transformed into the pathetic 'Confusio', a pejorative appellation that underscores the pseudo-religious direction of his psychotic retreat from unbearable reality. Santiuste reacts defensively to the real horror of war by coming to personify brotherly love. Armed, moreover, with his 'filón inagotable de ternura', he embarks on a desperate search for feminine comfort. Both the psychotic transformation and the overpowering urge for feminine (maternal) companionship are characteristic of Santiuste's pathological reaction to life.

The novel, as we have noted, is completely episodic. As Fajardo's private correspondent, Santiuste is permanently committed to a search for newsworthy events. The device for incorporating history is obvious, but credible in a character whose inability to face reality presupposes brief encounters with successive environments. Santiuste activates an episodic adventure in each setting, and these, in the end, come to interest as much as he.

Aided by a Celestina figure, who is magnificent in the medieval setting of Tetuan's Sephardic colony, Santiuste wins the love of the beautiful Yohar. His initial success is undeniable, but

Yohar eventually returns to the paternal roof and the embrace of a rich merchant. The pattern of Santiuste's love-affairs is thus established, for Yohar's decision reinforces that taken by Teresita in the previous Episodio. In Moorish Tangiers, Santiuste initiates the courtship of one of his host's several wives. Gonzalo Ansúrez, a Spaniard turned Moor, squashes the affair. On his return to Spain, Santiuste encounters a new failure. Lucila, towards whose maternal embrace he flies, has already remarried.

The final episode takes place in the second half of *Carlos VI en la Rápita*, in the peculiar world of the archpriest Juan Hondón. The inevitable female conquest is one of the several young women who live under the 'protection' of the medieval, semi-Moorish archpriest. Donata, too, falls under the spell of Santiuste, who is disguised as a seminary student for his escapades in Carlist territory. After a novelesque elopement, and the young lovers' capture by a jealous but magnanimous Juan Hondón, Donata abandons Santiuste for the service of a canon.

Santiuste's episodic passage through *Aita Tettauen* and *Carlos VI en la Rápita* has given rise to sharp criticism. Ricard, for example, sees a fundamental dichotomy in the structure of the latter, which incorporates both a segment of the war in Africa (1859-60) and an abortive Carlist rebellion. The critic views *Carlos VI en la Rápita*, consequently, as a combination of leftovers from *Aita Tettauen* and materials — essentially alien to those leftovers — that could not form the basis of a totally new Episodio; and he interprets the parallel structure of the two volumes (El Nasiry-Juan Hondón, Yohar-Donata, etc.) as an attempt to disguise the dichotomous juxtaposition noted above.[91]

Nevertheless, the parallelism mentioned, together with the active presence of Santiuste in both worlds, suggest a unified conception of the two volumes as a single novel. Galdós grasped the profoundly ironic possibilities inherent in a parallel reconstruction of the atmosphere surrounding the Carlist uprising, and this undoubtedly prompted his direct juxtaposition, in one volume, of the elements that were most susceptible of parallelism:

91 R. Ricard, "Structure et inspiration de *Carlos VI en la Rápita*," *Bulletin Hispanique*, LVII (1955), 70-83.

However, for a view that incorporates the Carlist uprising into the general context of the period, see T. García Figueras, *La guerra de Africa de nuestros abuelos* (Madrid, 1961), pp. 138-143.

El Nasiry's home in Tangiers and Juan Hondón's home in northern Spain. But even this source of irony, which might explain the structure of *Carlos VI en la Rápita*, must be viewed in the context of Santiuste's entire trajectory. In this broader perspective, both the parallelism and its ironic consequences may be seen as part of an overall parody of Alarcón's *Diario de un testigo de la guerra de Africa*.[92]

Galdós re-introduced Diego Ansúrez towards the end of *Carlos VI en la Rápita*, and the protagonist of *La vuelta al mundo en la Numancia*, middle-aged and married, has fulfilled the maritime vocation announced in *Narváez*. The novel begins with a quick review of Ansúrez's life in the intervening years. Most singular is the manner in which he found his wife, who fell on him one night while escaping from her convent. This humorous incident initiates the strong criticism of religious orders that characterizes the last Episodios of the Fourth Series.[93]

La vuelta al mundo en la Numancia relates a series of misfortunes that befall Diego Ansúrez. The itinerary of the plot is deliberately organized to incorporate several important historical events. In Andalusia, where he buries his wife, Ansúrez finds himself immersed in the peasant revolt of Granada. On his return trip to the sea, a unique source of strength and consolation for the sailor, Ansúrez and his daughter Mara meet the Peruvian Belisario. The young people fall in love, and much is made of Ansúrez's opposition to the match.

Galdós' devastating irony has Ansúrez place his daughter in the custody of nuns, but the lovers eventually escape and elope to America. The father's desperate persecution permits the author to incorporate the war between Spain and her ex-colonies. In time, and the Numancia's long voyage offers time in abundance, Ansúrez comes to identify himself with the happiness of the young couple. This gradual evolution symbolically projects the author's optimistic resolution of the fratricidal conflict. In general, the plot is thin and the symbolism rather obvious, for the physical restrictions of a naval vessel could hardly be overcome. Galdós attempted to compensate for the novel's short-

[92] See J. Casalduero, "Galdós y la Edad Media," *Asomante*, IX (1953), 19-20; and for the exaggerated religious and patriotic views that may have provoked the parodist's attitude in Galdós, reading all this in the twentieth century, see P. A. de Alarcón, *Diario de un testigo de la guerra de Africa* (Madrid, 1931), I, 21-25; II, 100-102, 277.

[93] See, e.g., Pérez Galdós, *Obras completas*, III, 438-439, 696-697.

comings with the tangential values of a travelogue, and the Numancia's circumnavigation of the earth offers the novelist's only artistic reconstruction of an exotic world.

The final volumes of the Series focus on Santiago Ibero, a name familiar to the readers of the Third Series. The boy protagonist, willful and naive, is the son one might have expected from Gracia and Santiago Ibero. A long sickness, followed by a long convalescence, prepare the boy's extensive readings in the Spanish adventure of the sixteenth century, and the heroic past drives Santiago to action. The Cervantine process is deliberately attenuated to avoid the suggestion of outright perturbation from excessive reading, and Santiago's initial quixotism is the believable consequence of a country bumpkin's profound ignorance of contemporary Spanish history. The confusion of sixteenth-century goals with nineteenth-century activities is sheer irony on the part of Galdós, his way of stressing the unbelievable character of the present when viewed in conjunction with the past.

Santiago escapes from home in the hope of joining Prim's Mexican expedition, a replica, to his mind, of the sixteenth-century exploit. His picaresque wanderings in search of Prim bring him into contact with the sad reality of modern Spain. The prosaic pessimism of the masses, the spineless dandyism of the students, and the vegetative complacency of the upper classes are all equally repugnant to the young warrior. His first steps in Madrid, taken in the more attractive company of rebellious non-commissioned officers, result in political imprisonment, a completion course, as it were, in nineteenth-century realities.

Santiago disappears for a time, but his family's fruitless search keeps him in the reader's eye and even affixes an attractive aura of mystery to his person. When he re-appears, Santiago has identified himself completely with Prim's revolutionary efforts. Galdós' ironic parallel is broken, and the protagonist's quixotic dream is streamlined by life into the truly heroic enterprise of the nineteenth century. Santiago has been hardened and wisened by adversity — the African imprisonment and the ordeal of his escape — and his crude will has been shaped and directed under the guidance of the humane captain Lagier.

The protagonist's subsequent activities are wedded to Prim's unsuccessful pronunciamentos, and plot interest would certainly have fallen off if Teresita Villaescusa had not been re-activated in the Series' last Episodios. Her latest lover is himself an active 'primista', and her world is thus suited to the presentation of the clandestine political movement. Teresita's unilateral attraction toward the young 'primista' of incorruptible faith suffices to inject a new level of interest into Santiago's political activities.

A casual fling prepares the 'cocotte's' definitive assault upon Santiago, and the affair ends up by altering both lives. The woman, whose essential goodness has been stressed throughout, changes her life completely, and Santiago, without a personal existence to speak of, falls deeply in love. After the young warrior's participation in Prim's successful coup, the ex-revolutionary and the ex-cocotte settle into a productive and happy life beyond the pale of a Spanish environment that would reject them.

Several other life trajectories — although not novels in their own right — may be added to give a more precise idea of the Fourth Series' novelistic richness. These are not tangential growths, which might hamper the development of the novels outlined, nor elements that are essentially superfluous to the overall development of the work. Eufrasia Carrasco, whose person links the Third and Fourth Series, can serve as an example. Her role in the latter includes an important affair with Fajardo and a major political conspiracy against Narváez. Despite her prominent place in the Series, however, neither her life nor her actions are organized as a dynamic novelistic development. There is no attempt or intent to alter her initial position in the world of fiction. Other lives in this same category (Domiciana Paredes, Bartolomé Gracián, Leoncio Ansúrez, Juan Hondón, and Gonzalo Ansúrez) will more profitably be studied, along with Eufrasia Carrasco, as characterizations.

Characterization

Fajardo establishes a basic human pattern of the Fourth Series: an inherent yearning for freedom and fulfillment, tied, paradoxically, to a fundamental incapacity to meet the demands of either. Young Fajardo's ecclesiastical education dissociated him from life, from vital activities. Later, a false erudition, which Galdós employed to satirize the shallow ignorance of Madrid's upper classes, creates a tolerant condescendence about the protagonist. Finally, the crude nepotism of the epoch — a subject satirized at length in the person of Don Segundo Cuadrado[94] — allows Fajardo a government sinecure, thus prolonging his spiritual lethargy. These precedents ill prepare Fajardo for the day when he must face reality, and he is incapable of dodging a convenient marriage, a last postponement, as it were, before coming face to face with himself.

The marriage of interest is not itself tragic, for his wife, however ugly, becomes Fajardo's only escape valve, the main outlet for his stagnant energies. The tragedy of unfulfillment lies in the protagonist himself. His economic redemption only outlines a fundamental 'abulia' more clearly, and precipitates anxiety-laden conflicts with the fervent desire for fulfillment that surges within him. Galdós masterfully emphasized the tragic lack of will that characterized a whole generation, leaving a gaping hole in a personality that is otherwise endowed with excellent qualities. Fajardo's numerous attributes are wasted in frustration, as were those of the period in which he lived.

The protagonist's cumulative anxieties lead to periods of derangement, manifest in moments of depression, indicative of his profound discontent, or in hallucinatory phases, which are a form of psychic compensation. Long voyages, varied diversions, and the passage of time serve to attenuate Fajardo's spiritual lesion, but the protagonist never completely overcomes the periodic anguish which stems, despite its various names, from a profound disgust with his useless life.[95]

Fajardo's characterization is convincingly effected through his own memoirs. This is striking because the first-person narrative usually offers formidable limitations in dealing with a subject's psychopathological derangement; and even when it is done in retrospect, the protagonist-narrator could hardly be expected to offer the full process of his own mental breakdown. Galdós overcame and compensated for this psychological limitation by taking full advantage of the possibilities of suggestion inherent in the memoir as a document; a mental breakdown

---

[94] See, e.g., Pérez Galdós, *Obras completas*, II, 1393-1395.
[95] See Casalduero, *Vida y obra*, p. 188.

is vividly manifest in such unconscious phenomena as temporal confusion, narrative discontinuity, and nonsensical digression.[96]

Lucila Ansúrez is a simple creation by comparison. The tender altruism of a first love is basic to the characterization, for it transforms the mute and listless nomad encountered initially into an active and expressive woman. Lucila's character is immensely enriched, moreover, by the novelist's simultaneous probe into the fundamental egoism of love. The character, whose primitive simplicity veils nothing of what she feels, manifests an uncompromising drive to retain undisputed possession of what is imagined to be universally desirable. This essential self-centeredness forges a very feminine composite of innate simplicity and wary suspicion, with a twist of Galdosian irony making the latter altogether justified.

Lucila's major appearance is prepared for in *Narváez,* where she is set in a primitive nomadic context. This image of the beautiful semi-savage, later augmented by the mystery inherent in Fajardo's 'lucilian' obsession, is made to contrast sharply with the Lucila depicted in the first pages of *Los duendes de la camarilla.* The jarring difference, emphasized by an impressionistic medium, is amazingly effective.[97] Galdós was equally successful in placing his fundamentally candid creation opposite Domiciana Paredes, a wily connosseur of human nature. The prolonged confrontation of *Los duendes de la camarilla* brings the nature of each character into sharp relief, and in the silent struggle over Gracián each resorts to characteristic means.

Lucila's marriage of escape, unlike that of Fajardo, produces no damaging after-effects. When she again appears after *Los duendes de la camarilla,* long married and mother of several children (as devastating a stroke, to the sentimental reader, as any in Galdós' work), Lucila is presented as the strong prosaic woman, happily adjusted to her routine existence. In *Aita Tettauen,* Galdós momentarily revived the Lucila of her first young love. Her crippled son Vicentito, perhaps the only fruit of her passionate affair with Gracián,[98] is astounded at her knowledge of military insignia; and the knowing reader perceives a melancholy recollection which is immediately smothered by the

96 See, e.g., Pérez Galdós, *Obras completas,* II, 1520 ff., and III, 99.
97 Ibid., II, 1569.
98 Ibid., III, 949.

presence of an aged, invalid, and moribund Halconero.[99] Lucila never ceases to disillusion the sentimental reader, for nothing could be more prosaic than her second marriage.[100]

Before *La revolución de julio*, Virginia Socobio is the typical upper middle-class young woman of the day, sweet but grounded in the meaningless superfluities that trammel her human fulfillment. The loveless marriage to Rementería is expected and a subsequent extra-marital affair, just short of public scandal, would not have shocked the reader, for it is the path trodden by her sister Valeriana. What shatters the character's prepared image is her flight with Leoncio Ansúrez, for it abruptly suggests a personal development that has been withheld from the reader. In effect, Galdós chose an initial shock of surprise as the basis of Virginia's novel.

The evolution between the two Virginias is only gleaned retrospectively, and even then from a limited unilateral correspondence with Fajardo. This lone avenue of expression often compensates, nevertheless, for the characterizational restrictions of the plot structure. Virginia's letters evince a valor in the face of adversity which gives rise to sympathy, and a strength and clarity of purpose that is a welcome relief after Fajardo and Lucila. Most of all, however, they manage to express an almost ineffable euphoria, which is considerably heightened by the disarmingly gentle and unsophisticated quality of their expression.[101] The bliss of self-realization permeates ever syllable written by the protagonist, and even effects the crystallization of a 'vital' morality, which overshadows any other ethical consideration.

The use of the epistolary form within a first-person narrative, confidential letters that break into Fajardo's memoirs, is a penetrating psychological device. It gives incomparable expression to Virginia's inner happiness, to her healthy rapport with life and reality, factors which constitute a break with sophisticated artificiality and social facade and are, on occasion, a magnificent saving grace of Galdosian sinners. Virginia's frequent appearances after *La revolución de julio* invariably confirm, despite mounting difficulties, the happiness found in a meaningful existence beside Leoncio Ansúrez.

99 Pérez Galdós, *Obras completas*, III, 229.
100 Ibid., p. 370.
101 See Ibid., p. 39 ff.

Teresita Villaescusa is unique in the Series in that she only realizes her full literary potential after two plot sequences. Her initial 'fall' must be viewed, as we must view Virginia's, in the light of what other feminine characters do in similar circumstances. This procedure, which is prescribed by Galdós' parallel presentations (Valera, Eufrasia, Manolita Pez), attenuates hasty judgments by the reader.

Galdós, whose women are ensnared by vice in the midst of uncontrollable passions or when corrupted by materialism, offers in Teresita a rather unusual 'sinner'. Her moves are calculated and wilfully implemented. She treats her men with almost maternal concern, but does not love them; she accepts the fruits of her specialized trade, but with no inkling of insatiable materialism. Teresita's outstanding traits are readily deduced from this pattern of behaviour: reason and will. These stand out at once, but are paradoxically immersed in a genuine feminine tenderness.

The latter always qualifies the former; and these paradoxical facets offer a dynamic conflict that is the heart of the characterization, a tension that constantly requires a new equilibrium. Her wilful decision to become a 'cocotte' is prompted by a cold, rational appraisal of her world; but the character soon seeks a vital equilibrium in charity, an inner conflict that lends verisimilitude to the paradoxical flow of good works that stem from her equivocal role. On the other hand, the charitable acts themselves — although the fruits of direct, personal sympathy, and quite unlike the impersonal formula of organized charity — are conditioned throughout by a powerful rationale: taking from the rich to give to the poor.

Reason and will clearly prevail in Teresita's first crisis of equilibrium, involving Santiuste; but these are much weaker in the second phase of her development, within the world of Santiago Ibero. A new equilibrium, in which emotion prevails, is reflected in the feminine charm, the deep passion, with which Teresita attracts and holds Santiago. The final synthesis is an exceptional woman: a clear intelligence and a powerful will serving a profoundly feminine tenderness.

Santiuste is similar to Fajardo in that his youth and intelligence are paralyzed by spiritual lethargy. The protagonist of *Aita Tettauen* is even more extreme, since a form of schizoid regression, almost catatonic at times, tends to dissociate him from the real world. Less severe psychological mechanisms permit Santiuste to function, for a time, in society: fantasy-poetization, which is momentarily effective in altering the face of unbearable reality, and escape into the maternal security of feminine companionship. These mechanisms are naturally subconscious, as indicated by the fact that the only one surprised by the contrast between real war and its poetic evocation from Madrid is Santiuste, the distorter himself.

The drive for feminine companionship is the most manifest and effective mechanism, even capable of drawing Santiuste from his catatonic spells.[102] The specific nature of Santiuste's urge, its maternal connotations, is masterfully underscored by the character's subconscious desire to eliminate Vicentito Halconero, Lucila's favorite son.[103] This compulsive drive for feminine companionship determines Santiuste's peculiar novelistic trajectory. A pathological Don Juan, he invariably fails to control the women he attracts. These, strong women as might be expected, gather about him in search of new horizons, or are maternally drawn to the needy child. All soon fathom his emptiness, and Santiuste is successively abandoned by four women. He ends in a state of chronic withdrawal, inevitable from the moment that his inability to face reality is recognized.

The dazed Santiuste discovered by Teresita — in *O'Donnell* — already reveals his basic flaw, and all subsequent treatment is in the manner of a clinical study. He emerges, therefore, as one of the most thorough of Galdós' psychopathological creations. Like Maximiliano Rubín, Santiuste is extremely apt at rationalizing away an unbearable reality; and creates, like the other, a religious system that accommodates a solution to his particular frustration. The one great difference between the characters is Santiuste's lack of antecedents. Galdós omitted a careful biography of Santiuste, a sketch of the traumatic experiences that might account for his flight from reality, and this differentiates Maxi's comprehensible irrationality from that of the problematical 'hero' of *Aita Tettauen*.

The omission noted, undoubtedly deliberate, is in keeping with Galdós' two-fold intent. The less individualized the

102 Pérez Galdós, *Obras completas*, III, 190 ff., 321 ff.
103 Ibid., pp. 274, 279.

characterization, that is, the fewer personal causes explaining Santiuste's derangement, the more extensive its representational value; and Santiuste's dearth of will, his ineptness in the face of reality, were probably associated in the author's mind with the period of Spanish history reconstructed. Besides, Santiuste actually constitutes a myth inversion, and one that the following generation of writers would exploit extensively. Myth figures, even when inverted by generational changes in sensibility, are invariably weakened, as universal ens, by too personal a causality for the human qualities they personify.

All this notwithstanding, Santiuste is credibly rendered, and his peculiarities made adequate to the historical environment depicted. His obsessive poetization of reality, for example, often has, ironically enough, a distinct Castelarian ring, and his religious syncretism takes place in a world in which Judaism, Christianity, and Mohammedanism are simultaneous in time and space: the chronological ambivalence of three calendars, for example, or the alternating perspectives from the Moorish and Spanish camps, the former even paradoxically entrusted to a renegade Spaniard.[104]

Santiago Ibero offers a sharp contrast to the other important male protagonists of the Series. Fajardo and Santiuste, characters polished by book knowledge and sophisticated practitioners of the social amenities, lack will altogether; while Santiago, devoid of intellectual and social refinements, is alone capable of forging an independent existence for himself.

Two elements, religion and love, function actively in the personal development that spells Santiago's gradual humanization. Galdós' oft-noted spiritual propensities, especially in this late period of his life, are nowhere more apparent than in the characterization of Santiago Ibero. A rather sophisticated system of spiritualist beliefs takes root in a crudely simple creature; but the paradox involved is instrumental in scoring the religious facet, and Spiritualism's core of philanthropy is thus highlighted in its effect upon the character's evolution toward maturity.[105] Teresita's love, even before it crystallizes as such, has a powerful

104 Pérez Galdós, *Obras completas*, III, 282-317.
105 For Galdós' spiritualistic beliefs, see Casalduero, *Vida y obra*, p. 144, Pattison, *Galdós and the Creative Process*, p. 48, and Gullón, *Galdós, novelista moderno*, pp. 105-112; and see, e.g., Pérez Galdós, *Obras completas*, III, 580.

effect upon Santiago, breaking through his characteristic taciturnity and softening his coarse individualistic exterior. Later, in one of the author's most delicate expressions of love, Santiago the introvert, reserved in his inner strength, finds the intimate human relationship that spells fulfillment, learns of a valued existence beyond his own.

Although perfectly suited to the maritime environment of *La vuelta al mundo en la Numancia*, Diego Ansúrez evolves no further than the change of mind normally experienced by a parent opposed, at first, to his child's marriage. This trite generational conflict lacks the dramatic tension — despite the play on Ansúrez's feelings of guilt — requisite to a more vital character development. The historical parallel (Spain-colonies; father-daughter) is effective symbolism, but its very existence precludes the protagonist's development beyond the traditional pattern.

Other characters, with less extensive roles in the Series, are more interesting and even more fully developed than Diego Ansúrez: Eufrasia Carrasco, Domiciana Paredes, Bartolomé Gracián, Gonzalo Ansúrez, and Juan Hondón.

The Eufrasia Carrasco encountered in the Fourth Series has evolved considerably from the tempestuous young lady of *Bodas reales*. Long experience, never clarified in retrospect, has added the repugnant duplicity of a corrupt society to the impulsive immorality of the dazzled countrygirl. Throughout the Series, Eufrasia leads a double life, married but with no moral restraint other than a careful attention to appearances. She is, for this reason, the very heart of the corrupt upper classes depicted in the Series. And although a carefree and vehement Eufrasia — reminiscent of the passionate and willful character of *Bodas reales* — breaks forth on occasion, it is the mask of circumspect hypocrisy that invariably prevails. Vivacious and cunning in affairs of the heart, sly and deceptive in politics, there is limitless literary appeal to Galdós' only direct characterization of sham and immorality on the highest social levels.

Gonzalo Ansúrez, the Moorish Spaniard from *Aita Tettauen*, reflects the intrinsic ambivalence of the renegade, made acute in the novel by the presence of invading Spaniards (including his own brother). Although never hesitant in his allegiance to an adopted culture — favoring family and fulfillment over the abstraction of 'patria' — Gonzalo reveals his Spanish characteristics at every turn. It is clear that the personage was not intended to project a vital anguish, but is presented, mainly, for his uniquely objective position. Gonzalo Ansúrez can perceive and underline the basic weaknesses of the culture he has adopted, but without ceasing to value the qualities that had prompted his free choice in the past.

Bartolomé Gracián, a modern replica of Don Juan — and a powerful contrast, in the Series, to Santiuste's deviations from the traditional outline — is a magnificent exercise in Galdosian irony. His combination of military rebelliousness and donjuanism, a fusion of two traditional Spanish attitudes that seek an undisciplined subversion of established order, offers an ironical insight into the Spanish psyche. Gracián's uncomplicated psychological make-up permits a direct and clear expression of those two complementary attitudes, and all his behavior is patterned according to the novelist's humorous projection of 'Spanishness' in the Series.

Domiciana Paredes projects the most negative aspects of a monastic existence beyond the convent walls. Her pattern of behavior, of which deviousness and hypocrisy are the outstanding traits, is conditioned by a long religious experience that includes a direct tie to Sor Patrocinio. Set in the midst of society, in the light of day, these traits are rendered accessible to the novelist's scalpel, and serve as an effective introduction to a period of history imbued with the figure of the stigmatic nun.

In another of the author's ironical parallels, the characterization is directly associated with that of Celestina. Like the traditional figure, whose basic traits she parallels, Domiciana appeals through her diabolical enterprises. In the telling atmosphere of a profitable cosmetics industry, and while dispensing maternal counsel, Domiciana's frustrated egoism pursues its twisted ends. The character is not at all weakened by its obvious similarities to Celestina, since the novelist emphasized a realistic setting, the wax shop through which countless figures pass, and a believable pattern of motivations, a frustrated being's desperate reactions to the opportunities left in a waning existence.

Juan Hondón, or Ruiz, is a perfect example of the ecclesiastic 'cacique,' but captivates, above all, by means of the paradox inherent in his presentation. Hondón's political sagacity and willful control of men are projected from within an ironical evocation of the 'cantor del buen amor': name, ecclesiastical office, hedonistic philosophy, sensual life, and drumming repetition of Hita's litany to the Virgin.

Galdós achieved an extraordinary characterization, as well as a masterful projection of the medieval Arcipreste into the nineteenth century. Hondón is a grand patriarchal figure, magnanimous or brutally cruel, but always the superior being and the profound connossuer of human nature. As Galdós intended, there is no end of wonder, of sobering wonder, in the fact that so nineteenth-century a personage should remain perfectly believable while evoking so much that is recognizably medieval.

A number of characters, one is led to feel, might have profitably been elaborated at greater length. Leoncio Ansúrez, for example, is convincing as the dynamic man of the people who finds a life for himself with Virginia, but there is a dimension to his personality, an explosive urge to 'darle al gatillo', that often appears extreme even for a man bent on a subversion of all social values. It is unfortunate, as well, in view of their potential as characters, that Yohar and Donata are given such limited roles as 'victims' of Santiuste's particular brand of donjuanism. Both women are patterned on a behavioral contradiction: initially capable of tender and submissive devotion, but soon drawn away by inner compulsions. An inborn set of economic criteria is only temporarily obscured in Yohar by her passion for Santiuste. When she is unable to move the indecisive and lethargic protagonist to economic activity, Yohar departs as serenely as she had come. Donata's second nature is a compulsive attraction to the service of clergymen, a criterion of social status and importance that is still not uncommon among the serving classes of rural Spain. This second nature is again but temporarily displaced by love, and Donata represents, in this sense, an addition to Galdós' repertoire of Spanish creations.

Some important secondary characters are neither new to the *Episodios Nacionales* nor to Galdós' repertoire of characterizations; and can serve, for this reason, as proof of the novelist's creative power in his late years. All fit into characterizational patterns repeated countless times in Galdós' work, yet each leaves the writer's pen anew with an extraordinary degree of individuality. Centurión, for example, has the sad role of a 'cesante', and the novelist's exploration of the fears, suspicions, and angers of the political 'outs' is only surpassed in *Miau*. Even Centurión's dreams are employed to emphasize the tragi-comical corrosion of that social predicament.[106] Segismunda, Fajardo's sister-in-law, personifies the economic impulse of the lower middle-class; a feminine Torquemada, but definitely more sophisticated and scientific. She is best described, in fact, as the combination of Torquemada and Cruz Aguila that created a new aristocracy. Guillermo de Aransis, the latter a name that resounds throughout Galdós' world of fiction, aptly depicts the decadent aristocracy that they replaced. Endowed with the most attractive personal traits, Aransis' incorrigible fatuousness, his adamant refusal to alter a useless existence, inexorably lead to the grasping talons of Madrid's numerous Segismundas.

In general, the Fourth Series is unequalled in the rich variety of its secondary characterization. María Ignacia, Fajardo's wife, is a marvelous penetration by Galdós into the heart of an ugly duckling; and her development in the work reveals, not without an element of surprise, the core of good humor, of good sense, and human sympathy that lies behind a crude defensive mask of pathological timidity and awkwardness. Jerónimo Ansúrez, patriarch of the nomadic family that lends so many protagonists to the Series, also offers a surprising, although thoroughly realistic development: from a primitive, anti-social attitude to a calm and mellow old age in direct contact with nature. The character's initial rage, that of an outcast from over-sophisticated society, is slowly assuaged within the peaceful rural atmosphere of the Halconero home; and it is the becalmed patriarch who expresses, on occasion, the wisdom garnered from having been everywhere and having seen everything. Telesforo del Portillo, ironically known as 'Sebo', is the policeman whose first duty is to his own pocket. The Series traces his logical development from servant-like submission to the role of exacting usurer. Manolita Pez, Teresita's mother, and for all practical purposes her procuress, is the extreme

106 Pérez Galdós, *Obras completas*, III, 123-124.

personification of the era's materialistic degeneration; but she is believably depicted as an amoral rather than an immoral personality.

There are very good characterizations even among the secondary figures whose limited roles permit a less extensive development. The Hermosilla sisters, victims of Gracián and already prostitutes when they appear in the Series, add popular flavor to the work. Their candid brutality is indispensable to the depiction of the epoch's popular movements.[107] Buenaventura Miedes' erudite babblings, his angelic impracticality, and his tragic life — in ironic contradiction to the name he bears — generate a sympathy reminiscent of that induced by Pío Coronado. Mazaltob, an appropriate name in Hebrew, is Galdós' version of a medieval Jewish Celestina, a meaningful characterization in view of some modern theories concerning the ethnico-religious background of Rojas' famous character. Emparán, Fajardo's father-in-law, is the insufferable bore who manages to combine religious fervor and financial shrewdness: with one hand he beats his breast, as it were, and with the other he picks up all sorts of confiscated church property. Socobio, Eufrasia's cuckold husband, is similar to Emparán, but adds a ridiculous pretension to nobility. He is the 'vergarista' whose stock phrase, 'evoluciono, luego soy', summarizes the cynical attitude of a powerful segment of Isabel's Spain. Together, Emparán and Socobio personify the combination of political, socio-economic and religious interests that determined the politics of that age. Binondo, from *La vuelta al mundo en la Numancia,* is another of Galdós' many versions of a man broken by intense guilt. The anguish generated by the death of his daughter, whose love he had opposed, seeks relief in the company of Diego Ansúrez; and Binondo's longing to share that guilt, his needling attempts to implant similar feelings in Ansúrez, represents a profound insight into human nature.

The Fourth Series offers an exceptional number of child characters. The very first novel highlights the picaresque adventures of Fajardo and his young friends in Rome. Other memorable scenes are the war games of Lucila's children, the terrible frustration of her crippled boy Vicentito, young Ibero's disillusioned wanderings through the Spanish countryside, and

107 See, e.g., Pérez Galdós, *Obras completas,* III, 115-119.

the incipient sexuality of Ezequiel Paredes. Much space is dedicated, as well, to reconstructing the daily life of Prince Alphonse, believably related through his playmate Agustín Fajardo.

The great historical figures of the period are again closely linked to fictional protagonists. Fajardo's visits with Narváez and Ibero's contacts with Prim and Topete, for example, prepare lengthy and sometimes very familiar presentations.[108] The most extensively elaborated historical characterization is that of the priest Merino, a relatively minor figure, to be sure, but a psychotic personality that permitted Galdós the intuitive presentation of an abnormal development. Merino is woven into the novels of Fajardo and Lucila, revealing a greater accumulation of anti-social rancor with each successive appearance. The cumulative process reaches paranoic proportions in *La revolución de julio,* at which time Merino bursts into History.

The historical characterization of the Fourth Series offers a degree of innovation in the extent to which personages are presented before their moment of historical importance. This device is, as we have seen, widespread in the *Episodios Nacionales,* but it appears nowhere else with such wealth of detail as here. The reader is taken, for example, to the homes in exile of the young men who helped make the Revolution of 1868, men who later perpetuated themselves in Spanish politics with the Restoration. Some are envisioned in a youthful bohemia that provides a touch of human warmth to the cold silhouettes found in the pages of history.[109] They retain, in the midst of serious political tasks, a fresh quality, a youthful elan that may actually reflect the nostaglic recollections of the very personages involved.

MISCELLANEOUS

1. *Comical elements*

Unlike the Second and Third Series, the Fourth reveals no overall pattern of comedy. Satire, although no one Episodio is conceived and developed primarily as such, appears in isolated

108 See, e.g., Pérez Galdós, *Obras completas,* II, 1499 ff., 1538-1549.
109 See, e.g., ibid., III, 704-707.

incidents,[110] but there is, of course, no world-view like Romanticism to parody. The absence of a specific outline of comedy is compensated for, in part, by an unprecedented display of irony, an irony that was never before so intense or so consistently negative in the *Episodios Nacionales*.

This irony is often expressed in the work through disturbed characters, who are themselves pathetically comical: Buenaventura Miedes' identification of Spain with a band of nomadic cutthroats, however numerous their primitive qualities; or Santiuste's demented correction of nineteenth-century Spanish history.[111] The most cutting irony, however, passes directly from author to reader in such characterizations as Domiciana Paredes, Bartolomé Gracián and Juan Hondón.[112]

The Fourth Series contains, as do all others, a number of comical characters and incidents. Centurión, 'Sebo', Miedes, and many others like them, evoke moments of laughter, but a general curtailment of comedy is nevertheless felt; and it is attributable, largely, to a novelistic content that rarely overcomes the tenor of disillusionment and frustration set by the first Episodios. No previous Series accumulates so many negatively resolved plots, which explains an aura of dejection that is not even attenuated by the work's revolutionary culmination.

2. *Symbolism*

There is no noticeable reduction in name symbolism, but the character of the device appears somewhat altered. The incidence of problematical names, that is, of names offering a less direct and more difficult symbolic association, appears greater. Villaescusa, Virginia, Domiciana Paredes, Socobio, etc., are highly suggestive names, for example, but must be studied for meaning. In general, however, the degree of difficulty does not substantially change the functions of name symbolism outlined earlier.

In every other sense, the Fourth Series is perhaps the most densely symbolic of the five. Particularly evident are the parallels established between history and fiction. The period between 1848 and 1868 is a prolonged conflict between liberty

---

110 See, e.g., Pérez Galdós, *Obras completas,* II, 1405, 1450.
111 Ibid., III, 619-620, 678-679.
112 See above, pp. 158-159.

and order, and it is novelized in a series of plots that polarize phases of an individual dimension of this conflict: freedom, marriage, struggle, and security. The movements of the political pendulum are reflected in successive plot developments, as was specifically noted in the cases of Fajardo, Lucila and Virginia Socobio de Rementería.[113] The remaining plots of the Series can, for the most part, be arranged within the framework of order (marriage, security) and rebellion (adultery, promiscuity); a fundamentally ironical relationship, as we have had occasion to note, when considered from the standpoint of conventional ethics.[114]

This parallelism between history and fiction often gives expression to a more precise manner of historical illustration. Fajardo, for example, avoids the limiting security of a religious life, but only to fall into the stagnant materialism of the money aristocracy. Lucila, who represents Spain in the symbolic scheme of the Ansúrez family, lives her conflict between a fickle army (Gracián), toward which she is naturally attracted, and the drab middle-class (Halconero), to which she eventually retreats in search of security. Virginia's trajectory represents the revolutionary alliance of middle-class and masses; and Teresita Villaescusa personifies a program of economic reform.

There are also a number of direct relationships between history and fiction. The most obvious is found in *La vuelta al mundo en la Numancia,* in which the father-Spain, daughter-colonies parallel transcends the immediate historical presentation and offers a plot culmination in which filial love would have replaced fratricidal animosity. Another parallel of this kind is established between the life of Santiago Ibero and the historical role of Prim: from exotic overseas adventure to the serious focus on the problem of Spain. Somewhat less direct in its symbolic possibilities, but not unwarranted here, is the 'tira y afloja' involving Santiuste's acceptance of the money offered by Yohar's family as a balm to his wounded feelings after her departure. From an adamant position of rejecting the money in exchange for his pride and honor, Santiuste comes to accept it outright, a possible allusion to the bargaining over Tetuan itself before the treaty of Wad Ras.[115]

113 See above, p. 144.
114 See above, p. 145.
115 See Alarcón, *Diario de un testigo,* II, 222-246.

A new form of symbolism, which is essentially ironical, occurs in the endings of *Aita Tettauen, O'Donnell,* and *La de los tristes destinos.* These volume endings either emphasize an ideal belied by historical reality or stress the negative aspects of what appears to have a positive historical value. In *Aita Tettauen,* an example of the first, Santiuste conquers by love, while Spanish troops enter Tetuan in military parade. In *La de los tristes destinos,* Teresita and Santiago, the couple symbolically identified with revolutionary Spain, find it necessary to accompany Isabel II into exile. In this setting, the revolutionary cries of 'España con honra' begin to take on a negative meaning. These symbolic extensions indicate the writer's perspective from a later historical period, but make possible an adverse judgment without distorting the history reconstructed.

The Fourth Series also abounds in immediately suggestive symbolism: the change of name undergone by the wife of Diego Ansúrez — from Angustias to Esperanza — coincides with her exchange of convent for outside life and represents a subtle reversal of the normal process of name alteration; O'Donnell focused upon as he reads his wife a 'folletín', just moments before he is called to power by Isabel II; and the suicide of captain Villaescusa, which exemplifies the nature of military solutions.[116] And although commented upon as early as *Gerona,* in the First Series, animal symbolism is, in terms of quantity and quality, an innovation of the Fourth Series.[117]

3. *Geographical determination*

Entire volumes of the Fourth Series have foreign settings. The history depicted clearly encourages the practice; but it is noteworthy that Galdós had consistently refrained from extensive foreign interpolations in earlier *Episodios Nacionales.* The Second Series, for example, does not deal with the numerous Spanish groups living in exile, even when important historical events issued from beyond the frontiers of Spain. The change noted here illustrates Spain's re-entry into the world community following the death of Ferdinand VII and the defeat of Carlism; but it also reflects Galdós' preoccupation with the question of

116 Pérez Galdós, *Obras completas,* III, 150-151, 185-186.
117 See, e.g., ibid., pp. 94, 298.

Spanish reality, which had come to occupy an important place in Spanish thought after 1898.

The new direction is established by *Las tormentas del '48*, a novel partially set in Italy and a title which suggests European rather than Spanish history. But nothing produced by Galdós before this first volume of the Fourth Series prepares the reader for the phenomenon under discussion, and this in itself accentuates the novelty of a historical reconstruction in which Spain is opened to the three directions that constitute its history, its essential reality: Africa, Europe, and America.

Of special interest, of course, are the novelist's presentations of Africa and Europe, the two solutions for modern Spain that had already been the subject of heated polemics when the Fourth Series was written.[118] Galdós, like all the leading figures of his generation, stressed a European solution.[119] It is to France, in the end, that his ideal couple flees, anxious for a European way of life that Galdós deliberately contrasted to that of Spain. There would be no great novelty if this position, more or less expected of Galdós, were inflexibly maintained; but the fact is that Galdós' approach was pointedly syncretic. Although Teresita and Santiago move to France, a Series climax that is suggestive in the extreme, it is nevertheless true that the novelist had already presented the opposite phenomenon in Gonzalo Ansúrez, the Spaniard who found fulfillment in Africa.

Galdós is not averse to stressing what Spain and Africa have in common. On the contrary, the combined Episodios *Aita Tettauen* and *Carlos VI en la Rápita,* bound by the trajectory of Santiuste, assimilate the two sides of the Straits of Gibraltar: the symbolic projection of a fratricidal war (Leoncio and Gonzalo Ansúrez), the superimposition of geography, religion, calendars, spiritual attitudes, and even sexual habits.[120] This essential identification, especially effective in the parallel characterization of Juan Hondón, appears to suggest, in view of the Series' definitive European orientation, a more comprehensive outlook: Africa is already in us, let us now enrich ourselves with Europe.

[118] See, e.g., R. Ricard, *Etudes Hispano-Africaines* (Tetuan, 1956), pp. 181-198.

[119] See J. Ferrater Mora, *Unamuno* (Buenos Aires, 1957), p. 21; and A. Jiménez, *Juan Valera y la generación de 1868* (Oxford, England, 1956), pp. 13-25.

[120] See, e.g., Pérez Galdós, *Obras completas,* III, 292-293, 331, 389.

With the presentation of the New World, depicted as an expression of 'Spanishness',[121] Galdós completed the outline of Spain at the crossroads of modern times: a unique synthesis of the past, present, and future; ethnically and culturally related to Africa, historically and geographically a part of Europe, and the mother of a world clearly emerging from infancy.

.4. Subconscious content

The Fourth Series offers an even greater incidence of dreams and hallucinations than the Third Series.[122] Some interesting but minor innovations are the coincidence of dream-hallucinations in two separate individuals,[123] the extension of a hallucinatory state to an entire fictional situation,[124] and the presentation of subconscious phenomena through historical figures.[125] The only substantial difference from the Third Series lies in a marked emphasis on the more direct forms of subsconscious externalization: hallucinations and directly narrated dreams.[126]

This change in emphasis brings about a corresponding alteration in the literary functions of the Series' subconscious content. The subjective distortion of reality, which is most effectively carried out by the direct forms of subconscious externalization, takes precedence over the function of dreams and hallucinations in characterization and plot development (anticipation, wish fulfillment), functions best implemented by the indirect or retrospective presentation of dream content.[127]

This functional shift must be understood, however, within the complex of literary effects associated with any form of subconscious presentation. Dreams, whether they be directly or indirectly presented, are related, as a rule, to the plot context,

---

121 See, e.g., Pérez Galdós, *Obras completas*, III, 471-472; and for other facets, see A. Del Río, "Notas sobre el tema de América en Galdós," *Nueva Revista de Filología Hispánica*, XV (1961), 291-294.

122 See Pérez Galdós, *Obras completas*, II, 1425, 1434, 1549, 1577, 1604, 1614, 1637, 1639, 1647; III, 123-124, 151, 159-160, 176, 201, 264, 268, 274, 279, 287, 312, 323, 387, 469-470, 490, 497-498, 523, 664, 749-750, et passim.

123 Ibid., III, 264.

124 Ibid., pp. 497-498.

125 Ibid., pp. 159-160.

126 Ibid., II, 1425, 1549, 1577, 1604, 1614, 1637, 1639, 1647; III, 123-124, 151, 159-160, 268, 274, 279, 498, 523, 664, 749-750.

127 See above, pp. 134-136.

and always complement plot development to one extent or another; they issue, of necessity, from specific individuals, and always add, whether presented in retrospect or not, to the reader's understanding of the character involved.

5. *Literary tradition*

Galdós' customary use of traditional materials is again evident here, although little is made in the Fourth Series of traditional plot outlines. The one clear example, the obvious affiliation of Santiuste's trajectory to the Don Juan theme, constitutes an ironical departure from the traditional norm. Some similarities to more contemporary works — Galdós' humorous association of the Teresita-Santiago affair to the theme of Dumas fils' best known work, and the vague association possible between Fajardo's novel and Flaubert's *l'Education sentimentale* — do not warrant further study here.

The emphasis in this area lies in the re-elaboration of traditional characters. This practice, common to all the *Episodios Nacionales*, takes on an ironico-symbolical function in addition to those previously studied.[128] The 'celestinism' that accompanies Domiciana Paredes projects the devious machinations of the powerful religious groups of the period. The most anti-social figure in Western literature, Don Juan, is unerringly selected to embody the disruptive spirit behind the series of pronunciamentos that characterizes nineteenth-century Spain. The evocation of Juan Ruiz ironically underscores the medievalism that persists in Spain and the African roots of much that is Spanish.

Equally important is the overall literary effect of an unprecedented accumulation of such figures. Gracián, Domiciana Paredes, and Hondón, like the Marcela studied in the Third Series, give the impression of complete projections from the past; more, in any case, than the many other Galdosian characterizations that take a trait or two from traditional models. This does not necessarily mean, as noted earlier, that they are totally anachronistic in the world of the Fourth Series; but it does indicate that a certain amount of deliberate literary distortion is attributable to their presence in the work.

[128] See above, pp. 136-138.

6. Theatrical elements

The interpolation of theatrical devices characterizes a great deal of Galdós' novelistic production. Frequent in the *Novelas contemporáneas,* the practice has no apparent relation to the completely dialogued novels or to the plays. In the *Episodios Nacionales,* oddly enough, theatrical devices are rarely employed before the Fourth Series, at which point their copious use begins.[129]

The interpolation of a theatrical segment generally involves one or two devices: captions resembling stage-directions, which sporadically replace the descriptive narrative, and scenic dialogue, which differs in typographical presentation from normal narrative dialogue, or both. Each device has some immediate effects. The captions promote linguistic economy; and scenic dialogue invariably emphasizes, by contrast within a narrative sequence, the literary segment thus presented. Despite these obvious literary effects, the practice of introducing theatrical elements remains problematical. The limited number of captions precludes long-range economy, and the relief provided by scenic dialogue does not always coincide with the plot culmination of the particular Episodio.[130]

The intermittent appearance of the aforementioned devices may be more meaningful if the practice is considered essentially stylistic, if its effects on the tone and pace of the literary expression are noted. To begin with, it can be pointed out that the theatrical interpolations actually represent periods of rest from the cumulative oppression of any one of the standard narrative forms. But the extreme character of the variation in tone and rhythm effected by this small scale generic superimposition must also be borne in mind. By suddenly interpolating a theatrical segment into a narrative sequence, Galdós qualitatively differentiated contiguous parts of a reading unit, thus producing a calculated disarticulation of the reality depicted.

C) Summary of Chapter II

Although written within the specifications of the *Episodios*

---

129 See, e.g., Pérez Galdós, *Obras completas,* III, 472, 483-484, 560-562, 634, 757-758.
130 Ibid., pp. 483-484.

Nacionales,[131] the Third and Fourth Series incorporate the experience acquired by Galdós in the creation of the *Novelas contemporáneas*. Like the latter, the late Series possess a wide range of formal flexibility, which facilitated a greater degree of plot independence within the literary unit and insured a novelistic complexity capable of enhancing the literary possibilities of the work. Furthermore, there is a corresponding decrease in the number of limited plot developments (subplots, novelistic microcosms) and in the elemental devices (surprising blood relationships, periodic encounters and separations, etc.) which were essential to the sustained interest of Series-wide unitive plots.

A number of innovations in novelistic development and conception also tend to enhance the literary quality of the Third and Fourth Series. Areas of fiction hitherto untapped in Galdós' historical novel are emphasized and literary practices common to all the *Episodios Nacionales* are raised to unprecedented levels of artistic polish. The most obvious example of the first is the author's extensive and intensive probe into the subconscious world, which makes these Series virtually comparable, in this respect, to the *Novelas contemporáneas*. An example of the second is the greatly expanded use of traditional literary elements.

Galdós' characterization, an area of creativity enriched by every positive innovation,[132] is a reliable measure of the artistic superiority ascribed to the Third and Fourth Series.[133] A multitude of independent plots accounts for the extraordinary number of characters requiring an extensive presentation. These literary protagonists, often the heart of a complete novel, were further enriched, relative to characters of earlier Series, by a variety of additional factors. One group, for example, develops with only sporadic connections to the history reconstructed. Calpena and Fajardo, unlike the protagonists of the First and Second Series, are hardly inhibited in their development as individuals by the limiting functions of historical representation. Another group of important characters is enriched by the author's probe into psychic depths untouched in the first two Series. Fago,

---

131 See above, p. 108.
132 See S. H. Eoff, *The Modern Spanish Novel*, (New York, 1961), p. 121.
133 For opinions to this effect see Gómez de Baquero, *Novelas y novelistas*; and Casalduero, "Galdós y la Edad Media," *Asomante*, IX (1953), 17.

Nelet, Leandra, and Santiuste, for example, are pathological entities unmatched by anything offered in earlier *Episodios Nacionales*. They are wholly credible individuals, despite psychic peculiarities that Galdós expressed without undue recourse to the recondite symbolism of psychiatry.

The secondary characters of the Third and Fourth Series also reveal a wealth of new facets, all attributable to the author's emphasis on psychopathological development and traditional literary re-elaborations. Churi, Negretti, Juan Hondón, and Domiciana, to mention but a few, exemplify Galdós' success in this area. The first two, from the Third Series, offer as meaningful, detailed, and extensive a psychological development as can be found in any of the author's secondary characters. The last two, from the Fourth Series, project a definite literary impression with a paradoxical forcefulness unequalled anywhere in Galdós' work.

As a rule, historical characterizations are more functional here than elsewhere in the *Episodios Nacionales*. For one thing, they are more closely linked to literary protagonists and consequently intervene more often in plot development. This, together with the fact that a larger segment of the historical reconstruction is offered directly through them (a consequence of the freedom some literary protagonists enjoy from historical representation), accounts for the fact that the Third and Fourth Series contain Galdós' best efforts at historical characterization.[134]

The most important single innovation of the Third and Fourth Series is the experimental impressionism noted by Casalduero.[135] But the critic's significant discovery must be viewed in the overall context of the work. As Gullón has stated in commenting on Galdós' efforts to transcend the objective transcription of reality:

> Naturalmente, en su época y en su momento Galdós no quiere someter la realidad al proceso de deformación posteriormente realizado por los 'ismos'; no pretende destruir la apariencia . . . su propósito es mostrarla en sus relaciones y correspondencias con otros estratos, para que pueda entenderse la complicada red de acontecimientos y la diversidad de significaciones contenidas en ellos.[136]

134 See above, pp. 129-131, 162.
135 See *Vida y obra*, pp. 173 ff.
136 *Galdós, novelista moderno*, p. 227.

Galdós implemented his search for new perspectives on reality by massing subconscious matter to project an impression of ambivalence. Other practices that blur the precise outline of an objective reality are the cumulative interpolations of traditional themes and characters, which invariably leave a residual anachronism, and the intermittent insertions of theatrical vignettes, which periodically contort the narrative. Finally, both novelistic development and characterization complement this with cumulative doses of paradox.[137]

Style

It is not surprising to find, given the novelist's experimental intentions, that the Third and Fourth Series entail an important stylistic change. Subconscious externalization required a highly suggestive literary medium, a language capable of richer imagery and less precision than Galdós' usual narrative prose.[138] This was true, as well, of the work's repeated projections of traditional literary elements.[139] It is obvious, in view of all that has been said, that a number of stylistic judgments — Boussagol's with respect to *Zumalacárregui*, for example—must be re-evaluated.[140]

Galdós' experimental impressionism altered the objective quality of reality in order to stress essential aspects of the real. This goal, to the limited extent pursued by the author, necessarily excited a new interest in experimenting with the expressive capacities of language, transformed from a reflector of reality into an instrument for capturing its essence. Consequently, the Third and Fourth Series often present a type of literary expression which is relatively rare in the rest of Galdós' work:

A las diez, la embocadura de la calle de Rodas por la de Embajadores era tenebrosa, siniestro el espacio que la oscuridad permitía ver entre las dos filas de casas negras, gibosas, mal encaradas. El farol de la esquina dormía en descuidada lobreguez; el inmediato pestañeaba con resplandor agó-

137 See above, pp. 112, 115-116, 122-123, 125-126, 144, 154, 59.
and see, e.g., Charles Bally, Elise Richter, Amado Alonso, Raimundo Lida, *El impresionismo en el lenguaje*, 2ed. (Buenos Aires, 1942), p. 142.
138 See, e.g., Pérez Galdós, *Obras completas*, II, 372, 820, 868; III, 201, 279, 312, 387.
139 See, e.g., ibid., II, 1583, 1599-1600; III, 397, 401-402.
140 For opposed views on a single work (*Zumalacárregui*), see G. Boussagol, "Sources et composition du *Zumalacárregui*," *Bulletin Hispanique*, XXVI (1924), 241-264; Sainz de Robles, "B. Pérez Galdós: su vida, su obra y su época," p. 156.

nico; sólo brillaba, despierto y acechante, como bandido plantado en la encrucijada, el que al promedio de la calle alumbraba el paso a una mísera vía descendente: la Peña de Francia. Animas del purgatorio andarían de fijo por allí; las vivientes y visibles eran: un ciego, que entró en la calle apaleando el suelo; el sereno, cuya presencia en la bajada del Rastro se advirtió por la temblorosa linterna, que hacía eses de una a otra puerta, hasta eclipsarse en el despacho de vinos; una mendiga seguida de un perro, al cual se agregó otro can, y siguieron los tres calle abajo . . . En el momento de mayor soledad, una mujer dobló con decidido paso la esquina de Embajadores y puso cara y pecho a la siniestra calle, metiéndose por la oscuridad, afrontando animosa las molestias y peligros del suelo, que no eran pocos, pues donde no había charcos había resbaladizas piedras, y aquí y allá objetos abandonados, como cestos rotos o montones de virutas, dispersos bultos que figuraban en la oscuridad perros dormidos o gatos en acecho.[141]

Galdós' literary style is not altered completely in these late Series; in fact, the new stylistic pattern fails to predominate anywhere. The precise clarity associated with the prose of earlier *Episodios Nacionales* continues to be the distinguishing quality of the style since historical reality — still the main subject matter of the literary work — requires the same essentially objective approach of the author. Galdós did not alter his basic criteria of historical presentation — in the impressionistic manner of Valle-Inclán, for example — and he could hardly be expected to transcend those criteria stylistically.[142] Once the primary demands of historical reconstruction were satisfied, however, the novelist exercised a degree of stylistic innovation in the Third and Fourth Series that is not found elsewhere in his work.

The Series produced after a lapse of nineteen years reveal a more paced rhythm of development and narration. The stylistic experimentation noted above accounts for this, to a certain extent, as do the unprecedented number of retrospective characterizations, the denser imagery of these Series,[143] and the extensive use of the epistolary form. In effect, the change is visible in the length of the individual Episodios of these

141 Pérez Galdós, *Obras completas*, II, 1569; and for further examples, see Casalduero, *Vida y obra*, pp. 173-176.
142 See, e.g., Pons, *Hommage a Ernest Martinenche*, pp. 381-389.
143 See, e.g., Pérez Galdós, *Obras completas*, II, 324, 330, 335, 1353; III, 95, 96, 122, 202, 277, 534.

Series, which average from fifteen to twenty pages more than the volumes of the first two.

The greater stylistic richness of the Third and Fourth Series is due to a fuller exercise of the author's extraordinary aptitude for the epistolary form. An extended use of letters is not a novelty to the *Episodios Nacionales* since lengthy correspondence is found as early as the First Series.[144] But the difference noted here is both quantitative and qualitative: more letters and in a greater number of apt artistic functions.[145] Letters provide some of Galdós' most successful depictions of psychological nuances. Pilar's reflect an irony born of despair, Virginia's express almost ineffable human feelings, Calpena's letters capture the tone of a weakened and discouraged romantic, and those of Librada, Fajardo's mother, express the comical self-deceit with which mothers see their sons.[146]

In these late *Episodios Nacionales* Galdós remained a master at accommodating language to character. As a device of realistic characterization, a function that dialogue always serves in Galdós, the Third and Fourth Series offer the most varied linguistic inflections of nineteenth-century Spain.[147] Moreover, the novelist even improved his mastery of the dramatic possibilities of dialogue, which is effectively employed for such different purposes as setting a specific emotional tone (the baby language of Lucila and Bartolomé Gracián), stressing insensitivity (the semi-articulate babbling of Churi), and even creating a mood of anguished inarticulateness.[148]

---

[144] Pérez Galdós, *Obras completas*, I, 1051-1056.

[145] See above, pp. 110, 119-120, 133; and for different opinions concerning Galdós' use of the epistolary form, see Alas, *Galdós*, pp. 356-357, Darío, *España contemporánea*, pp. 235-236, and Gullón, *Galdós, novelista moderno*, pp. 254-256.

[146] Pérez Galdós, *Obras completas*, II, 1454-1455.

[147] Ibid., pp. 336-337, 371-372, 421, 435, 478, 777, 1275; III, 534-535.

[148] Ibid., pp. 710, 1571, 323.

CHAPTER III

FIFTH SERIES

The Fourth Series reconstructs a segment of history (1862-1868) subsequent to Galdós' arrival in the Peninsula, but the chronological scope of the entire literary unit (1848-1868) can hardly be identified with Galdós' personal experience of Spanish history. The Fifth Series, however, actually fictionalizes an era (1868-1880) that forms part of the novelist's own life. In the years preceding the Revolution of 1868, Galdós forsook the free and marginal existence of student and novice playwright,[1] and all the history that stems from that memorable date is an intrinsic part of the mature writer's active participation in Spanish life.

All the *Episodios Nacionales* are equally historical as far as the modern reader is concerned; but the author's relation to the subject matter of each Series, a crucial factor in literary elaboration, must interest the critic. The Fifth Series, clearly dealing with a phase of the writer's own life, evidences an autobiographical projection, for example, that might have conditioned the creative process.[2] In fact, Galdós' personal involvement in the history depicted would suffice, in some quarters, to bar the last *Episodios Nacionales* from the category of historical fiction: "Llamamos 'novelas históricas' las que cuentan una acción ocurrida en una época anterior a la del novelista."[3]

The six Episodios of the Fifth Series were written in the four years between 1908 and 1912, a length of time which suggests a diminishing of Galdós' normal rate of composition. The novelist, almost blind at this point, produced them under the burden of intense political activity and mounting economic difficulties.[4]

---

1 Berkowitz, *Pérez Galdós*, pp. 66-68.
2 Pattison, *Galdós and the Creative Process*, p. 8.
3 Anderson Imbert, *Estudios*, p. 26; but for a rejection of such limitations, see Sheppard, *The Art and Practice of Historical Fiction*, p. 17.
4 Berkowitz, *Pérez Galdós*, pp. 346 ff.

Galdós had identified himself more actively than ever with the aspirations of modern Spain; but too late to be effective in politics or to hold aloft the succeeding generation's banner of rebellion.[5] There is unconcealed bitterness, furthermore, in Galdós treatment of an epoch (1869-1880) — a period of obvious decline when viewed from the vantage-point of 1908 — with which he may well have identified his own life.

A) *Fifth Series*

The Fifth Series reconstructs the succession of crises that resulted in the failure of the Revolution of 1868, an extraordinary expenditure of energy that led back to the point from which it had started. This futility marks every page of Galdós' last historical novels; but it is intensified by the author's perspective from the twentieth century, which revealed the catastrophic proportions of a generation's failure to solve its basic problems and cast overtones of caricature on the various regimes between 1868 and 1881.

Literary form

Ten volumes is too well-established a literary unit for the Fifth Series, with its six volumes, to be considered complete. The novelistic structure of the unfinished Series is such, however, that no unesthetic amputation is noticeable; and only the foreknowledge of the proposed historical scope of the unit, which was to have reached the first years of the twentieth century, suggests its incompleteness.[6]

Like all preceding Series, the Fifth offers a chronological sequence of historical events. In almost every other respect the last set of *Episodios Nacionales* differs substantially from the rest. Its six volumes constitute an unbalanced dichotomy, in which the first two volumes, which are relatively independent novels, recall the dissociated novelistic structure of the preceding Fourth Series; and the last four volumes, narrated in the first-person by a single protagonist, offer a degree of formal unity not employed so extensively since the First Series.

5 Berkowitz, *Pérez Galdós*, pp. 381-382; and see M. de Unamuno, "Galdós en 1901," *De esto y aquello*, I (Buenos Aires, 1950); and Casalduero, *Vida y obra*, p. 187.

6 See M. Enguídanos, "Mariclío, musa galdosiana," *Papeles de Son Armadans*, XXI (June, 1961), 245.

This reversion to the formal unity of the very first *Episodios Nacionales* is even compounded in the last four by a distinct lack of subplots, which, it will be remembered, were a dissociative factor in the First Series. This dearth of independent elements is even more surprising in that the four Episodios in question do not reconstruct an era as inherently unitary as the War of Independence. A plausible explanation may lie in the accelerated historical presentation of the four Episodios, which encompass more historical time (1871-1881) than is usually reconstructed in four volumes of the work. Galdós' biography would certainly support the hypothesis of a writer struggling against time and exhaustion in a bid to present as full a historical background to 1898 as he had to 1868; a task that required a minimum of novelistic elaboration while incorporating a maximum of history, that is, the direct narration of a single protagonist who is unencumbered by simultaneous subplots.

This sharp drop in novelistic elaboration,[7] under the urgency noted above, goes a long way towards explaining still other radical innovations of the last four volumes: autobiographical projection and fantasy content. A protagonist like Tito Liviano, who is delineated within an autobiographical framework, reduced the need for fictional elaboration, for which Galdós compensated by interpolating a fantasy dimension that provided magical connections between persons, places, and things.

Plot development

The post-revolutionary world depicted here is consciously disfigured by the greater accumulation of successively larger portions of caricature and burlesque.[8] An overinsistence on mediocrity, disenchantment, and vulgar dissipation marks the novelist's increasing disgust as he moved away from 1868. What optimism Galdós retained after 1898[9] had dwindled considerably by 1908, and was probably dissipated by the crisis of 1909 and its aftermath. These basic chronological relationships are particularly useful in dealing with the last four volumes of the Fifth

7 See Gómez de Baquero, *Novelas y novelistas*, pp. 34, 51, 57.
8 For a comparison to both Quevedo and Valle-Inclán, see Enguídanos, "Mariclío, musa galdosiana," *Papeles de Son Armadans*, XXI (June, 1961), 235.
9 See Pérez Galdós, *Memoranda*, pp. 237-245.

Series and in explaining the abrupt termination of the *Episodios Nacionales* in 1912.

The first of the Series' three plots, complete in *España sin rey*, is of unusual complexity for a work with a minimum of novelistic development. It is centered on Fernanda Ibero's tragic love for Don Juan de Urríes and enriched with the lives of Nicéfora, the necessary third party to the triangle, and Wilfredo de Romarate, the supposedly objective but really quite subjective observer. All three dimensions are skillfully arranged to create an aura of disenchantment and precipitate a climactic distortion of reality.

Novelistic economy, essential as we have seen to the conception of the Fifth Series, justifies a plot centered on Santiago Ibero's daughter and a setting that is familiar. Fernanda's love, offered by Galdós in full lyrical bloom, is disenchantingly wasted on the novelist's cheapest version of Don Juan. Urríes follows the established pattern of promiscuity, but gains his fleeting sexual triumphs by means of political influence and money instead of charm and valor.

Don Juan's philanderings are given special relief in his affair with Nicéfora, whose twisted complexity contrasts with Fernanda's rural simplicity. Nicéfora is a paradoxical combination of mysticism and voluptuousness, although she is conveniently over-simplified, at first, as seen through the eyes of Romarate. This naive country gentleman, whose sad experiences round out the plot, feels himself capable of furthering the Carlist cause in the babylonic Madrid of 1869. His staid traditionalism is laughable and anachronistic in that environment. Romarate must eventually do violence to his provincial candor, to the proud ethic that is the mainspring of his being; and an anguished effort to restore a semblance of accord between his real existence and his idealized self-image results in a siege of madness.

Galdós directed these interrelated lives to a theatrical climax, replete with Calderonian echoes. The catalyst is provided by Romarate's perturbed condition, which permits an allegorico-ethical perspective to become an intrinsic part of the world of fiction. Platonically attracted to Fernanda, Romarate envisions her as the Good, and proposes, in quixotic fashion,[10] to aid her against Nicéfora, the personification of evil in his view. The

---

[10] Pérez Galdós, *Obras completas*, III, 851 ff.

stage is set, literally, when Urríes decides to elope with Nicéfora from the convent to which she has been led in a moment of mystic frenzy. Romarate, the self-appointed champion of religion, morals, and Fernanda, prepares an ambush and then leaves his sword behind. Fernanda is morbidly attracted to the scene of her misfortune, confronts Nicéfora and, quite beside herself, uses the sword to kill the 'Enemy'.

The trappings are unmistakably theatrical, even Calderonian: the allegorization and polarization of ethical values, the fateful succession of coincidences that precipitate the final action, and the dramatic technique of the ending.[11] For a moment Fernanda actually incarnates the abstraction she represents in Romarate's mind, executing justice upon sacrilegious Evil.

The second plot of the Series, complete in *España trágica*, is centered on the Vicentito Halconero encountered in previous Series. An understandably depressed Fernanda also re-appears, and the economy of plot elements is complete. Slowly, as Fernanda and Vicentito begin to reciprocate in affection, the Series is brought to a new pitch of lyricism. Everything is made to suggest a happy ending, and the reader anticipates a positive resolution to the disenchantment of *España sin rey* in the propitious development of *España trágica*. Fernanda's sudden death brings new depths of disillusionment to the work.

This disappointment is but the first indication of Vicentito's paradoxical fate: an intelligent, good, and brave young man who always fails. An emphatic discrepancy between the protagonist's ideal possibilities and his real mediocrity is a permanent source of disenchantment. Vicentito fails to alter Fernanda's tragic destiny, nor could he have reasonably been expected to overcome tuberculosis. But the inescapable fact remains that carefully instilled hopes are defrauded, and the protagonist appears, reasonably or not, in the role of a plaything of whimsical chance with no control over his destiny. The long courtship of Pilar Calpena — whose name indicates a new economy of novelistic elements — is insipid, unenthusiastic, and only ends in marriage because it could lead nowhere else.

Despite quasi-heroic efforts, Vicentito never overcomes his burden of mediocrity. This is most strikingly emphasized when he is moved by a courageous concept of personal honor to

11 Pérez Galdós, *Obras completas*, III, 868-869.

challenge José Paul y Angulo, the wildest agitator of the Prim era. Vicentito is wounded, but not, ironically enough, in the fulfillment of his mission. On the contrary, he is the ridiculous victim of a political streetfight. Galdós compounded this juxtaposition of the sublime and the ridiculous by having the protagonist's ludicrous accident — wounded over a cause whose leader he detests — coincide with Prim's fatal wound.

The last plot of the Series consists of Liviano's personal account of his movement through the Spain left by Prim. Other episodic plots in the *Episodios Nacionales,* those centered on Araceli, Monsalud, and Fajardo, for example, differ substantially from Liviano's personal escapades. Although accommodatingly rootless, the protagonists mentioned were moved by specific goals which brought even the least related adventures into essential unity. Tito Liviano has no specific trajectory, no set of personal goals. There is no passion, no ideal to provide cohesion and meaning to his fragmentary existence.

Liviano's random movement across four volumes only produces a long if unimpressive list of feminine 'conquests', for he is Galdós' least discriminating donjuanesque creation. His energies, and the reader's time, are invariably expended on servant girls and women of easy reputation. The fact is that the process of rendering a woman accessible is of little import, since Liviano has no aversion to employing a procuress. The interest created by the adventures of a genuine Don Juan is missing, as is the pathos associated with even the most routine love relationship, so that the prominent sensual vein of Liviano's novel merely creates a mood of cheap debauchery. Accumulated sexual experiences project an empty, indiscriminate sensualism, which Galdós uses to debase an era of history.

Nevertheless, Tito Liviano's life is more complex than has been suggested in the preceding sketch of his 'infra-real' existence. Galdós' irony has the ultrasensual being paradoxically introduce the 'super-real' dimension of the work. Liviano is the exclusive channel for a world of mythological fantasy that is never quite assimilated into the basic realism of the *Episodios Nacionales.*[12] This extraneous matter, which Galdós originally

---

[12] C. Clavería, "La veta fantástica en la obra de Galdós," *Atlante,* I (1953), 137.

felt compelled to justify in realistic terms, as dream content,[13] soon becomes an independent element of the work. The device of Liviano's fantastic pension, received for services rendered to Clio (Mariclío), is absolutely essential to the protagonist's movement in the Series, whether it be on the 'infra-real' level of his appetites or on the 'super-real' level proper to the muse of History.[14]

The fantasy dimension, unassimilated as it may remain in the general context of Galdós' historical novel, provides Liviano with an itinerary if not a personal trajectory. As Mariclío's official witness, his presence in the work acquires a meaning that his personal existence altogether lacks.[15] The result, however, is an open bifurcation of novelistic activities: one direction represented by the dissipated woman chaser; the other by the official historical observer. The two activities, even when simultaneous, coincide but superficially, thus weakening the novelistic fibre of the last Episodios.

Clearly, the existent volumes of the Fifth Series do not measure up to those of the previous four as novels. Neither Halconero's disenchanting biography nor Liviano's aimless movements command a high level of interest, which does not necessarily detract from their successful projection of mood. The last four volumes are hampered as novels, moreover, by the two innovations that made possible an accelerated historical presentation and which were indispensable complements, besides, to Galdós' deliberate creation of a burlesque atmosphere: autobiographical interpolation and fantasy content (Mariclío, etc.). Both represent radical departures from the literary norms of the *Episodios Nacionales*.

Characterization

The Fifth Series has few protagonists, few extensively developed characterizations of any kind. This may be traced, in part, to the fact that the Series is incomplete; but it is even more directly related to the work's obvious reduction in novelistic density.

---

13 See, e.g., Pérez Galdós, *Obras completas*, III, 1149-1151.
14 See, e.g., ibid., pp. 1281, 1362.
15 See Gómez de Baquero, *Novelas y novelistas*, p. 51.

España sin rey, the most elaborate plot in the Series, contains the greatest number of thorough characterizations. Fernanda Ibero resembles the women of her family (Demetria, Gracia). She is, on the one hand, exactly what that ready-made association presupposes: sensible and innocent. Her occasional deviations from this pattern of behaviour — a phase of morbid curiosity and a latent violence that explodes into climactic action — are understandable, on the other hand, in the daughter of Santiago Ibero (Third Series) and the sister of Santiago Ibero (Fourth Series). The two facets of Fernanda, superimposed rather than successive stages in her development, retain a basic logic despite an element of paradox. They represent a human synthesis conveniently prepared by Galdós in earlier Series.

Nicéfora is a more patent and less explainable paradox. So contradictory is her behaviour, in fact, that Galdós avoided thrusting her upon the reader, and Romarate's simple judgments, prejudiced and confused as they may be, facilitate a gradual assimilation of the character's complexity. As Nicéfora gains prominence in the work, the reader replaces Romarate's judgment of deliberate hypocrisy with direct perceptions of what appears to be an authentic personality split: a pendular movement between mysticism and sensuality that is strengthened by a Jewish-Carlist genealogy and compounded by name confusions reminiscent of Cervantes.[16]

The juxtaposition of ascetic fervor and sexuality, at times almost simultaneous in Nicéfora, creates an impression of diabolism that remains an essential part of the characterization.[17] This falls perfectly into line, of course, with the allegorico-ethical development of *España sin rey*. Nicéfora is morally repulsive, which is her intended literary effect, but as a character she is all the more exciting for it.

Wilfredo de Romarate is more realistically developed as a personality. His ridiculous accumulation of outmoded political and social values is tied to a specific formative background, so that the naive human being issues logically from a stale provincial aristocracy.[18] The 'bailio' is a knight of sorts in the

---

16 Pérez Galdós, *Obras completas*, III, 773-774, 840.
17 See, e.g., ibid., p. 858.
18 Ibid., pp. 763-765.

nineteenth century, a fact that underscores his fundamental anachronism and links him directly to the renowned literary figure he resembles.

Romarate undergoes crisis after crisis in the chaotic environment of Madrid, but his brittle pride — a defensive reaction to inner weakness — injects comical overtones into personal conflicts that are tragic. His first encounter with loose women, for example, leads to an unbridled passion for 'La Africana,' a ludicrous development for such a stale figure. Unlike Cervantes' hero, Romarate fails to transform the antithesis of his knightly ideals, and 'La Africana's' disdain for hallowed tradition preys incessantly on the protagonist's mind. Another disruptive factor is political in nature. Firm in his outmoded political convictions, Romarate attends almost every session of the 'Cortes' of 1869. He listens, day after day, to the grandiloquent speeches of Castelar, until an irresistible attraction begins to sap the foundations of his idealized world-view.[19]

In short, Romarate succumbs ignominiously. Contradictions destroy his self-image and generate an unbearable tension. He is too old and too simple to change, and the accumulated tension is consequently dissipated in lunacy. Romarate only recovers his senses by evolving a new quixotic self-image, which is both understandable in its psychological implications and indispensable to the theatrical denouement of *España sin rey*.

Don Juan de Urríes, the cheapened Don Juan, is a weak unidimensional characterization, but his membership in the 'Cortes' of 1869, which incidentally facilitates the introduction of important historical figures, may entail a representational function. The boss-controlled puppet, an immoral and insignificant human being, immediately appears unworthy of that assembly's lofty mission, yet one cannot help identifying him to some extent with the political efforts sparked by the Revolution of 1868.

Vicentito Halconero, sole protagonist of *España trágica*, is catalogued by the age in which he lived:

De cuanto pudiera decirse acerca de Vicentito Halconero, lo más fundamental es que provenía espiritualmente de la Revolución del 68. Esta y las ideas precursoras le engendraron a él y a otros muchos, y como los frutos y las criaturas

19 See, e.g., Pérez Galdós, *Obras completas*, III, 796.

de aquella revolución fueron algo abortivos, también Vicente llevaba en sí los caracteres de un nacido a media vida.[20]

The protagonist who is destined to fall disappointingly short of his own potential presents special characterizational problems. Galdós had to strike an artistic balance between the credibility of Halconero's personal traits, which set a high potential, and the credibility of a series of actions that subvert his potential and produce a disenchanting mediocrity.

The novelist chose unerringly for the desired effect from his stock of characters. Halconero is the enthusiastic but hopelessly crippled boy from the Fourth Series, a frustrating contradiction that the biographical plot of *España trágica* carried over into the spiritual realm.[21] An overpowering maternal bond, which must also be appreciated through data supplied in the Fourth Series,[22] restrains the young protagonist's idealism, leading him to an exasperating lack of personal direction, to a solid if passionless marriage, and to political compromise.

Pattison has noted the similarity between the readings ascribed to Halconero and those of the young Galdós.[23] Other autobiographical insertions are the visits to Duran's bookstore and to the parliamentary sessions, but these actvities were normal in a youth of that period and merely suggest a casual association between author and character. The powerful maternal influence and the nature of Halconero's political compromise (Sagasta) are more suggestive,[24] but the character, known to the reader from earliest childhood, is far too well established a personality to suffer from such coincidences.

Neither Pilar Calpena, giddy and superfluous, nor Bravo, Halconero's spineless friend, evoke any interest as human beings. The few personalities that stand out in *España trágica* belong, in fact, to another literary generation: Lucila Ansúrez, the protagonist's overprotective mother, and Santiago Ibero, Fernanda's distraught father.[25]

20 Pérez Galdós, *Obras completas*, III, 872.
21 See ibid., pp. 223-225.
22 Ibid.
23 *Galdós and the Creative Process*, p. 9.
24 See D. F. Brown, "More Light on the Mother of Galdós," *Hispania*, XXXIX (1956), 403-407.
25 See Pérez Galdós, *Obras completas*, II, 874-875, 877.

The last four Episodios are exclusively dedicated to the extravagant existence of Tito Liviano, who introduces himself as follows:

> Yo, con paciencia y saliva, quiero decir tinta, he reconstruí-do mi árbol, y en él tengo señoras linajudas, títulos de Castilla, que casi se dan la mano con logreros y mercachifles de baja estofa; tengo un obispo católico, un cura protestante, una madre abadesa, dos gitanos, una moza del partido, un caballero del hábito de Santiago y varios que lo fueron de industria . . . Soy, pues, un queso de múltiples y variadas leches. Debo declarar que de la heterogeneidad de mis fundamentos genealógicos he salido yo tan complejo, que a menudo me siento diferente de mí mismo.[26]

The picaresque format (lineage) stresses a proteic quality, a combination that recalls the *Golden Ass* or the anonymous continuation of *Lazarillo de Tormes*.

In effect, Liviano is sufficiently malleable to function amid metamorphoses and mythological connections while living an 'infra-real,' burlesque caricature of his age. He is at home, on the one hand, with magic pens, telepathy, and all the fantastic paraphernalia of a visionary historian; and embodies, on the other, a unique brand of donjuanesque roguery.

Except for a few episodes in the traditional vein, which highlight the protagonist's 'picardía,'[27] Liviano's 'infra-real' existence revolves about women. Galdós employed an endless round of cheap donjuanesque adventures (instead of the traditional succession of masters) as the rotating mechanism for a multiple perspective on society, an innovation that doubles as a device of artistic disfiguration. Liviano's specific point of view varies somewhat with each successive sexual adventure, thus providing a wide vista of society and a total vision that is qualitatively predetermined by the sordidness which all the particular perceptions have in common.

The characterization is totally devoid of realism. There is nothing in Liviano's background, nor in his immediate environment, to justify or explain his peculiar aberrations: the 'infra-real' sexual obsession and the 'super-real' communication with mythological elements. The novelist's conception of the character is perfectly clear, however, for true to his burlesque intentions,

---

26 Pérez Galdós, *Obras completas*, III, 983-984.
27 See, e.g., ibid., pp. 1038-1044.

Galdós invented an appropriate chronicler: from Titus Livy to the caricaturesque Tito Liviano, alias Proteo Liviano, alias Prometeo Liviano. The character's physical being and his pattern of behavior appear to grow out of the author's caricatural distortion of name. 'Liviano' suggests promiscuous behavior, which has no basis in the protagonist's psychological make-up, and abnormal smallness, for which no hereditary explanation is given. 'Tito,' on the other hand, sets the flippant tone of the character's memoirs. The tiny woman-chaser and visionary historian is a fictitious being through and through, and he is superbly adequate, for this reason, to the function of bridging incongruous worlds.

These last four Episodios offer characterizations that are unique in Galdós' historical novel: beings who move, in the narrator's view, between a real world and a world of fantasy. Floriana is an example of one type. The facts concerning her real life are imprecise, whereas her existence within the fantasy dimension is strengthened by direct ties to Mariclío and by a specific role (Education) in the work's allegorical scheme. Graziella is somewhat different. A promiscuous woman in the real world and a playful nymph in the other, she is strongly anchored in the former while performing no special allegorical function in the latter. Graziella is a picaresque contact between Mariclío and Liviano, injecting a timely Italian note into the last Episodios.

Mariclío is the most prominent allegorical characterization, moving freely on the various levels of the work. The personification of History is too well established to be weakened, as such, by appearing among real people and in real places. Her personality is too fixed, on the other hand, to allow characterizational changes; but there remains her physical appearance, which is constantly adapted to variations in the tenor of history.[28]

It is clear from the first that Mariclío is not a mere allegorization of History, a pseudonym for Clio. Two new factors attend Galdós' re-elaboration of the classical muse: vulgarization and hispanization. The first is clearly indicated by the use of 'tía,' and heavily underscored in the various descriptions of

[28] See, e.g., Pérez Galdós, *Obras completas*, III, 1008, 1025.

Mariclío. The popularization of the figure may have been intended to reflect on the nature of the history reconstructed, or to present an ultimate, personified expression of the novelist's popular view of the past.[29] In addition, Galdós limited the allegorical range of the character by hispanicizing her name: Mariclío, Doña Mariana. She is the muse of a Spanish history, or as suggested by her attitude, a Spanish muse of History.[30]

Most of the Fifth Series' secondary characters have a complementary function in the work's overall burlesque intent. Celestina Tirado, for example, possesses just enough of her namesake to suggest an unfavorable comparison: not the malevolent grandeur of a true Celestina, nor even of a Domiciana Paredes, but the 'ramplonería' of a vulgar procuress. Tapia, from *España sin rey*, has enough of the rogue to induce the cynical perversion of Romarate and sufficient knowledge of human nature to lead the innocent gentleman to a point of no return; but he is never more than a pint-sized Satan, malicious but without grandeur. Segismundo Fajardo — another of the author's characterizational expedients — offers a unique inversion of the prodigal son theme. He is first encountered in open rebellion against the stark materialism of his home. In this revolt against Segismunda, his mother and the Torquemada of the *Episodios Nacionales*, the insignificant student from the Fourth Series achieves a degree of prominence. With his ultimate return to the home, Galdós inverted the spirit of the parable. In succumbing to the temptations of materialistic mediocrity, Segismundo personifies the weakness of an entire generation.

As a rule, the women left in the wake of Liviano's amorous exploits are scarcely more than names. Only the following attain anything like a clear delineation of personality. Obdulia recalls the character of the same name in *Misericordia*, and a pseudo-romantic mellifluousness common to both suggests an inadvertent duplication by Galdós. María de la Cabeza Ventosa sports masculine traits that account for her success in the world of business. She rules Liviano with an iron hand, but her inflexible 'pundonor,' masculine in its demands, inevitably leads to a break with the lecherous protagonist. Chilivistra brings

29 See Enguídanos, "Mariclío, musa galdosiana," *Papeles de Son Armadans*, XXI (June, 1961), 238-239.
30 See, e.g., Pérez Galdós, *Obras completas*, III, 1362-1363.

Nicéfora to mind, but a Nicéfora devoid of demoniacal qualities. Both oscillate between religiosity and voluptuousness, but Chilivistra's hypocritical nature is unmistakable and detracts from her paradoxical forcefulness. Penélope is the novelist's humorous version of the politically active woman: vain, stupid, and immoral. Casiana is Liviano's most permanent feminine companion, and she is accordingly denied a true self. Her complacency is such that she neither questions nor doubts the protagonist's dual existence.

The Fifth Series is also exceptional for its extended use of characters from the *Novelas contemporáneas,* added proof of Galdós' deliberate economy of novelistic factors. It is not surprising, in this sense, to find that he selected only typed characters, figures requiring virtually no further development. Basilio Andrés de la Caña remains an exaggerated and comical personification of the 'arbitrista.' Estupiñá and Ido del Sagrario also remain faithful to models drawn years before.

Ido's is the most functional role. Galdós omitted the peculiar madness and the squalor that are his comical levers in other major appearances,[31] but the same simple and timid creature plays out another of his many pathetic roles. Ido must consent, however unwillingly, to his daughter's liaison with a priest. The use of Ido del Sagrario to underscore the moral nadir of an epoch is well calculated, for an action that might stamp any other character as singularly evil, and thus lose some of its representational value, is conceivable in a being long identified with the terrible anguish of living.

Many historical figures delineated in the Fifth Series have a special value in being drawn from first-hand knowledge. Personages like Cánovas del Castillo and Sagasta appear almost as extensively as their counterparts from earlier Series, but with one substantial difference. The novelistic thinness of the Fifth Series often precludes their integration in a plot sequence, which makes it impossible for Galdós to proceed in his accustomed manner, offering intuited familiar aspects through plot connections. He is obliged, in fact, to improvise fantastic devices to this end: Liviano's impish transformation in order to relate the private life of Amadeo I, a magic pen in the case of Elena

---

[31] See W. H. Shoemaker, "Galdós' Literary Creativity: D. José Ido del Sagrario," *Hispanic Review,* XIX (1951), 204-237.

Sanz, and telepathy in that of Cánovas del Castillo. These are effective enough for conveying information, but their use does irreparable damage to the historicity of the personages involved. Three historical figures stand out in the work, being largely unaffected by its vein of fantasy: Nieves de Borbón, José Paul y Angulo, and Nicolás Estébanez. The first two are violent extremists, a characteristic brought almost to the point of outright caricature in Galdós' rendition. Paul y Angulo retains but one saving contact with conventional humanity, his gentleman's code of honor; but Nieves de Borbón is altogether de-humanized in her behaviour. The Carlist princess, a feminine Cabrera, is the novelist's most effective portrayal of petulance and sadism.[32] On the other hand, Nicolás Estébanez is an ideal combination of politician and man of action, whose acts are rational and tempered by a fundamental humanity.

When compared with the first four Series, the Fifth seems less effective in characterization. This is most evident in the last four volumes where the predominance of an unrealistic protagonist determines the quantitative and qualitative nature of the characterization. Liviano's rapidity of movement in time and space, his completely self-centered narration, allow only a sketchy presentation to those whom he encounters. He himself, however, and the various protagonists of *España sin rey* and *España trágica*, fully satisfy Galdós' illustrative intent, living a disenchanting mediocrity and expressing an era's dissipation and lack of vigor.

MISCELLANEOUS

1. *Comical element*

The entire Fifth Series was written in a satirico-burlesque vein. This phenomenon has already been traced through its effects on plot development and characterization, and the resulting degree of humor — an expected by-product of caricaturesque distortion — is a fair measure of its effectiveness.

Galdós' main formula of burlesque rendition is the deliberate juxtaposition of the sublime and the ridiculous. This may be effected either separately within each of the work's literary

32 See Pérez Galdós, *Obras completas*, III, 1264-1266.

levels (history, 'infra-reality', and 'super-reality') or in a cross pattern of these levels. Some examples of the first are the insertions of Figueras' flight in the history of the Spanish Republic, or of the sleepy Olympus in the amazing world of allegorized fantasy.[33] Examples are even more numerous of a sublime-ridiculous juxtaposition involving two or more of the levels offered in the work: Romarate's humorous perception of the 'Cortes' of 1869,[34] or Halconero's wound being made to coincide with the assassination of Prim; not to mention the innumerable adventures of Liviano, who straddles the mythological and the base.

The fictional world that revolves about Liviano, that of the last four Episodios, simply overflows with humorous incidents. Besides the comedy inherent in his many sexual escapades, in his equally numerous encounters with a fantasy dimension, there are moments of picaresque humor (the 'papist' speech, for example) and of raucous comedy (his courtship of the huge peasant girl). Another source of humor appears, moreover, if Liviano is viewed as a deliberately contorted autobiographical creation, a likely possibility in view of the Cervantine method of presentation, which stresses while obscuring the identification.[35]

2. Symbolism

Name symbolism prevails to the end, and even appears here with an exceptional creative function. We have seen it supplant causal development in the characterization of Tito Liviano, a protagonist that required little beyond an initial baptism. The only other novelty in this area is the visible increase in name-surname combinations: Don Juan de Urríes, Cándido Palomo, Angel Cordero, Leona Brava, and others. The redundance of such combinations adds, however minutely, to the burlesque quality of the Fifth Series.

The work's allegorico-mythological apparatus is clear in meaning. The symbolic references to Spain and Spanish history are either direct or immediately clarified by Mariclío's com-

---

[33] Pérez Galdós, *Obras completas*, III, 1126-1127, 1137.
[34] Ibid., pp. 780-786.
[35] Ibid., pp. 992, 996; and for an enlightening parallel, compare the beginning of Liviano's memoirs with Galdós' *Memorias*, p. 35.

ments, while Education and Work are allegorized in unmistakable terms and in much the same manner employed in Galdós' allegorical novels. What ambivalence appears is a function of Galdosian irony. Such elements of the fantasy world as bulls, nymphs, and subterranean caverns, for example, have a sexual connotation if considered figments of Liviano's mind, but they may express, as symbols in their own right, the beauty and nobility that is latent in the heart of Spain.

The Fifth, like all previous Series, contains plots or plot segments that invite symbolic interpretation. Some examples of the latter have already been noted: the evolution of Segismundo Fajardo and the pathetic role of Ido del Sagrario. *España sin rey* is an example of an entire plot with symbolic possibilities. Fernanda Ibero is readily identified with Spain, which would then find itself — in 1869 — caught between unscrupulous politicians (Urríes) and religious diabolism (Nicéfora). Her only defender — in an added twist of Galdosian irony — is an anachronistic and confused Quijote figure (Romarate). One must emphasize, as always, the supplementary character of such an interpretation, which is in no way essential to the development of the novel as such.

A number of other symbolic relationships merit some comment. The title *De Cartago a Sagunto* prompts a historical comparison that is unqualified satire, and it is immediately compounded by a mock-epic opening. The creation of 'las tres Parcas', a direct attack on religious hypocrisy, fits perfectly into the allegorized scheme of the work. The combined effect of Domiciana Paredes, Rafaela Milagro, and Donata is extraordinary. The emphasis on mystico-sensual characterizations — Donata, Nicéfora, Chilivistra — is undoubtedly directed to the same end.

3. *Subconscious content*

The Fifth Series contains numerous dreams and hallucinations, which function, for the most part, in the manner outlined in previous studies.[36] The only novelty of importance is the extent to which Galdós fused the unconscious and conscious levels. In dealing with Romarate, for example, the two dimensions successively complement each other in creating a mood of

[36] See above, pp. 134-136, 167-168.

ambivalence proper to the plot of *España sin rey*.[37] In the last
four volumes of the Series, however, the effect of subconscious
externalization is considerably reduced. Dreams and hallucinations appear in a world of fiction that is already distorted by
extraneous fantasy elements, and they often retain no con-
sistency whatever.[38]

The two unreal dimensions found in the Fifth Series — subconscious and fantasy — differ basically. Dreams and hallucinations always remain an integral part of the dreamer's world,
an extension of its boundaries, and never attain a literary direction alien to him. The allegorico-mythological content of the
Series cannot be effective, on the other hand, in subordinate
relationship to the real particulars of the fictional world. It consists, largely, of universal symbols, which are only obscured by
close ties to concrete realities. In effect, the allegorico-mythological dimension of the Fifth Series is minimally assimilated into
the real world about Liviano. Floriana and Mariclío, despite
numerous contacts with the protagonist, are independent of the
novelistic content of *La primera República* and *De Cartago a
Sagunto*.

4. Mood

Each Series of *Episodios Nacionales* projects a specific mood
in its combination of plots, characters, and history. Some of
these moods, it may be recalled, express a negative disavowal:
the picaresque opportunism of the Second Series or the
asphyxiating 'abulia' of the Fourth. None of them compare, however, with the piercing negative quality of the Fifth Series, of
the last four volumes especially. It is a disturbing surprise in
a writer of Galdós' usual serenity.

The anguish that can be detected may suggest the novelist's
conscious identification with the history reconstructed. There
seems little doubt that the novelist was personally affected —
and more so with every year that passed after 1898 — by the
tragic events that ultimately sprang from the policies or lack
of policies that characterized the era fictionalized in the Fifth
Series:

---

[37] Pérez Galdós, *Obras completas*, III, 853-858.
[38] See, e.g., ibid., p. 1133.

Produjo ciertamente la Gloriosa medias voluntades, inteligencias en tres cuartos de madurez, con incompleto conocimiento de las cosas, por lo que la gran procesión histórica partida de Cádiz y de Alcolea se desordenó a mitad de su camino, y cada pendón se fue por su lado. La razón de esto era que buena parte de la injundia revolucionaria se componía de retazos de sistemas extranjeros, 'procedentes de saldos políticos'. La fácil importación de vida emperezó en tal manera a los directores de aquel movimiento, que no extrajeron del alma nacional más que los viejos módulos de sus ambiciones y envidias, olvidándose de buscar en ella la esencia democrática y el secreto del nuevo organismo con que debían armar las piezas desconcertadas de la nación.[39]

The similarities to Unamuno's position after 1906 are interesting, but Galdós' views were probably more directly influenced by theories expressed for years by Joaquín Costa.[40] Nevertheless, there are indications of a coincidence of thought and feeling between Galdós and the Generation of 1898.[41] The novelist's burlesque distortion, an artistic judgment upon history, may stem from an attitude similar to that which would in time account for the 'esperpento'.[42]

In the case of Galdós, however, it would be misleading to suggest that the intensely negative mood elicited by caricaturesque distortion precludes any other attitude. Despite the anguish, and the resultant negativism outlined above, the novelist himself is never overwhelmed by the hopelessness he depicts. On the contrary, he appears to have identified himself closely with Mariclío, inserting the ordinal in *La primera República* and closing the *Episodios Nacionales* with a call to revolution.

B) *Summary of Chapter III*

The incomplete Fifth Series is characterized by a formal dichotomy. The first two volumes are patterned, for the most

39 Pérez Galdós, *Obras completas*, III, 872.

40 See E. Tierno Galván, *Costa y el regeneracionismo* (Barcelona, 1961), pp. 179-180.

41 Casalduero, *Vida y obra*, pp. 186-187; and Gullón, "Cuestiones galdosianas," *Cuadernos Hispanoamericanos*, XXXIV (1958), 237-238.

For a more detailed study of this relationship, see J. M. Monner Sans, "Galdós y la Generación del 98," *Cursos y Conferencias*, XXIV (1943), 57-85; and H. C. Berkowitz, "Galdós and the Generation of 98," *Philological Quarterly*, XXI (1942), 107-120.

42 See P. Salinas, "Significación del esperpento o Valle-Inclán, hijo pródigo del '98," *Cuadernos Americanos*, VI (1947), 218-244.

part, on the dissociative norms established by the Fourth Series, but the last four revert as a unit to the structural cohesiveness of the First Series. An aging, blinded Galdós found it urgent to accelerate his presentation of nineteenth-century Spanish history, which was to include the following titles: *Sagasta, Las colonies perdidas, La reina regente,* and *Alfonso XIII.* This explains the unitive devices that expedite the formulation of the last four volumes, rapidly incorporating nearly ten years of history: first-person narration, unipersonal and episodic plot, and autobiographical framework.

Galdós achieved a rapid reconstruction of history, but at the expense of novelistic complexity, by thinning the fictional background normal to the *Episodios Nacionales.* Moreover, what plot content remained was further weakened by an allegorico-mythological vein, which substituted for novelistic complexity while lending itself to Galdós' distortive intent. The first two Episodios are better developed as novels, but also reveal the effects of the novelist's desire to work partly in caricature.

An impoverished characterization is the immediate consequence, for without the framework of a cohesive plot, characters tend to lack complete and understandable development. This applies most, of course, to Liviano, who monopolizes the last four volumes. But the protagonists of *España sin rey* and *España trágica,* although more realistic, are themselves divested of complexity in the interest of historical illustration. It is clear that Halconero, with his discouraging mediocrity, is a more telling representative of post-revolutionary Spain than a dynamic Araceli, a wilful Monsalud, or a courageous Santiago Ibero could be.

The secondary characters of the Fifth Series are clearly functional in Galdós caricature of an age, but they are less affected as literary creations by this illustrative task. Except for extreme cases like Graziella and Leona Brava, the secondary characters do not vary greatly from those of earlier Series, since they depend little, for literary fulfillment, on extensive appearances or thorough plot integration.

The novelistic thinness of the work put a greater burden of historical representation on the historical figures themselves. Galdós was often dealing, moreover, with people known to him personally. Both these factors facilitate an extensive and exact portrayal of the historical characters presented in the Fifth Series. As literary elaborations, however, these often lack the completeness and the verisimilitude of their counterparts from earlier Series. Two reasons for this are immediately evident. The lack of novelistic complexity prescribed the use of fantastic devices in their presentation; and Galdós' intuitive apparatus was apparently curbed in dealing with figures still very much in his and the public's memory.

Style

The stylistic variations found in the Fifth Series reflect the formal dichotomy noted earlier. The first two volumes remain largely within the stylistic configuration of the Fourth Series, albeit with a visible decrease in the impressionism noted there.[43] The language of *España sin rey* and *España trágica* is for the most part direct and unlabored, with few expressions reminiscent of the previous Series' modernistic flights and only the slightest indications of the flippant tone that would prevail in the last four volumes.[44]

With the advent of Tito Liviano in *Amadeo I*, both mood and style change rather abruptly. The radical alteration is prepared by the change effected in the narrative form. A first-person narration is not in itself a novelty to the *Episodios Nacionales*, but Liviano's expression in that subjective medium does constitute a stylistic innovation. The first-person is usually employed by Galdós in letters or memoirs, which imply, of course, that the character is conscious of using an established literary format. Liviano's narration, despite an ironical attempt at justifying a literary vestiment,[45] is far more verbal than written, more flippant than literary. [46]

Periods of heroism and ideals may be directly fictionalized in the first-person, for the character who lives the history and represents the period can narrate without the contortions induced by guilt or shame (First Series). When the epoch, or some part of it, is lacking in positive qualities, a first-person narrative often results in satire. The narrator, representative of

---

43 See above, pp. 172-173.
44 See, e.g., Pérez Galdós, *Obras completas,* III, pp. 775-778.
45 Ibid., p. 996.
46 See, e.g., ibid., pp. 983, 993, 1038, 1079, et passim.

what he is describing, feels the need to defend the indefensible (Second Series). The Fifth Series offers a third possibility, which results when author and fictional first-person narrator coincide in their relationship to a negative age. Then, a conscious irony delights in the burlesque distortion of a historical reality that both author and narrator reject as an intrinsic part of themselves.

Burlesque distortion, as a function of style, is particularly evident in the last four *Episodios Nacionales*. The language and the concepts it expresses form a ludicrous potpourri of values. The loftiest allegorical descriptions are interlaced with common speech and even earthy idiomatic expressions. Important historical narrations are interrupted by observations that stem from the narrator's 'infra-real' experiences.[47] The interpolation of a 'super-real,' allegorico-mythological dimension would normally effect a corresponding stylistic adjustment; but instead of raising the linguistic level, Galdós deliberately employed a familiar, conversational first-person narrative. To this can be added a measure of 'forgetful' repetition,[48] both a stylistic and conceptual emphasis on the monotonous dissipation of the period. In short, the overall process of burlesque distortion is augmented by a stylistic configuration that often renders 'un Lepanto en zapatillas,' to use the author's own expression.

The effectiveness of the last four *Episodios Nacionales* is questionable. The degree of disfiguration achieved encumbers the reading and occasionally impedes comprehension. To a literary work already burdened with fusing three distinct dimensions ('infra-real,' historical, 'super-real'), Galdós added such disruptive devices as interpolated theatrical elements and subconscious externalizations.[49]

---

[47] See, e.g., Pérez Galdós, *Obras completas*, III, 1137.
[48] See, e.g., ibid., pp. 1116, 1321.
[49] Ibid., pp. 990, 1110, 11177; and pp. 768, 803, 853-855, 883, 1065, 1132-1133, 1210, 1234-1235, 1236, 1320-1325, et passim.

CONCLUSION

This study has been conceived as an introduction to the *Episodios Nacionales;* consequently, every literary aspect stressed in it (characterization, humor, symbolism, etc.) is susceptible of further analysis. A number of important facts and relationships pertinent to the volumes studied and to Galdós' work in general have been examined. There are, however, features that have not been discussed in the chapter summaries and must be stressed here.

The *Episodios Nacionales* are historical novels; yet no 'a priori' definition of that literary 'genre' can satisfactorily include all forty-six volumes. These may only be classified therein if the term 'Historical Novel' is broadened to include their special characteristics. But one finds, however, that the necessary process of classification blurs the most essential differences that might be thought to exist between Galdós' historical novels and the rest of his novelistic production.[1]

Galdós' treatment of History—a subject matter that holds the work within the broad category of historical fiction—is everywhere conditioned by the philosophical attitudes and artistic perspectives of the realist writer, so that no inflexible definition of 'Historical Novel,' especially if based on the norms established by the literature of the Romantics, could possibly incorporate the *Episodios Nacionales.*

> Los *Episodios* no pertenecen al subgénero de la novela histórica, que toma la historia como un marco externo donde encuadra el desenvolvimiento de unas vidas humanas; en ellos son las vidas humanas mismas las que, en su despliegue, tejen la historia; y ésta, sobre la única materia de las pobres existencias individuales, proyecta su sentido más allá de cada una, hacia un plano transcendente.[2]

Ayala's statement—despite its generic stipulations, with which no general agreement can be reached—may serve as a penetrating insight into the fundamental difference betwen Galdós'

---

1 See above, pp. 12-25.
2 F. Ayala, "Conmemoración galdosiana," *Histrionismo y representación* (Buenos Aires, 1944), p. 195.

historical novel and that of most traditional writers in the 'genre.' The deliberate insistence that human beings make up the substance of History, the literary expression of 'historia e intrahistoria',[3] sets Galdós apart from all but the greatest historical novelists of any age.

It is their rigid formal outline, far more than any stylistic, thematic, or procedural criteria that might be applied, that distinguishes the *Episodios Nacionales* from the rest of Galdós' work. Because they deal with a specific constant (historical time), and with a subject matter for which the novelist's perspective required a specific order of treatment, the *Episodios Nacionales,* unlike any other segment of the novelist's work, are fixed into a set literary form: ten volume Series unit, progressive sequence of time, and prescribed quantitative limitations.[4]

This external fixation of form can be quite misleading. In fact, the study of plot structure and development in the various Series reveals that the 'set' formal outline of the literary unit may condition but rarely inhibits the novelistic variety or richness of the content. On the contrary, it is evident that the *Episodios Nacionales* offer the widest range of novelistic forms encountered anywhere: objective narrations, memoirs, both immediate and retrospective, epistolary novels, and varied combinations of these. The flexibility of the individual Episodio, even within the formal outline of the Series, is extraordinary.

Galdós' use of varied novelistic forms to project the variety of historical circumstances, the specific and distinct character of each period, is an important factor in the success of the *Episodios Nacionales.* One need only recall, in this connection, the novels of the Second Series which feature Bragas or those in the Fourth in which Santiuste is the protagonist. Nowhere else in Galdós are the alterations in literary temperament and expression so evident as in these forty-six volumes: from the epic drive of the first Episodios to the caricaturesque distortion of the last. And each stage of this evolution is made viable in the literary guise of a distinct form of novelistic expression.[5]

---

3 See above, pp. 40-49.
4 See above, pp. 51-52, 108.
5 For the qualitative differences in the extremes mentioned, see Gilman, *Homenaje a A. M. Huntington,* pp. 171-192; and Enguídanos, "Mariclío, musa galdosiana," *Papeles de Son Armadans,* XXI (June, 1961), p. 235.

The study of plot development also scores the progressive dissociation of novelistic content in successive literary units. This evolution within the formal outline of the Series, prompted both by qualitative variations in the historical subject matter and by the author's directed efforts to allow greater literary flexibility,[6] accounts for the greater degree of novelistic complexity that enhances the artistic potential of each successive Series. This concept of progressive literary enrichment runs counter to most general evaluations of the *Episodios Nacionales*.[7] Casalduero, however, has seen this:

> Se comprende, pues, que la primera serie haya contado con el favor del público; más extraño parece que arrastrados por el asunto hayan creído que estaban leyendo una narración épica; por último, es difícil de comprender que no vieran la superioridad novelística de las otras series, especialmente de las dos últimas.[8]

Another established view of Galdós' historical novel—its characterizational poverty—is disproved by a detailed analysis of character presentation and development in the *Episodios Nacionales*. The novelist's primary interest in human development is definitely not diluted or altered when he approaches a historical subject. Whatever shift may take place between contemporary novelist and historical novelist—from people to events—is more than offset by the wealth of new characterizational possibilities opened by a perspective on the past.

In effect, the *Episodios Nacionales* boast as wide a variety of characterizations as may be found anywhere in Galdós, even wider, in fact, if historical personages are included. Characters like Salvador Monsalud, 'El Empecinado,' José Fago, Trijueque, Maroto, Bragas, and Juan Hondón, to mention but a few of the myriad human patterns represented in the forty-six volumes, are both the product of one or more of Galdós' penetrating perspectives on human nature and the reflection, simultaneously, of some specific element of the historical situation depicted. And it is precisely this combination that accounts for the universal quality of a mere historical reconstruction.

---

6 See above, pp. 77-78, 109-110, 139-140.

7 See, e.g., L. B. Walton, *Pérez Galdós and the Spanish Novel of the 19th Century* (London, 1927), p. 61.

8 Casalduero, "Galdós y la Edad Media," *Asomante*, IX (1953), p. 17.

In spite of the somewhat limiting representational function that most characters perform in the *Episodios Nacionales*,[9] these reveal characterizations that are comparable, in the quality of their presentation and development, to the better creations found in the *Novelas de primera época* or the *Novelas contemporáneas*. Fajardo, for example, experiences intensely dramatic human conflicts that make him one of the novelist's most memorable protagonists; and José Armengol or Navarro are as tragic in their fundamental human make-up as the Polo Corteses found in other segments of Galdós' work. As for feminine characterizations, always a specialty of the author, it was first in the *Episodios Nacionales*, with Jenara, that the author sketched the prototype of his most expressive feminine creations. And any group of novels that boasts Pilar Loaysa, Domiciana Paredes, Teresita Villaescusa, and Sor Teodora de Aransis, to mention but a few, needs little defense in terms of feminine characterization.

The depiction of secondary figures, in which the characterizational opportunities offered by a perspective on the past are most readily implemented, represents one of Galdós' major successes in the *Episodios Nacionales*. Characters almost too numerous to mention project the attitudes and feelings of every stage in Spain's nineteenth-century history, and they do so as believable human beings, anguished, overjoyed, or disheartened by the life that pulsates within or about them.

Here too the techniques are, to say the least, as varied as in any segment of Galdós' work: Pepe Pellejos, 'Pujitos', Marcial, 'Pelambres', and countless other types taken from Ramón de la Cruz or Mesonero Romanos; Hillo, 'El Gran Capitán', Malespina, and innumerable other comical figures from the molds of Plautus and Cervantes; Lobo, the Requejos, Romo, and many others whose very physical being projects the twisted substance of their souls; and people like Negretti, Churi, and María Ignacia Emparán, whose cursory presentation as secondary figures suggests all the dense complexity of more extensively developed characters.

One fact is made progressively clearer in this study: Galdós' imaginative creativity is substantially less inhibited in the *Episodios Nacionales* than elsewhere in his literary production. This, perhaps more than any single factor, makes the forty-six Epi-

9 See above, pp. 102-103.

sodios both a magnificent discovery for the reader of Galdós and an incalculably rich expression, perhaps the richest, of the novelist's creative abilities. This is true to a great extent, as we have seen, of plot development and characterization, but it is most evident in studies of specific areas of Galdós' historical novel.

A study of the comical elements in the *Episodios Nacionales* reveals almost every conceivable degree and avenue of humor, a range and flexibility of comical devices and conceptions that is not found in Galdós' other novels.

Galdós, as Casalduero has noted:

> Nunca va tras el chiste por el chiste, de aquí que su visión cómica comparte tanta simpatía, tanta comprensión, tanta ternura. Su ironía, sin embargo, se adapta al ritmo de su pasión y llega a restallar como un látigo de indignación.[10]

True. But the outline of comedy, as extracted from the *Episodios Nacionales*, is far more complex: the humorous quality of a pathetic being, whose weaknesses the humane novelist fathoms through laughter; the mildly comical disdain projected by the parody of a specific world-view, a humorous conception of an age that conditions an entire novelistic development; the unqualified satire of a period, in which the author's bitter perception of Spanish reality is expressed with the doubly effective serenity of a controlled artistic medium; and irony, the varying intensities of which can most rewardingly be traced in Galdós' historical novel: from the mild 'literarization' of Spanish history in *La batalla de los Arapiles*, via the ethical subversion of *O'Donnell*, to the projection of Tito Liviano as the soul of Spain. To this broad outline might be added, as a final indication of the author's daring flexibility in the *Episodios Nacionales*, Galdós' humorous autobiographical projections in the last two Series.[11]

The study of symbolism in the forty-six volumes again reveals a remarkable diversity of practices and devices. Name symbolism—Galdós' most characteristic didactic device[12]—pre-

10 Casalduero, "Galdós y la Edad Media," *Asomante*, IX (1953), p. 17; and see Del Río, *Estudios galdosianos*, p. 18.

11 See above, pp. 184, 190, and Casalduero, *Vida y obra*, pp. 184-191.

12 See, e.g., A. Alonso, "Lo español y lo universal en la obra de Galdós," *Materia y forma en poesía* (Madrid, 1955), p. 238; and Ayala, "El realismo en literatura con referencia a Galdós," *La Torre*, VII (April, 1959), 118.

vails, as nowhere else, in the five Series, replete throughout with the most varied comical, illustrative, and characterizational functions. Galdós availed himself, for the purpose of symbolism, of every conceivable literary element: titles like *La segunda casaca, Un faccioso más y algunos frailes menos, De Oñate a la Granja, Los duendes de la camarilla, La de los tristes destinos,* and *De Cartago a Sagunto;* mock literary openings like that which introduce the memoirs of Bragas or that which initiates Liviano's narration in *De Cartago a Sagunto;* and even animals, as many long passages from *Gerona*—and many shorter ones throughout the work—well indicate.

Moreover, Galdós' historical novel offers unique examples of an extraordinary ability to have believable characters and realistic plot situations (whole plots or segments thereof) project the qualitative essence and the human composition of specific historical moments. His artistic projection of historical relationships as concrete human problems and situations is his most effective illustrative device. But it is much more than that, for the characters and plot situations are themselves subtly affected by a suggestive association with transcendental historical realities. It is an esthetic interaction that endows the *Episodios Nacionales,* and simultaneously, with a humanized historical transcendence and a visibly 'historicized' human content.

A wealth of characters on all levels of development express, in the *Episodios Nacionales,* the profound interest that Galdós reveals everywhere in the relatively hidden aspects of human personality. The difference is again a question of degree, of qualitative and quantitative flexibility. In no other segment of his work does the novelist accumulate a repertoire of 'strange' characters like Leandra, Nelet, Fago, Churi, and Negretti. And the phenomenon is by no means restricted to the Third Series, for the following group of Episodios offers Fajardo, Santiuste, Binondo, and Miedes. Nowhere else does Galdós present such an impressive array of distinct enigmatic personalities, for each of those mentioned above—and many others besides—is a rule unto himself.

The subconscious externalizations and the aberrational behaviour that stem from Galdós' emphasis on the abnormal in the *Episodios Nacionales*—yet to be studied with the care with which similar phenomena have been examined in the *Novelas contemporáneas*—are as rich and varied as any to be found in the novelist's work. As is usually the case in Galdós, dreams, hallucinations, and other psychic phenomena play important roles in characterization and plot development. In the *Episodios Nacionales,* moreover, these are often made to reflect, in the crisis of an individual being, the turbulent character of a historical situation or the pathological condition of an entire age.

The study of Galdós' use of traditional literary themes and characters in the *Episodios Nacionales* suggests that it may be necessary to modify certain widely held opinions:

> More important is the fact that Galdós' creative methods, especially in fictional materials as distinct from historical ones but even also in the *Episodios,* tended to use more recent personal experience and observation of his own rather than literary materials.[13]

There are numerous indications of the novelist's use of a great variety of literary materials: primarily Spanish, to be sure, but with occasional foreign sources such as Shakespeare, Balzac, and Dickens.

Traditional Spanish themes and characters abound everywhere in the novelist's literary production: Don Quijote, Don Juan, the picaresque, Celestina, and Juan Ruiz. But it is in the historical novel, once again, that the full impact of Galdós' re-elaboration of literary materials is felt.

The novelist's use of Cervantes, especially of the *Quijote,* has already drawn the attention of scholars.[14] Nevertheless, the *Episodios Nacionales* allow further comparative studies, particularly in connection with Cervantine works other than the *Quijote.* Most of these interesting re-elaborations have been overlooked by critics; yet themes like that of *Celestina* provide Galdós' historical novel with many characterizations and even an occasional plot outline.

Surprisingly enough, the Don Juan theme has not been studied in Galdós. When such a study is undertaken, the *Episodios Nacionales* will undoubtedly figure prominently in it, for nowhere in Spanish literature, not even among the modern generations that have cultivated the Don Juan theme with spe-

13 W. H. Schoemaker, "Galdós' Classical Scene in *La de Bringas,*" *Hispanic Review,* XXVII (1959), 432.
14 See titles listed under Obaid and Warshaw in the Bibliography.

cial intensity, is there a repertoire comparable to the 'byronized' Lord Gray, the pathetic Falfán de los Godos, the broken Nelet, the 'calibanized' Churi, the genuine Gracián, the pathological Santiuste, and the fantastic Liviano.

The literary outline most employed by Galdós is the picaresque. This is especially true in the *Episodios Nacionales*, in the study of which there has been occasion to note that the episodic character of novels that must incorporate widely dispersed historical events encouraged Galdós' use of the picaresque-like protagonist, rootless, and forever wandering. The fact is, however, that the picaresque stamp set upon numerous Galdosian characters entails something more than a mere literary expedient. More often than not the negative attributes of the rogue reflect the essential truth, off-repeated by modern thinkers, that a Spaniard without a vital 'quehacer' instinctively reverts to a picaresque world-view.

The separate interpolations of these literary re-workings are always esthetically and functionally viable. Numerous pages in this study point out the realistic quality of a characterization or the essential verisimilitude of a plot outline, and indicate, as well, the important novelistic, characterizational, comical, stylistic, and symbolical functions they perform in the work. But it is the cumulative effect that is perhaps of greatest interest, for without its picaresque, donjuanesque, celestinesque, and quijotesque elements the *Episodios Nacionales* would be completely altered. These elements constitute, if they are statistically arranged, a secondary background to the entire work, providing the primary historical background with unmistakable universal overtones.

Finally, the *Episodios Nacionales* reveal a variety and range of geographical settings that is unique in Galdós. Nothing in the novelist's previous production, nor in that of the generation with which he is most often linked, prepares the reader for the foreign settings of the Fourth Series. In fact, one would have to go to Baroja or Valle-Inclán for anything comparable. Of course the uniqueness of this phenomenon—which is nevertheless meaningful and appropriate in the historical context of the *Episodios Nacionales*—adds powerfully to the notion of Galdós' historical novel as that segment of his work in which he is least restricted in the conception and use of literary elements.

Appendix: Galdós on Spain and Spaniards

Me representé a mi país como una inmensa tierra poblada de gentes, todos fraternalmente unidos; me representé la sociedad dividida en familias, en las cuales había esposas que mantener, hijos que educar, hacienda que conservar, honra que defender; me hice cargo de un pacto establecido entre tantos seres para ayudarse y sostenerse contra un ataque de fuera, y comprendí que por todos habían sido hechos aquellos barcos para defender la patria, es decir, el terreno en que ponían sus plantas, el surco regado con su sudor, la casa donde vivían sus ancianos padres, el huerto donde jugaban sus hijos, la colonia descubierta y conquistada por sus ascendientes, el puerto donde amarraba su embarcación fatigada del largo viaje, el almacén donde depositaban sus riquezas; la iglesia, sarcófago de sus mayores, habitáculo de sus santos y arca de sus creencias; la plaza, recinto de sus alegres pasatiempos; el hogar doméstico, cuyos antiguos muebles, transmitidos de generación en generación, parecen el símbolo de la perpetuidad de las naciones; la cocina, en cuyas paredes ahumadas parece que no se extingue nunca el eco de los cuentos con que las abuelas amansan la travesura e inquietud de los nietos; la calle, donde se ven desfilar caras amigas; el campo, el mar, el cielo; todo cuanto desde el nacer se asocia a nuestra existencia, desde el pesebre de un animal querido hasta el trono de reyes patriarcales; todos los objetos en que vive prolongándose nuestra alma, como si el propio cuerpo no le bastara. (*Trafalgar*, I, 241)

Pero es de advertir que entre nosotros es muy común el intento de arreglar las más difíciles cuestiones mandando vivir o morir a quien se nos antoja, y somos tan dados a los gritos, que repetidas veces hemos creído hacer con ellos alguna cosa. (*El 19 de marzo y el 2 de mayo*, I, 403)

—¡Esos países no tienen vergüenza! —gritó con furor don Santiago Fernández, levantándose otra vez de su asiento. —En Austria y Prusia habrá lo que usted quiera; pero no hay Valdesogo de Abajo ni un Navalagamella.

Discretísimo lector, no te ríes de esta presuntuosa afirmación del Gran Capitán, porque bajo su aparente simpleza encierra una profunda verdad histórica. (*Bailén*, I, 475)

El pueblo español . . . es, de todos los que llenan la tierra, el más inclinado a hacer chacota y burla de los asuntos serios. Ni el peligro le arredra, ni los padecimientos le quitan su buen humor; así vemos que, rodeado de guerra, muertes, miseria y exterminio, se entretiene en componer cantares, creyendo no ofender menos a sus enemigos con las sátiras punzantes que con las cortadoras espadas. (*Napoleón, en Chamartín*, I, 579)

Ayer barriendo a los franceses, y hoy dejándonos barrer; ayer poderosos y temibles, y hoy impotentes y desbandados. Contrastes y antítesis propias de la tierra, como el paño pardo, los garbanzos, el buen vino y el buen humor. ¡Oh España, como se te reconoce en cualquier parte de tu historia adonde se fija la vista! Y no hay disimulo que te encubra, ni máscara que te oculte, ni afeite que te disfigure, porque adondequiera que aparezcas, allí se te conoce desde cien leguas, con tu media cara de fiestas y la otra media de miseria; con la una mano empuñando laureles y con la otra rascándote tu lepra. (*Napoleón, en Chamartín,* I, 603)

El pueblo español, que con presteza se inflama, con igual presteza se apaga, y si en una hora es fuego asolador que sube al cielo, en otra es ceniza que el viento arrastra y desparrama por el bajo suelo. (*Napoleón, en Chamartín,* I, 624)

Así lo nuevo se había edificado sobre y entre los restos de lo antiguo en confuso amasijo, como la gente española se desarrolló y crió sobre despojos de otras gentes con mezcladas sangres, hasta constituirse como hoy lo está. (*Zaragoza,* I, 703)

Hombres de poco seso, o sin ninguno en ocasiones, los españoles darán mil caídas, hoy como siempre, tropezando y levantándose, en la lucha de sus vicios ingénitos, de las cualidades eminentes que aun conservan, y de las que adquieren lentamente con las ideas que les envía la Europa central. Grandes subidas y bajadas, grandes asombros y sorpresas, aparentes muertes y resurecciones prodigiosas reserva la Providencia a esta gente, porque su destino es poder vivir en la agitación como la salamandra en el fuego; pero su permanencia nacional está y estará siempre asegurada. (*Zaragoza,* I, 759)

Sucedía en Sevilla una cosa que no sorprenderá a mis lectores, si, como creo, son españoles, y era que allí todos querían mandar. (*Gerona,* I, 763)

Estaba formado su espíritu con uno de los más visibles caracteres del genio castizo español, que necesita de la perpetua lucha para apacentar su indomable y díscola inquietud y ha de vivir disputando de palabra u obra para creer que vive. (*Juan Martín, el Empecinado,* I, 975)

Los guerrilleros constituyen nuestra esencia nacional. Ellos son nuestro cuerpo y nuestra alma; son el espíritu, el genio, la historia de España; ellos son todo, grandeza y miseria, un conjunto informe de cualidades contrarias, la dignidad dispuesta al heroismo, la crueldad inclinada al pillaje. (*Juan Martín, el Empecinado,* I, 976)

A esta variedad en los pareceres y terquedad para sostenerlos llamo yo enjaezar los entendimientos a la calasera, es decir, a la española. (*Los cien mil hijos de San Luis,* I, 1616)

Lo que siempre está lo mismo es mi país, que no deja de luchar un momento por la misma causa y con las mismas armas, y si no con las mismas personas, con los mismos tipos de guerreros y políticos. Mi país sigue siempre a la calasera. (*Los cien mil hijos de San Luis,* I, 1621)

También era orador, que es casi lo mismo que ser español y español poeta. (*Los apostólicos,* II, 118)

Hay pueblos que se transforman en sosiego, charlando y discutiendo con algaradas sangrientas de tres, cuatro o cinco años, pero más bien turbados por las lenguas que por las espadas. El nuestro ha de seguir su camino con saltos y caídas, tumultos y atropellos. Nuestro mapa no es una carta geográfica, sino el plano estratégico de una batalla sin fin. Nuestro pueblo no es un pueblo, sino un ejército. Nuestro gobierno no gobierna: se defiende. Nuestros partidos no son partidos mientras no tienen generales. Nuestros montes son trincheras, por lo cual están sabiamente desprovistos de árboles. Nuestros campos no se cultivan, para que pueda correr por ellos la artillería. En nuestro comercio se advierte una timidez secular originada por la idea fija de que 'mañana' habrá jaleo. Lo que llamamos paz es entre nosotros como la frialdad en física: un estado negativo; la ausencia de calor, la tregua de la guerra. La paz es aquí un prepararse para la lucha, y un ponerse vendas y limpiar armas para empezar de nuevo. (*Los apostólicos,* II, 122)

En una palabra, cada español, al pedir libertad, reclama la suya, importándole poco la del prójimo . . . (*Los apostólicos,* II, 177)

La confusión de pareceres, el incesante conspirar con recursos misteriosos y fines mal determinados, las repugnantes connivencias de la Policía con los conspiradores de todas clases . . ., expresión morbosa de nuestra miseria . . . (*Un faccioso más y algunos frailes menos,* II, 238)

¡Así pagan su tenaz constancia celtíbera! ¡Así se derrochaba el tesoro inmenso de la energía española! ¡Es verdadero milagro que después de tan imprudente despilfarro del caudal por uno y otro bando, todavía quedara mucho, y quedará siempre, y quede todavía . . .! (*Zumalacárregui,* II, 336)

Pero algo trascendía siempre, como es natural, mayormente entre españoles, raza inepta para guardar secretos. (*Zumalacárregui,* II, 402)

Da dolor ver tanta energía empleada en la guerra de hermanos. Y cuando la raza no se ha extinguido peleando consigo misma es porque no puede extinguirse. (*Zumalacárregui,* II, 408)

. . . aquí, donde salimos de una zaragata para entrar en otra, donde nos peleamos por los derechos de la corona, por las juntas, por la milicia urbana, por una letra de más o menos en la Constitución, y por lo que dicen o dejaron de decir Juan y Manuela. (*Mendizábal,* II, 431)

Talento no les falta, buena voluntad tampoco. Y fracasan, no obstante, y continuarán fracasando unos tras otros. Es cuestión de fatalidad en esta maldita raza. Se anulan, se estrellan, no por lo que hacen, sino por lo que dejan de hacer. En fin, amiguito, nuestros mandarines se parecen a los toreros medianos: ¿Sabe usted en qué? Pues en que no 'rematan' . . . (*Mendizábal,* II, 431)

¡Hablar! La maldita palabra. Es la sarna del país. España llegará al fin del siglo sin haber hecho nada más que rascarse, es decir, hablar . . . (*Mendizábal,* II, 439)

. . . no ignoraba que, en nuestra tierra de garbanzos y pronunciamientos, el guerrero victorioso es el único salvador posible en todos los órdenes. (*Mendizábal*, II, 459)

En los empleos tiene usted la explicación de la inercia nacional, de esta parálisis, que se traduce luego en ignorancia, en envidia, en pobreza . . . los empleos, que son como el opio o el 'hascisch' para esta nación viciosa, indolente. (*Mendizábal*, II, 510)

La chismografía se ha tomado en esta desdichada tierra las atribuciones que en otros países corresponden a la opinión. Y que la manejan bien los españoles. Esto y las guerrillas son las dos manifestaciones más poderosas del genio nacional. (*De Oñate a La Granja*, II, 542)

Así hemos venido todo el siglo, navegando con sinnúmero de patrones, y así ha corrido el barco por un mar siempre proceloso, a punto de estrellarse más de una vez; anegado siempre, rara vez con bonanzas, y corriendo iguales peligros con tiempo duro y en las calmas chichas. Es una nave ésta que por su mala construcción no va nunca adonde debe ir: los remiendos de velamen y de toda la obra muerta y viva de costados no mejoran sus condiciones marineras, pues el defecto capital está en la quilla, y mientras no se emprenda la reforma por lo hondo, construyendo de nuevo todo el casco, no hay esperanzas de próspera navegación. Las cuadrillas de tripulantes que en ella entran y salen se ocupan más del repuesto de víveres que del buen orden y acierto en las maniobras. Muchos pasan el viaje tumbados a la bartola, y otros se cuidan, más que del aparejo, de quitar y poner lindas banderas. Son, digan lo que quieran, inexpertos marineros: valiera más que se emborracharán, como los ingleses, y que borrachos perdidos supieran dirigir la embarcación. Los más se marean y la horrorosa molestia del mar la combaten comiendo; algunos, desde la borda, se entretienen en pescar. Todos hablan sin término, en la falsa creencia de que la palabra es viento que hace andar la nave. Esta obedece tan mal, que a veces el timonel quiere hacerla virar a babor y la condenada se va sobre estribor. De donde resulta, ¡ay!, que la dejan adonde las olas, el viento y los discursos quieren llevarla. (*De Oñate a La Granja*, II, 572)

Era la enfermedad general, ya crónica, que se agravaba. Mas no por ello moriría el enfermo: España tenía fibra y agallas para resistir tanta calamidad; su sobriedad de mendigo le garantizaba la existencia; su pasividad fatalista le permitía seguir arrastrándose y dando tumbos, hasta que vinieran hombres y tiempos mejores, los cuales . . ., ¡ay!, también podría suceder que no vinieran. (*De Oñate a La Granja*, II, 643)

No te maravilles de esto: vivimos en el país de las recomendaciones y del favor personal. La amistad es aquí la suprema razón de la existencia, así en lo grande como en lo pequeño, así en lo individual como en lo colectivo . . . (*Luchana*, II, 656)

Allanad y afirmad el suelo sobre todo, y esto lo haréis con las artes de la paz, no con guerras y trapisondas. Haced un país donde haya todo lo contrario de lo que unos y otros, a quienes no se si llamar guerreros o bandidos, representáis; haced un país donde sea verdad la justicia, donde sea efectiva la propiedad, eficaz el mérito, fecundo el trabajo, y dejaos de quitar y poner tronos . . . Lo que va a resultar es que, cualquiera que sea el resultado, estáis fabricando una nación de bandolerismo, que en mucho tiempo, gane quien ganare, ha de seguir siendo bandolera, es decir, que tendrá por leyes la violencia, la injusticia, el favor, la holgazanería, el pillaje y la desvergüenza. En un pueblo a que dais tal educación, cualquier trono que pongáis será un trono figurado, de cuatro tablas frágiles y cuatro mal pintados lienzos . . . (*La campaña del Maestrazgo*, II, 849)

Será una manifestación aislada, como otras mil que vemos, del cansancio y pesimismo de la raza española, que indómita en su decadencia dice: 'Antes de que me conquiste el extranjero, quiero morirme. Me acabaré, en parte por consunción, en parte suicidándome con la espada siniestra de las guerras civiles. (*La estafeta romántica*, II, 883)

Tantas frases sonoras y campanudas se me ocurren para maldecir esta endiablada máquina de las sublevaciones militares, que prefiero no transcribir ninguna, seguro de que otras voces y plumas lo expresarán más campanuda y gravemente que yo en el curso infinito de nuestras políticas trapisondas. Es un hecho, es un vicio de la sangre, del cual participamos todos, y con él hemos de vivir hasta que Dios quiera curarnos. Yo no he de verlo, y se me figura que tú tampoco lo verás. (*La estafeta romántica*, II, 956)

Tanta iniquidad, injusticia tan cínica y desvergonzada, me sublevaron. Pero ¿España es así y ha de ser siempre así? ¿Es en ella mentira la verdad, farsa la justicia y únicos resortes el favor o el cohecho? (*Vergara*, II, 975)

La fatalidad había traído a esta pobre nación a un dualismo que sería manantial inagotable de desdichas por larguísimo tiempo. La idea absolutista, la intransigencia religiosa hallábanse tan hondamente incrustadas en los cerebros y en los corazones de una gran parte de los hijos de España, que era cequedad creer que podrían ser extirpados 'de un tirón' . . . ¿Era conveniente la transacción, aun siendo mala cosa? Sí, porque con ella, si España no mejoraba, al menos viviría, y los pueblos rehusan la muerte aun más que las personas. (*Vergara*, II, 1048)

Pero en España la oposición se forma en cuatro días después del éxito. Nace como la mala hierba y crece como la espuma. (*Montes de Oca*, II, 1081)

Yo voy viendo que la mejor de las paces es la guerra y que nunca están los españoles tan sosegados y contentos como cuando les encharcamos con sangre el suelo que pisan . . . pues no sé quiénes serán 'ellos' ni quienes seremos 'nosotros'; pero entre media España y la otra media andará el juego. A prepararse, digo, que aquí la paz es imposible, y, si me apuras, desastrosa, porque el español ha nacido eminentemente peleón, y cuando no sale guerra natural la inventa, digo que se distrae y 'da gusto al dedo' con las guerras artificiales. (*Montes de Oca,* II, 1085)

Comía el que tenía qué y todos hablaban cuanto querían de lo humano y de lo divino, derrochando su aptitud crítica, que era y sigue siendo la virtud o el vicio del siglo. (*Montes de Oca,* II, 1091)

¡Qué delicioso país y qué Historia tan divertida la que aquella edad a las plumas de las venideras ofrecía! Toda ella podría escribirse con el mismo cuajarón de sangre por tinta y con la misma astilla de las rotas lanzas. El drama comenzaba a perder su interés por la repetición de los mismos lances y escenas. Las tiradas de prosa poética y el amaneramiento trágico ya no hacían temblar a nadie; el abuso de las aventuras heroicas llevaba rápidamente al país a una degeneración epiléptica, y lo que antes creíamos sacrificio por los ideales no era más que instinto de suicidio y monomanía de la muerte. (*Montes de Oca,* II, 1135-1136)

La única fe que se trasluce entre tanta garrulería es la de los adelantamientos personales; el móvil supremo que late aquí y allí no es más que la necesidad de alimentarse medianamente, la persecución de un cocido y de unas sopas de ajo, ambiciones tras de las cuales despuntan otras más altas, anhelos de comodidades y distinciones honoríficas. Bien lo dice la profana Clío cuando, interrogada acerca de estas cosas tan poco hidalgas, nos muestra la imagen de la nación desmedrada por los hábitos de ascetismo a que le han traído los que durante siglos le predicaron la pobreza y el ayuno, enseñándola a recrearse en su escualidez cadavérica y a tomarla por tipo de verdadera hermosura. Dícenos también la diosa que no puede hacer nada contra los siglos que han amaestrado a nuestra raza en la holgazanería, imbuyéndole la confianza en que los hombres serán alimentados con semillitas que lleva y trae el viento de la Providencia. Añade que las necesidades humanas, eterna ley, despertaban, al fin, en el pobre español los naturales apetitos, sacándole del sueño de austeridad ascética, y al llegar esta situación, encontraba más fácil pedir a la intriga que al trabajo la mísera sopa y el trajecito pardo con que remediarse del hambre y del frío. (*Bodas reales,* II, 1266)

Desorientado y confuso se ve el narrador de estos acontecimientos al tener que decir que aquel cínico era simpático y airoso por extremo, que fuera de la política era un hombre encantador, que a todo el mundo cautivaba; ornado de sociales atractivos y aun de cristianas virtudes . . . ¡Oh! España, en todo fecunda, es la primera especialidad del globo para la cría de esta clase de monstruos. (*Bodas reales,* II, 1277)

Mejor estaríamos nosotros en Africa que en la Europa, si el Africa es, como cuentan, tan parecida a La Mancha . . ., y aunque en ella hay moros, mejor nos entenderemos con éstos que con tanto civilizado perverso de las Austrias y de las Inglaterras . . . (*Bodas reales,* II, 1313)

Es, a su juicio, que el pueblo español no quiere curarse de su principal defecto: la exageración . . . la exageración es lo que nos pierde a los españoles. Aquí el religioso cree que no lo es si no le damos inquisición, y el filósofo no ha de parar hasta la impiedad y descreimiento . . . (*Narváez*, II, 1535)

España vive siempre entre dos amos: el ejército y la clerecía; cuando el uno la deja, el otro la toma. ¿Duermen las espadas?, pues se despabila el fanatismo. (*Los duendes de la camarilla*, II, 1578)

¿La sedición qué es? El instinto de la raza española, que, por no caer en la barbarie, da un grito, pega un brinco y, en su entusiasmo, viene a caer un poquito más acá de la Ordenanza. (*Los duendes de la camarilla*, II, 1578)

No hay cosa, por desatinada que sea, que no pueda ser verdad en este país, mayormente si es cosa contra la justicia y contra la paz de los hombres . . . Aquí puede pasar todo, y la palabra 'increíble' debe ser borrada del libro ese muy grande donde están todas las palabras, porque en España nada hay que sea mismamente increíble . . . (*Los duendes de la camarilla*, II, 1635-1636)

Dentro de cada español, por mucho que presuma de cultura, hay un sayón o un fraile. La lengua que hablamos se presta como ninguna al escarnio, a la burla, y todo lo que no es caridad, ni mansedumbre. (*La revolución de julio*, III, 13)

. . . los militares, siguiendo la rutina histórica, no van a cambiar la ley, sino a restablecerla . . . Esto debe hacerlo el pueblo, la masa total; pero aquí nos hemos acostumbrado a que el pueblo delegue esa función en los militares, y ya no es fácil cambiar de sistema. (*La revolución de julio*, III, 39)

España es un mendigo que se aburre de estar siempre pidiendo en la misma esquina. 'Vámonos a la de enfrente que por ésta no pasa nadie'. España no necesita de la acción consolidadora del tiempo, porque no tiene nada que consolidar; necesita de la acción destructora, porque sus grandes necesidades son destructivas. Las revoluciones, que en otras partes desequilibran la existencia, aquí la entonan. ¿Por qué? Porque nuestra existencia es en cierto modo transitoria, algo que no puede definirse bien. Yo la veo como si el ser nacional estuviera muriendo y naciendo al mismo tiempo. Ni acaba de morirse ni acaba de nacer. (*La revolución de julio*, III, 54)

De todo hemos tenido modelos admirables. ¡Lástima grande que con modelos perfectísimos de cada una de las partes no hayamos tenido nunca el modelo sintético, integral! (*O'Donnell*, III, 173)

. . . el moro y el español son más hermanos de lo que parece. Quiten un poco de religión, quiten otro poco de lengua, y el parentesco y aire de familia saltan a los ojos. ¿Qué es el moro más que un español mahometano? ¿Y cuántos españoles vemos que son moros con disfraz de cristianos? (*Aita Tettauen*, III, 226)

Contra tal idea se rebelaba su fe cristiana, su fe española, virtud grande de una raza aventurera que confía en salir de todos los atascaderos que pone en su camino la fatalidad, y al fin sale; no se sabe

cómo, pero sale. Hay una providencia especial para los locos . . .
(*Aita Tettauen*, III, 270)

Sin duda, aquel noble señor y su familia obedecían a un impulso atávico inconsciente, y creían cumplir una misión social reduciendo a los inferiores a servil obediencia; procedían según la conducta y hábitos de sus tatarabuelos, en tiempos en que no había Constituciones encuadernadas en pasta para adornar las bibliotecas de los 'centros políticos'; no eran peores ni mejores que otros mandones que con nobleza o sin ella, con buenas o malas formas, caciqueaban en todas las provincias, partidos y ciudades de este vetusto reino emperifollado a la moderna. Los perifollos eran códigos, leyes, reglamentos, programas y discursos que no alteraban la condición arbitraria, inquisitorial y frailuna del hispano temperamento. (*La vuelta al mundo en la Numancia*, III, 433)

. . . conservaba en su carácter el dejo de las fierezas inquisitoriales, que en toda alma española están adheridas, como se adhieren a la lengua los sonidos del idioma. (*La vuelta al mundo en la Numancia*, III, 444)

Aunque políticamente no fueran aquellos nuestros hermanos, por el habla y los sentimientos no podían negar la casta. Prueba plena del parentesco daban los valientes americanos con su afición al juego de la guerra civil. Como nosotros, se dividían en furiosos bandos, y se perseguían y se fusilaban 'por dar gusto al dedo'. (*La vuelta al mundo en la Numancia*, III, 456)

Las venas de nuestra nación se están vaciando siempre; pero pronto vuelven a llenarse . . . Este pueblo heroico y mal comido saca su sangre de sus desgracias, del amor, del odio . . ., y de las sopas de ajo. (*La de los tristes destinos*, III, 638).

¡Oh, ferrocarril del Norte, venturoso escape hacia el mundo europeo, divina brecha para la civilización! . . . todo se te perdona por los inmensos beneficios que nos trajiste, ¡oh, grande amigo y servidor nuestro, puerta del tráfico, llave de la industria, abertura de la ventilación universal y respiradero por donde escapan los densos humos que aun flotan en el hispano cerebro. (*La de los tristes destinos*, III, 654-655)

Lo que llamamos pronunciamientos, los pequeños actos revolucionarios que amenizan dramáticamente nuestra Historia, no son más que aplicaciones heroicas de las providenciales sanguijuelas, sinapismos, ventosas o sangría que exige un agudo estado morboso. (*La de los tristes destinos*, III, 669)

En España es un hecho constante la realidad de lo contrario, o que cosas y personas actúen al revés de sí mismas. (*España sin rey*, III, 820)

Esta fidelidad a una casa en que predominaban ideas tan contrarias . . . se explica o por la atracción de los elementos opuestos, o por la simpatía personal que en España suele relegar las ideas a un lugar secundario. (*España sin rey*, III, 825)

Las ideas más altas pueden, hijo mío, convertirse de honradas en afrentosas al pasar de la mente de un grande hombre al magín desconcertado del vulgo . . . Y ya sabes, tú lo has dicho; en ciertos terrenos toda España es plebe. (*España trágica*, III, 916)

¡Oh, España mía, único país del mundo que sabe ser a un tiempo desgraciado y alegre! (*España trágica*, III, 934)

Sólo España, fecunda en ingenios, en héroes, en santos y en monstruos, nos da estos engendros de la razón y la sinrazón, de la fe mística y el orgullo marcial fundidos dentro de un alma. (*Amadeo I*, III, 1035)

En él veía yo la personificación vigorosa del espíritu de rebeldía que alienta en las razas españolas desde tiempos remotos, y que no tiene trazas de suavizarse con las dulzuras de la civilización . . . (*La primera República*, III, 1081)

¡Oh, España!, ¿qué haces, qué piensas, qué imaginas? Tejes y destejes tu existencia. Tu destino es correr tropezando y vivir muriendo . . . (*La primera República*, III, 1097)

El grave mal de nuestra patria es que aquí la paz y la guerra son igualmente deslavazadas y sosainas. Nos peleamos por un ideal, y vencedores y vencidos nos curamos las heridas del amor propio con emplastos de arreglitos y anodinas recetas para concertar nuevas amistades y seguir viviendo en octaviana mansedumbre. (*De Cartago a Sagunto*, III, 1207-1208)

Republicanos condenados hoy a larguísima noche: cuando veáis amanecer vuestro día, sed astutos y trágicos. (*De Cartago a Sagunto*, III, 1208)

En sinfín de páginas de la historia del mundo se ven hermosas querellas y tenacidades de una raza por éste o el otro ideal. Contiendas tan vanas y estúpidas como las que vio y aguantó España en el siglo XIX, por ilusorios derechos de familia y por unas briznas de Constitución, debieran figurar únicamente en la historia de las riñas de gallos. (*De Cartago a Sagunto*, III, 1236)

. . . los españoles no se afanan por crear riqueza, sino que se pasan la vida consumiendo la poca que tienen, quitándosela unos a otros con trazas y ardides que no son siempre de buena ley. (*Cánovas*, III, 1288)

La querella dinástica se hizo crónica, y la repugnante dolencia creció, invadiendo el cuerpo social en el curso del siglo. Todavía, ¡pobre España!, todavía tienes sarna que rascar por largo tiempo. (*Cánovas, III*, 1313).

¡Oh, desmedrada España! Cada día pesas menos, y si abultas más atribúyelo a tu vana hinchazón. (*Cánovas*, III, 1314)

No creo ni en los revolucionarios de nuevo cuño ni en los antediluvianos, esos que ya chillaban en los años anteriores al 68. La España que aspira a un cambio radical y violento de la política se está quedando, a mi entender, tan anémica como la otra. Han de pasar años, lustros tal vez, quizá medio siglo largo, antes que este regimen, atacado de tuberculosis étnica, sea sustituído por otro que traiga nueva sangre y nuevos focos de lumbre mental. (*Cánovas*, III, 1350)

Alarmante es la palabra revolución. Pero si no inventáis otra menos aterradora, no tendréis más remedio que usarla los que no queréis morir de la honda caquexia que invade el cansado cuerpo de tu nación. Declaraos revolucionarios, díscolos si os parece mejor esta palabra, contumaces en la rebeldía. En la situación a que llegaréis andando los años, el ideal revolucionario, la actitud indómita si queréis, constituirán el único síntoma de vida. Siga el lenguaje de los bobos llamando paz a lo que en realidad es consunción y acabamiento . . . Sed constantes en la protesta, sed viriles, románticos, y mientras no venzáis a la muerte, no os ocupéis de Mariclío . . . (*Cánovas*, III, 1363)

LIST OF WORKS CONSULTED

(An asterisk precedes works which refer directly
to the *Episodios Nacionales*)

Alarcón, P. A. de. *Diario de un testigo de la guerra de Africa.* 2 Vols. Madrid, 1931.
*Alarcón Capilla, A. *Galdós y su obra.* Madrid, 1922.
*Alas, L. *Galdós.* Madrid, 1912.
*Alberti, R. "Un Episodio Nacional: *Gerona,*" *Cursos y Conferencias,* XXIV (1943), 16-21.
*Alomar, G. "Galdós: I *Los Episodios,*" *Lectura,* XX (1920).
*Alonso, A. *Ensayo sobre la novela histórica.* Buenos Aires, 1942.
*———— *Materia y forma en poesía.* Madrid, 1956.
———— Charles Bally, Raimundo Lida, and Elise Richter. *El impresionismo en el lenguaje.* Buenos Aires, 1942.
*Alonso Cortés, N. *Quevedo en el teatro y otros ensayos.* Valladolid, 1930.
*Altamira y Crevea, R. *De historia y arte.* Madrid, 1898.
———— *La enseñanza de la historia.* Madrid, 1895.
*———— "La mujer en la novela de Galdós," *Atenea,* LXXII (1943), 145-159.
Anderson Imbert, E. *Estudios sobre escritores de América.* Buenos Aires, 1954.
*Arroyo, C. *Galdós.* Madrid, 1930.
Auerbach, E. *Mimesis.* Trans. Willard Trask. New York, 1957.
*Ayala, F. *Histrionismo y representación.* Buenos Aires, 1944.
*———— "Sobre el realismo en literatura con referencia a Galdós," *La Torre,* VII (April, 1959), 91-121.
*Balbín de Unquera, A. "Novelas y novelistas históricos en España," *Revista Contemporánea,* CXXXI (1905), 385-407.
Balzac, H. de. *Oeuvres Complètes.* 40 Vols. Paris, 1912-1932.
*Barja, C. *Libros y autores modernos.* Los Angeles, 1933.
*Baroja y Nessi, P. "Pérez Galdós y la novela histórica española," in *Divagaciones apasionadas.* Madrid, n. d.
*Barr, R. G. "A Census of Characters in the *Episodios Nacionales* of Pérez Galdós." Unpublished Doctoral Dissertation. University of Wisconsin, 1937.
*Barr, R. G. "Galdós, Modern Prophet," *Hispania,* XXII (1939), 357-360.
*Bataillon, M. "Les sources historiques de *Zaragoza,*" *Bulletin Hispanique,* XXIII (1921), 129-141.
Berkowitz, H. C. *La biblioteca de Galdós.* Las Palmas, 1951.
———— "Galdós and the Generation of 1898," *Philological Quarterly,* XXI (1942), 107-120.
*———— "Galdós and Mesonero Romanos," *Romanic Review,* XXIII (1932), 201-205.
*———— *Pérez Galdós, Spanish Liberal Crusader.* Madison, 1948.
———— "Unamuno's Relations with Galdós," *Hispanic Review,* VIII (1940), 321-338.
Berlin, I. *The Hedgehog and the Fox.* New York, 1957.
Bernbaum, E. "The Views of the Great Critics on the Historical Novel," *PMLA,* XLI (1926), 424-441.
*Boussagol, G. "Sources et composition du *Zumalacárregui,*" *Bulletin Hispanique,* XXVI (1924), 241-264.
*Bravo Moreno, F. *Síntomas de la patología mental que se hallan en las obras literarias de B. Pérez Galdós.* Barcelona, 1923.
*Brown, D. F. "More Light on the Mother of Galdós," *Hispania,* XXXIX (1956), 403-407.
Brown, R. *La novela española,* 1700-1850. Madrid, 1953.

Brunetière, F. *Honoré de Balzac*. Paris, 1906.
Burckhardt, J. *Judgments on History and Historians*. Trans. H. Zohn. Boston, 1958.
Bury, J. B. *The Idea of Progress*. New York, 1932.
Cam, H. *Historical Novels*. London, 1961.
°Cano, J. L. "Revisión de Galdós," *Insula*, LXXXII (1952).
°Carranza, M. *El pueblo a través de los Episodios Nacionales*. San José, Costa Rica, 1942.
°Casalduero, J. "Galdós y la Edad Media," *Asomante*, IX (1953), 13-27.
° ———— "Trayectoria de la creación galdosiana," *Cuadernos*, Paris, VI (1954), 39-44.
° ———— *Vida y obra de Galdós*. Madrid, 1951.
°Casona, A. "Galdós y el Romanticismo," *Cursos y Conferencias*, XXIV (1943), 13-24.
°Clavería, C. "Galdós y los demonios," in *Homenaje a J. A. van Praag*. Amsterdam, 1956.
° ———— "El pensamiento histórico de Galdós," *Revista Nacional de Cultura*, Caracas, XIX (1957), 170-177.
° ———— "Sobre la veta fantástica en la obra de Galdós," *Atlante*, I (1953), 78-86, 136-143.
Collingwood, R. G. *Historical Imagination*. Oxford, 1935.
———— *Idea of History*. New York, 1956.
°Contreras, R. A. de. "La evolución galdosiana," *Razón y Fe*, XX (1908), 82-92.
Croce, B. *European Literature in the Nineteenth Century*. Trans. Douglas Ainslee. London, 1924.
———— *La filosofia di Giambattista Vico*. Bari, 1922.
———— *Filosofia, Poesia e Storia*. Milano-Napoli, 1952.
°Darío, R. *España contemporánea*. Madrid, n. d.
°Del Río, A. *Estudios galdosianos*. Zaragoza, 1953.
° ———— "Los ideales de Galdós," *Revista Hispánica Moderna*, IX (1943), 290-291.
° ———— "Notas sobre el tema de América en Galdós," *Nueva Revista de Filología Hispánica*, XV (1961), 270-294.
° ———— "Trabajos recientes sobre Galdós," *Revista Hispánica Moderna*, XI (1945), 52-56.
°Dendariena, G. *Galdós: su genio, su espiritualidad, su grandeza*. Madrid, 1922.
Díaz-Plaja, G. *Introducción al estudio del romanticismo español*. Madrid, 1942.
°Díez Canedo, E. "España y Galdós," en *Conversaciones literarias*. Madrid, n. d.
Else, G. F. *Aristotle's Poetics: The Argument*. Cambridge, 1957.
°Enguídanos, M. "Mariclío, musa galdosiana," *Papeles de Son Armandans*, XXI (June, 1961), 235-249.
°Entrambasaguas, J. de. *Las mejores novelas contemporáneas*. 5 Vols. Barcelona, 1957-1961.
Eoff, S. H. *The Modern Spanish Novel*. New York, 1961.
° ———— *The Novels of Pérez Galdós*. St. Louis, 1954.
Ferrater Mora, J. *Unamuno*. Buenos Aires, 1957.
°Franco, D. *España como preocupación*. Madrid, 1960.
°Gamero y de Laiglesia, E. G. *Galdós y su obra*. 3 Vols. Madrid, 1933-1935.
°García Figueras, T. *Recuerdos centenarios de una guerra romántica*. Madrid, 1961.
Geyl, P. *Use and Abuse of History*. New Haven, 1955.
°Gilman, S. "Realism and Epic in Galdós' *Zaragoza*," in *Homenaje a A. M. Huntington*. Wellesley, Mass., 1952.
°Giménez, A. *Valera y la generación de 1868*. Oxford, 1956.
°Giusti, R. F. "La obra galdosiana," *Cursos y Conferencias*, XXIV (1943), 3-12.
°Gómez de Baquero, E. *De Gallardo a Unamuno*. Madrid, 1926.
° ———— *Novelas y novelistas*. Madrid, 1918.

*———— *El Renacimiento de la novela española en el siglo XIX*. Madrid, 1924.

*Gómez de la Serna, G. "El episodio nacional como género literario," *Clavileño*, XIV (1952), 21-32.

*———— *España en sus Episodios*. Madrid, 1954.

*Gómez de la Serna, R. *Nuevos retratos contemporáneos*. Buenos Aires, 1945.

*González Blanco, A. *Historia de la novela en España desde el romanticismo*. Madrid, 1909.

*Gooch, G. P. *History and Historians in the Nineteenth Century*. London, 1952.

Grierson, Herbert, Edwin Muir, G. M. Young, and S. C. Roberts. *Sir Walter Scott Lectures*. Edinburgh, 1950.

Gullón, R. "Cuestiones galdosianas," *Cuadernos Hispanoamericanos*, XXXIV (1958), 237-254.

*———— *Galdós, novelista moderno*. Madrid, 1960.

*———— "Lo maravilloso en Galdós," *Insula*, CXIII (1955).

*Hafter, M. Z. "Ironic Reprise in Galdós' Novels," *PMLA*, LXXVI (June, 1961), 233-239.

*Heros, A. "Galdós y el Nuevo Mundo," *Hispania*, XXIV (1941), 101-111.

Hilhouse, J. T. *The Waverly Novels and Their Critics*. Minneapolis, 1936.

*Hinterhäuser, H. *Los Episodios Nacionales de B. Pérez Galdós*. Madrid, 1963.

Hodges, A. A. The Philosophy of William Dilthey. London, 1952.

*Huerta, E. "Galdós y la novela histórica," *Atenea*, LXXII (1943), 99-107.

Kantor, Mackinlay, Irving Stone, and John O'Hara. *Three Views of the Novel*. Washington, 1957.

King, E. L. "What is Spanish Romanticism," *Studies in Romanticism*, II (1962), 1-11.

Laín Entralgo, P. *Menéndez y Pelayo*. Barcelona, 1945.

*Lázaro, A. *La verdad del pueblo español*. San Juan, Puerto Rico, 1939.

*Lhande, P. "Galdós: L'homme — l'oeuvre," *Etudes*, Paris, CLXII (1920), 281-295.

Livingstone, L. "Interior Duplication and the Problem of Form in the Modern Spanish Novel," *PMLA*, LXXIII (September, 1958), 393-406.

López Morillas, J. *El krausismo español*. México, 1956.

*Louis-Lande, L. "Le roman patriotique en Espagne. *Episodios Nacionales*, par Pérez Galdós, Madrid, 1873-75," *Revue des Deux Mondes*, XIV (1876), 934-944.

Löwith, K. *Meaning in History*. Chicago, 1949.

Lukacs, G. *The Historical Novel*. Trans. Hannah and Stanley Mitchell. London, 1962.

———— *Studies in European Realism*. Trans. Edith Bone. London, 1950.

*Madariaga, S. de. *De Galdós a Lorca*. Buenos Aires, 1960.

*———— *Semblanzas literarias contemporáneas*. Barcelona, 1924.

*———— *Spain*. New York, 1930.

Maigron, L. *Le roman historique à l'epoque romantique*. Paris, 1912.

Manzoni, A. *Opere*. Milan, 1953.

*Marañón, G. "El mundo por la claraboya," *Insula*, LXXXII (1952).

———— *Vida e historia*. Madrid, 1958.

*Martinenche, E. "Le théâtre de M. Galdós," *Revue des Deux Mondes*, XXXII (1906), 815.

Martínez Ruiz, J. *Doña Inés*. New York, n. d.

*———— *Lecturas españolas*. Madrid, 1920.

Marx, Karl, and Frederick Engels. *Revolution in Spain*. New York, 1939.

Maugham, W. Somerset. *Great Novelists and Their Novels*. Philadelphia, 1948.

Mendilov, A. A. *Time and the Novel*. London, 1952.

*Menéndez y Pelayo, Marcelino, Benito Pérez Galdós, and José María Pereda. *Discursos de la Real Academia Española, 7 y 21 de febrero, 1897*. Madrid, 1897.

*Mesa, R. de. "Génesis de los *Episodios*," *Revista de Libros*, III (1919), 33-46.

Mesonero Romanos, R. de. *Escenas Matritenses*. 2 Vols. Madrid, 1925.

*———— *Memorias de un setentón*. 2 Vols. Madrid, 1926.

*Monner Sans, J. M. "Galdós y la Generación del '98," *Cursos y Conferencias*, XXIV (1943), 57-85.
*Montesinos, J. F. *Introducción a una historia de la novela en España en el siglo XIX*. Madrid, 1955.
*———— *Costumbrismo y novela*. Los Angeles, 1960.
———— "Notas sueltas sobre la fortuna de Balzac en España," *Revue de Littérature Comparée*, XXIV (1950), 309-338.
———— *Pedro Antonio de Alarcón*. Zaragoza, 1955.
Nagel, E. *The Structure of Modern Science*. New York, 1961.
Navarro, T. "La lengua de Galdós," *Revista Hispánica Moderna*, IX (1943), 292-293.
*Obaid, A. H. "Galdós y Cervantes," *Hispania*, XLI (1958), 269-273.
*———— "La Mancha en los *Episodios Nacionales*," *Hispania*, XLI (1958), 42-47.
*———— "El Quijote en los *Episodios Nacionales*." Unpublished Doctoral Dissertation. University of Minnesota, 1953.
*———— "Sancho Panza en los *Episodios Nacionales*," *Hispania*, XLII (1959), 199-204.
Ollers, C. "Galdós y Balzac," *Insula*, LXXXII (1952).
Onís, F. de. "*El españolismo de Galdós*," in *Ensayo sobre el sentido de la cultura española*. Madrid, 1932.
———— "El humorismo de Galdós," *Revista Hispánica Moderna*, IX (1943), 293-294.
*Pattison, W. T. *Galdós and the Creative Process*. Minneapolis, 1954.
Peers, E. Allison. "Studies in the Influence of Sir Walter Scott in Spain," *Revue Hispanique*, LXVIII (1926), 1-160.
Pérez de Ayala, R. "Galdós," in *Divagaciones literarias*. Madrid, 1958.
———— *Principios y finales de la novela*. Madrid, 1958.
Pérez Galdós, B. *Arte y crítica*. ed. A. Ghiraldo. Madrid, 1923.
———— *Crónica de la quincena*. ed. W. H. Shoemaker. Princeton, 1948.
———— *Episodios Nacionales*. 10 Vols. Madrid, 1881.
———— *La Fontana de Oro*. Madrid, 1906.
———— *Memoranda*. Madrid, 1906.
———— *Memorias*. ed. A. Ghiraldo. Madrid, 1930.
———— *Obras completas*. 3rd ed. 7 Vols. Madrid, 1950-1951.
———— *Tormento*. Madrid, 1906.
———— Marcelino Menéndez y Pelayo, and José María Pereda. *Discursos de la Real Academia Española, 7 y 21 de febrero, 1897*. Madrid, 1897.
*Pérez Minik, D. *Novelistas españoles de los siglos XIX y XX*. Madrid, 1957.
*Pons, J. S. "Le roman et l'histoire. De Galdós à Valle-Inclán," in *Hommage à Ernest Martinenche*. Paris, 1939.
Portnoff, G. "Beginning of a New Idealism in the Works of Tolstoy and Galdós," *Romanic Review*, XXIII (1932), 33-37.
———— *La literatura rusa en España*. New York, 1932.
Poulet, G. *Studies in Human Time*. Trans. Elliott Coleman. Baltimore, 1956.
Reyes, A. *El deslinde*. México, 1944.
*Ricard, R. "Deux romanciers: Ganivet et Galdós," *Bulletin Hispanique*, LX (1958), 484-499.
*———— *Etudes Hispano-Africaines*. Tetuan, 1956.
*———— "Note sur la genèse de *Aita Tettauen*," *Bulletin Hispanique*, XXXVII (1935), 471-477.
*———— "Structure et inspiration de *Carlos VI en la Rápita*," *Bulletin Hispanique*, LVII (1955), 70-83.
*Rogers, P. P. "Galdós and Tamayo y Baus' Letter Substitution Device," *Romanic Review*, XLV (1954), 115-120.
*Romera, A. R. "Estampa de Galdós," *Atenea*, LXXII (1943), 108-120.
*Rosell, M. "Valoración de Galdós," *Atenea*, LXXII (1943), 121-135.
*Sainz de Robles, F. C. "Benito Pérez Galdós: su vida, su obra y su época," in Pérez Galdós, *Obras completas*, Vol. I. Madrid, 1950.

*Salaverría, J. M. "Galdós," in *Nuevos retratos*. Madrid, 1930.
*Salillas, R. *En las cortes de Cádiz*. Madrid, 1910.
Salinas, P. "Significación del esperpento o Valle-Inclán, hijo pródigo del '98," *Cuadernos Americanos*, VI (1947), 218-244.
*Sarrailh, J. "Quelques sources du *Cádiz*," *Bulletin Hispanique*, XXIII (1921), 33-48.
*Scatori, S. *La idea religiosa en la obra de Galdós*. Paris, 1927.
Schraibman, J. *Dreams in the Novels of Galdós*. New York, 1960.
———— "Dreams in the Novels of Pérez Galdós," *Literature and Psychology*, X (1960), 91-96.
*———— "Patria y patriotismo en los *Episodios Nacionales* de Galdós," *Boletín Informativo del Seminario de Derecho Político de la Universidad de Salamanca*, XXVII (August, 1962), 71-86.
Sheppard, A. T. *The art and Practice of Historical Fiction*. London, 1930.
*Shoemaker, W. H. "*La de los tristes destinos* and its Shakespearean connections," *Modern Language Notes*, LXXI (1956), 114-119.
*———— "Galdós' Classical Scene in *La de Bringas*," *Hispanic Review*, XXVII (1959), 423-434.
*———— "Galdós' Literary Creativity: D. José Ido del Sagrario," *Hispanic Review*, XIX (1951), 204-237.
*Soriano, R. "Don Benito," *Atenea*, LXXII (1943), 93-98.
Stone, Irving, Mackinlay Kantor, and John O'Hara. *Three Views of the Novel*. Washington, 1957.
*Swett, D. B. "A Study of the Carlist Wars as a Literary Theme in the *Episodios Nacionales* of Galdós." Unpublished Doctoral Dissertation. University of Southern California, 1948.
Tierno Galván, E. *Costa y el regeneracionismo*. Barcelona, 1961.
Tilgher, A. *Storia e antistoria*. Modena, 1928.
*Torres Bodet, J. *Tres inventores de realidad*. México, 1955.
Toynbee, A. J. *Greek Historical Thought*. New York, 1952.
*Trend, J. B. *Origins of Modern Spain*. New York, 1934.
*———— *A Picture of Modern Spain*. New York, 1921.
*Unamuno y Jugo, M. de. *De esto y aquello*. 4 Vols. Buenos Aires, 1950-1954.
*Varela Hervias, E. *Cartas de Pérez Galdós a Mesonero Romanos*. Madrid, 1943.
*Vázquez Arjona, C. "Cotejo histórico de cinco *Episodios*," *Revue Hispanique*, LXVIII (1926), 321-550.
*———— "Un *Episodio Nacional* de Benito Pérez Galdós: *El 19 de marzo y 2 de mayo*," *Bulletin Hispanique*, XXXIII (1931), 116-139.
*———— "Un *Episodio Nacional* de Galdós: *Bailén*," *Bulletin of Spanish Studies*, IX (1932), 116-123.
*———— "Introduction to the Study of the First Series of *Episodios*," *PMLA*, XLVIII (1933), 895-907.
*Villamil, E. F. "Comprobaciones sobre documentación en Pérez Galdós," *Correo Erudito*, II (1941), 20-24.
*Walton, L. B. *Pérez Galdós and the Spanish Novel of the Nineteenth Century*, London, 1927.
———— "La psicología anormal en la obra de Galdós," "*Boletín del Instituto Español*, IV (1948), 10-13.
*Warshaw, J. "Galdós' Indebtedness to Cervantes," *Hispania*, XVI (1933), 127-142.
Wellek, R. "The Concept of Realism in Literary Scholarship," *Neophilologus*, XLV (1961), 1-20.
*Yáñez, A. "Traza de la novela galdosiana," *Cuadernos Americanos*, II (1943), 122-140.
Zambrano, M. *Pensamiento y poesía en la vida española*. México, 1939.
Zellers, G. *La novela histórica en España, 1828-1850*. New York, 1928.
Zola, E. *Balzac*, Trans. Anon. Madrid, 1890.

INDEX